LIFE IN CHRIST

Register This New Book

Benefits of Registering*

- ✓ FREE accidental **loss replacement**
- ✓ FREE **audiobook** – *Pilgrim's Progress*, audiobook edition
- ✓ FREE information about new titles and other **freebies**

www.anekopress.com/new-book-registration

*See our website for requirements and limitations.

LIFE IN CHRIST

Lessons from Our Lord's
Miracles and Parables

The Miracles of Our Lord
Volume 10

Charles H. Spurgeon

We love hearing from our readers. Please contact us at www.anekopress.com/questions-comments with any questions, comments, or suggestions.

Life in Christ, Vol. 10
© 2023 by Aneko Press
All rights reserved. First edition 1891.
Revisions copyright 2023

Scripture quotations are from The Authorized (King James) Version. Rights in the Authorized Version in the United Kingdom are vested in the Crown. Reproduced by permission of the Crown's patentee, Cambridge University Press.

Cover Design: Natalia Hawthorne
Cover Painting: Matt Philleo
Editors: Ruth Clark and J. Martin

Aneko Press

www.anekopress.com
Aneko Press, Life Sentence Publishing, and our logos are trademarks of
Life Sentence Publishing, Inc.
203 E. Birch Street
P.O. Box 652
Abbotsford, WI 54405
RELIGION / Christian Life / Spiritual Growth
Paperback ISBN: 979-8-88936-258-6
eBook ISBN: 979-8-88936-259-3

10 9 8 7 6 5 4 3 2 1
Available where books are sold

Contents

Chapter 1

Bankrupt Debtors Discharged

And when they had nothing to pay, he frankly forgave them both. (Luke 7:42)

The two debtors differed very considerably in the amounts which they owed: the one was in arrears five hundred pence, and the other fifty. There are differences in the guilt of sins, and in the degrees of men's criminality. It would be a very unfair and unrighteous thing to say that all men are exactly alike in the extent of their transgressions. Some are honest and upright, kind and generous, even though they be but natural men; while others appear to be of a malicious, envious, selfish disposition, and rush into evil, sinning, as it were, with both hands greedily. The man who is moral, sober, and industrious is only a fifty-pence debtor as compared with the vicious, drunken blasphemer whose debt is written at five hundred pence.

Our Savior recognizes the distinction because it exists and cannot justly be overlooked. There are distinctions among unconverted men, very great distinctions. One of them, a young man, came to Jesus, and he had so many fine traits in his character that the Lord, looking upon him, loved him; whereas when the Pharisees gathered around him, our Lord looked upon them with indignation. The soil, which was none of it yet sown with the good seed, varied greatly, and some of it was honest and good ground before the sower came to it. Sinners differ from each other.

But I call your particular attention to this fact – that though there was one point of difference in the two debtors, there were three points of similarity, for they were both debtors. So, firstly, all men have sinned, be it little or be it much. Secondly, they were both alike bankrupt and neither of them could meet his debt; the man who owed fifty-pence could no more pay than he who owed five hundred-pence, so they were both insolvent debtors. But what a mercy it is that they were alike in the third point! For *when they had nothing to pay,* their creditor *frankly forgave them both.*

Oh, my dear friends, we are all alike in the first two things! Oh, that we might be all of us alike in this last point also, that the Lord our God may grant to every one of us the free remission of sins according to the riches of his grace through Christ Jesus! Why should it not be so, since Jesus is exalted on high to give repentance and remission of sins? There is forgiveness with God. *He delighteth in mercy* (Micah 7:18). He can cast all our sins into the depths of the sea, that they may not be mentioned against us anymore forever. While we are compelled to go together down two-thirds of the road, what a pity it would be that we should be divided in the third portion of it!

That first two-thirds of the road is a very muddy, boggy piece of way, and we sorrowfully wade along it in company – all in debt and all of us unable to pay; but that next part of the road is well made, smooth, and good for travelers, and it leads into the gardens of joy. Oh, that we may travel it, and find the free pardon of God! Oh, for free remission for all of us without exception! Why not? May God send it of his great mercy at this good hour! To that end I wish to speak with you, dear friends, for I believe that the Lord Jesus has something to say unto you, and I pray that your hearts may be open to him, crying gladly, "Master, say on!"

Our first point for consideration is *their bankruptcy – they had nothing to pay;* the second is *their free discharge – he frankly forgave them both;* and the third is *the connection between these two things,* for that little word *when* marks the connection – **when** *they had nothing to pay, he frankly forgave them both* (emphasis added).

First, let us think of their bankruptcy. This was their condition. They were unquestionably in debt. If they could have disputed the creditor's claim, no doubt they would have done so. If they could have pleaded

2

that they were never indebted, or that they had already paid, no doubt they would have been glad to have done so; but they could not raise a question; their debt could not be denied. Another fact was also clear to them, namely, that they had nothing to pay with. No doubt they had made diligent search; they had emptied out their pockets, their cash-boxes, and their lockers, and they had found nothing; they had looked for their household goods, but these had vanished piece by piece.

They had nothing at home or abroad that they could dispose of. Things had come to such a pass with them that they had neither stock nor money, nor anything in prospect which they could draw upon; they were brought to the last extremity, reduced to absolute beggary. Meanwhile, their great creditor was pressing them for settlement. That idea lies in the heart of the text. The creditor had evidently brought his overdue accounts, and had said to them, "These claims must be met. There must be an end to this state of affairs; your accounts must be discharged." They were just brought to this condition – they must confess the debt, and they must also humbly acknowledge that they had nothing to meet it with. The time for payment had come, and it found them without a penny. No condition could be much more wretched.

So far, I have stated the parable, and it most truly sets forth *the condition* of every man who has not come to Jesus Christ and received the frank forgiveness of his sins. Upon this we will elaborate. We are all by nature and by practice plunged into debt, and this is the way in which we came to be so. Hear it and mark it well. As God's creatures we from the very first owed to him the debt of obedience. We were bound to obey our Maker. It is he that made us, and not we ourselves; and we were, therefore, bound reverently to recognize our Creator, affection-ately to worship him, and dutifully to serve him. This is an obligation so natural and reasonable that nobody can dispute it. If you are the creatures of God, it is nothing more than right that you should honor him. If you receive daily the breath in your nostrils and the food that you eat from him, then you are bound to him by the ties of gratitude and should do his will.

But, dear friends, we have not done his will. We have left undone the things we ought to have done, and we have done the things we ought not to have done, and so we have come in a second sense into his debt.

3

We now stand liable to penalty, yes, we are condemned already. There is due from us to God, in vindication of his broken law, both suffering and death; and in the Word of God we find that the righteous penalty for sin is something utterly overwhelming. *Fear him,* says Christ, *which is able to destroy both soul and body in hell* (Matthew 10:28).

Yes, I say unto you, fear him! Very terrible are the metaphors and symbols by which the Holy Spirit sets forth the misery of a soul upon which the Lord pours forth his fiery indignation. The pain of loss and pain of woe that sin at last brings upon guilty men are inconceivable: they are called "the terrors of the Lord." There is not one among us, apart from the Lord Jesus Christ, but who owes to God's law a debt that eternity cannot fully meet, even though it be crowded with agonizing regrets. A life of forgetfulness of God and breaking of his law must be recompensed by a future life of punishment. That is where we stand. Can any man be at rest while this is his condition before God? We are debtors: the debt is overwhelming; it brings with it consequences tremendous to the last degree.

And we are utterly unable to make any amends for this. If he should meet with us and call us to account, we cannot answer him one of a thousand. We cannot excuse ourselves, and we cannot by any possibility render to him his righteous due. If any think they can, let me remind them of this, that to cancel the debt that we owe to God we must pay it all. God demands – righteously demands – from us the keeping of his entire law. He tells us that he that is guilty in one point is guilty in all, for God's law is like a fair vase of alabaster, lovely in its entireness, but if it be chipped in any part, it may not be presented in his court; the least flaw in it mars its perfection and destroys its value.

A perfect obedience to a perfect law is that which is required by the justice of the Most High; and is there any one of us who can render it, or who can attempt to pay the penalty due for not rendering it? Our inability to obey comes from our own fault and is part of our crime. Ah me! may none of us ever have to bear the penalty! to be banished from his presence, and from the glory of his power! to be cast away from all hope and light and joy forever! Why, there are those at this moment in the abyss of woe who have for thousands of years endured the heavy hand of justice, and yet their debt remains undischarged even now; for they have yet to appear before the judgment seat of Christ at the last day and answer for their transgressions. It is certain that to meet the whole payment is impossible; neither in the form of obedience, nor in the form of penalty may we ever hope to meet it – it would be all in vain to make the attempt.

Remember, too, that if there is anything that we can do for God in the way of obedience, it is already due to him. All that I can do if I love God with all my heart and soul and strength, and my neighbor as myself, throughout the rest of my life, is already due to God; I shall but be discharging new duties as they occur – how will this affect old disobediences? In what way can I cleanse myself from my former stains by the resolve that I will not be defiled with fresh ones? If your hand be bloodred can you make it clean by the mere resolution that you will not plunge it again into the dye? You know it is not so: past sin cannot be removed by future carefulness.

> Could my tears for ever flow,
>   Could my zeal no respite know,
> All for sin could not atone;
>   Christ must save, and Christ alone.

We have nothing with which to meet our liabilities because everything that we can possibly earn or obtain in the future is already due to justice, and so we have nothing left unmortgaged, nothing of our own.

Moreover, the debt is immense and incalculable! Fifty-pence is but a poor representation of what the most righteous person owes; five hundred-pence is but an insignificant sum compared with the transgressions of the greater offenders. Oh friends, when I think of my life, it seems to be like the sea, made up of innumerable waves of sin; or like the seashore, made up of sands that cannot be weighed nor counted. My faults are utterly innumerable, and each one deserving death eternal.

Our sins, our heavy sins, sins against light and knowledge, our foul sins, our repeated sins, our aggravated sins, our sins against our parents, our sins against all our relationships, our sins against our God, our sins with the body, our sins with the mind, our sins of forgetfulness, our sins of thought, our sins of imagination – who can reckon them up in order unto God? Who knows the number of his trespasses? Now, to think that we can ever meet such a debt is indeed to bolster up ourselves with a notion that is utterly absurd – we have nothing to pay.

Moreover, I will go a little further. Even if these sins were somewhat within range, and if we were not indebted for the future as to all we can even do, yet what is there that we *can* do? Does not Paul say of himself that he was not sufficient to think anything of himself? Did not the Lord tell his Israel of old, *From me is thy fruit found* (Hosea 14:8)? Did not Jesus say to his disciples and even to his apostles, *Without me ye can do nothing* (John 15:5)? Then, O bankrupt sinner, what is there good that you can do of yourself? You must first of all get the good work from God before you can perform it yourself. It is true that you are to *work out your own salvation with fear and trembling* (Philippians 2:12), but what must come first?

Read the passage: *For it is God which worketh in you both to will and to do of his good pleasure* (Philippians 2:13). If the Lord does not work salvation in us, we cannot work it out. Every good thing in man is the work of God, the product of the Spirit of God operating upon the heart and mind. Men are dead in trespasses and sins, dead to all that is holy and acceptable with God, and life itself is a gift. What then can sinners do? Their bankruptcy is utter and entire; and this is true of every man that is still outside of Christ – he is a debtor, and he has nothing to pay.

This being the case, I want to spend a minute in noticing *certain temptations* to which all bankrupt sinners are much subject. One of these is to try and forget their spiritual state altogether. Some of you here today have never given serious thought to your souls and to your condition before God. It is an unpleasant subject. You suspect that it would be still more unpleasant if you looked into it. You want amusement, something to while away the time, because you do not care to examine the state of your heart before God. Solomon exhorts the diligent man to know the state of his flocks and look well to his herds; but he that is careless and idle would rather leave such probing, and let things go as they please.

The man who is going backward in business has no pleasure in stocktaking. "Oh," says he, "don't bring me my books; I shall not sleep at night if I look into them." He knows that he is sinking lower and lower, and will soon be a ruined man; and the only way in which he can endure his life is to drive himself dull, carry himself away by drink, or by going into company, or by idle amusement. He labors to divert the hours that he may conceal from himself his true condition. But what a fool he is! Would it not be infinitely wiser if he would look the thing in the face and have it out, and know his actual state? Such ignorance as he chooses is not bliss to a right-hearted man, but suspense and misery.

I have often prayed this prayer – "Lord, let me know the very worst of my case, for I do not wish to entertain a hope that will at last deceive me." Disappointment will be bitter in proportion as false hope was sweet. This is the temptation of the bankrupt soul, to shut its eyes to unwelcome truth. Legend has it that the ostrich, when hunted, buries its head in the sand and conceives that the hunter is gone when he is no longer seen. But of course he is not hidden; the unseen danger is quite as real as if it stared us in the face. However forgetful you may be, God does not forget your sins.

Another temptation to a man in this condition is to make as good a show as he can. A man who is very near bankruptcy is often noticed for his impressive behavior. What a horse he drives as he comes up to business! What fashionable parties he gives! Just so, he desires to keep up his credit as long as ever he can. He is going to make a ruin of it by and by, but for a season he assumes the airs of my lord, and everybody near him imagines that he has money enough and to spare. The governor of a besieged city threw loaves of bread over the wall to the besiegers to make them believe that the citizens had such large supplies that they could afford to throw them away; yet they were starving all the while.

There are some men of like manners; they have nothing that they can offer unto God, but yet they exhibit a glittering self-righteousness. Oh, they have been so good, such superior people, so praiseworthy from their youth up; they never did anything much amiss; there may be a little speck here and there upon their garments, but that will brush off when it is dry. They make a fair show in the flesh with morality and formality, and a smattering of generosity. Besides, they profess to be religious: they attend religious services and pay their quota of the expenses. Who could find any fault with such good people? Just so; this profession is the fine horse and trap with which they too are behaving impressively just before going through the court. There is nothing at all in you, and there never was, if you are as nature has made you; why then do you try to defy it, and make yourself to seem something when you are nothing? You may by this means deceive yourself, but certainly you will not deceive God.

Another temptation that lurks in the way of a bankrupt sinner is that of making promises of what he will do. Men in debt are generally very promising men; they will pay next week for certain. But when that next week comes, they meant the next week further on, and then payment shall be doubly certain; yet they put in no appearance even then, or, if they do, they give a bill. Is not that a precious document? Is it not as good as the money itself? They evidently think so, for they feel quite as easy as if they had really paid that debt. But when the bill falls due, what then? It falls, unknown, to rise again. Ah me! a bill is often just a lie with a stamp on it. So will debtors go on as long as they can.

This is what every sinner does before he becomes cleared by the sovereign grace of God. He cries, "I mean to do better." Never mind; tell us no more what you mean to do, but do it. To promise and vow so falsely is only adding to your sins! "Oh! but you know I do not intend to go on in this way always. It is a long lane that has no turning. I shall come up short one of these days, and then you will see." What shall we see? We shall see what we shall see; and that will not be much. Yes. We shall see the dew of promise disappear, and the morning cloud of resolution pass away.

Dear sir, you cannot raise our hopes now. Neither God nor man will trust you; you have promised these twenty years, and in no one year have you made a real move in the right direction. You have not lied unto men only, but also unto God, and how will you answer for it? Know you not that every promise that you make to God that you do not keep is a great addition to your transgressions, and helps to fill up the measure of your iniquities? Give up the way of lying, I pray you.

Another temptation is to always ask for more time, as if this was all that was needed. When the debtor, in another parable, was arrested, he said to his creditor, *Have patience with me, and I will pay thee all* (Matthew 18:26). We cannot pay any of our debt today, and yet we dote upon tomorrow. Yes, it does seem such a relief to get a little longer time;

somehow a vague, shadowy hope seems to pervade the months to come. The sinner cries, *Go thy way for this time; when I have a convenient season, I will call for thee* (Acts 24:25). It is not convenient just now, but do wait a little bit, for a suitable hour will come.

With this temptation Satan has destroyed multitudes of men, tempting them to ask for more time, instead of coming up to the mark at once and asking for immediate pardon. What are the fictitious virtues of tomorrow? Why do men dote upon the unknown future? To an immediate decision I would press you at this moment; and may God by his divine Spirit deliver you as a bird from the hand of the waterfowl hunter, that you may no longer procrastinate and waste your life in disobedient delay.

This being the temptation, let me hint to those of you who are bankrupt what *your wisdom* is. It is your wisdom to face the business of your soul. The matters of your soul are the most important things you will ever have on hand, for when your wealth must be left, and your estate shall see you no more, and when your body is dead, your soul will still be living in eternal happiness or endless woe; therefore, do not let your state in reference to God be ignored. It is the most important matter; give it the first place. Settle this business before you attend to anything else.

Take care that you face it, like an honest man, and not as one who makes the best of a bad story. Though it be bad, yet still the best thing you can do is to go right through with it in truth and soberness before the Lord. Hope lies that way. Do not let your danger be concealed like a thief who hides in the good man's cupboard until the hour to rob his house. Do not permit the sparks to smolder where they may consume your all. Quench the fire before you sleep. When you face the matter, be very true and sincere with yourself and with God, because you are not now dealing with creditors who may be cheated, but you are dealing with One who knows the secret thoughts and intents of your heart. Before God nothing but truth can stand; the painted hypocrite is spied out immediately. The Lord takes off all masks, and men stand before him as they really are, and not as they would seem to be; so be true with yourself. Do not take your pen and write down sixty if you owe a hundred; but put the fair hundred down. Tricks and falsehoods had better be put away once and for all when you deal with God.

One thing more: it will be your wisdom to give up all attempts to pay, because you have nothing to pay with. Do not delude yourself into the idea that you will pay one day, for you never will. Do not make the slightest attempt at paying, for you cannot do it; but take quite another course, and plead absolute poverty, and appeal to mercy. Say, "Lord, I have nothing, I am nothing, I can do nothing. I must throw myself upon your grace." Of this grace I am now going to speak. May I so speak as to encourage you who are bankrupts to come to the Lord, that he may frankly forgive you all.

Our second topic is their free discharge. *He frankly forgave them both*. What a blessing they obtained by facing the matter! These two poor debtors, when they went into the office, were trembling from head to foot, for they had nothing to pay, and were deeply involved; but see! they come out with light hearts, for the debt is all disposed of, the bills are receipted, the records are destroyed. Even thus the Lord has blotted out the handwriting that was against us, and has taken it out of the way, nailing it to his cross.

In this free discharge I admire, first of all, *the goodness* of the great creditor. What a gracious heart he had! What kindness he showed! He said, "Poor souls, you can never pay me, but you need not be cast down because of it, for I freely cancel your debts." Oh, the goodness of it! Oh, the largeness of the heart of God! I was reading of Caesar the other day. He had been at fierce war with Pompey, and at last he conquered him, and when he conquered him, he found among the spoil Pompey's private cabinet, in which were contained letters from the various noblemen and senators of Rome who had sided with him.

In many a letter there was fatal evidence against the most prominent Romans, but what did Caesar do? He destroyed every document. He would have no knowledge of his enemies, for he freely forgave them and wished to know no more. In this Caesar proved that he was fit to govern the nation. But look at the splendor of God when he puts all our sins into one cabinet, and then destroys the whole. If the sins of his people are sought for, they cannot now be found. He will never mention them against us anymore forever. Oh, the goodness of the infinite God, whose mercy endures forever! Bow before that goodness with joy.

But then, observe *the freeness* of it – *He frankly forgave them both*. They did not stand there and say, "Oh, good sir, we cannot pay," and plead and beg, as for their lives; but he freely said to them, "You cannot pay, but I can forgive. You ought never to have gotten into my debt, and you ought not to have broken your promises to me; but behold, I make an end of all this weary business. I freely blot out all your obligations!" Did not this open a fountain in their eyes? Did they not hasten home to their wives and children, and tell them that they were out of debt, for the beloved creditor had forgiven it all most freely? This is a fair picture of the grace of God. When a poor sinner comes to him bankrupt, he says, "I forgive you freely; your offense is all gone. I do not want you to earn a pardon by your tears, and prayers, and anguish of soul. You do not have to make me merciful, for I am merciful already; and my dear Son Jesus Christ has made such an atoning sacrifice that I can be just and yet can forgive you all this debt. Therefore, go in peace."

Furthermore, this debt was *fully* discharged. The creditor did not say, "Come, my good fellow, I will take fifty percent of the account if you find the remainder." As they had nothing by which to pay, they would not have been a bit the better if he had reduced them ninety percent. If he had taken half the debt, the one would have owed two hundred and fifty and the other twenty-five; but still their case would have been hopeless, since they had not a farthing of their own. Now the Lord, when he blots out his people's sin, leaves no trace of it remaining. My own persuasion is that when our Lord Jesus died upon the cross, he made an end of all the sins of all his people, and made full and effective atonement for the whole of those who ever shall believe in him. I can sing with all my heart –

> Here's pardon for transgressions past,
>   It matters not how black their cast;
> And, O my soul, with wonder view,
>   For sins to come here's pardon too.

All the sin of believers has been once and for all carried into the wilderness of oblivion by our great Scapegoat, and none shall ever find a sin by which to condemn one soul of the chosen band. There is no debt left against a believer; no, not one single penny's worth of debt remains upon the score. Does not the Spirit of God himself ask the question, *Who shall lay any thing to the charge of God's elect?* (Romans 8:33). The

Lord has frankly forgiven their debt, and he has not done so in part, but as a whole. As for our sins, *the depths have covered them* (Exodus 15:5); there is not one of them left. Hallelujah!

Observe that it was a very *effective* forgiveness too. The only person that can forgive a debt is he to whom the debt is due. God only can forgive sin, seeing it is a debt to him. What do you think of those folks who are said to be able to forgive you for a shilling? Why, I say that to pay them their fee would be eleven-pence three farthings and another farthing thrown away. When you have gotten their forgiveness, what is the good of it? Suppose I were to forgive you for injuries done by you to the queen; of what value would my forgiveness be? He against whom I have transgressed is the only one that can pronounce my pardon; but if he absolves me, how effective is the sentence!

When the creditor said, "I freely forgive you both," why, the deed was done. His lips had power; he had finished the debt by his word. And so, when the Lord Jesus Christ is looked unto by the eye of faith, there comes a voice from his dear wounds that cries to the poor trembling bankrupt sinner, "Your sins, which are many, are all forgiven. I have blotted out your sins like a cloud, and like a thick cloud your iniquities." What an effective pardon it is! How it charms the heart and lulls every fear to rest! He frankly, he fully, he freely, he effectively forgave them both.

And I believe that when this is done, I may add another adjective – it is an *eternal* discharge. That creditor could never summon those debtors again for debts that he had remitted. He could never think of such a thing with any show of justice. He had frankly forgiven them, and they were forgiven. God does not play fast and loose with his creatures and forgive them and then punish them. I never shall believe in God's loving a man today and casting him away tomorrow. The gifts and calling of God are without repentance on his part. Justification is not at all an act that can be reversed and followed with damnation. No, no; *whom he justified, them he also glorified.*

> If sin be pardoned I'm secure,
>   Death has no sting beside;
> The law gave sin its damning power,
>   But Christ my ransom died.

By his death our Redeemer effectively swept away sin once and for all, and all the curse of the law he removed. In the offering of bulls and lambs there was a continual remembrance made of sin, for the blood of bulls and of goats could not take away sin; but the apostle writes, *This man, after he had offered one sacrifice for sins for ever, sat down on the right hand of God* (Hebrews 10:12), because his work was effectively and eternally done.

Only one more remark on this point. This frank forgiveness *applied to both debtors – he frankly forgave them both.* The man that owed only fifty-pence needed a free discharge as truly as the debtor who owed five hundred; for though he was not so deep in the mire, yet he was as truly in the swamp. If a man was lying in prison for debt, as men used to do under our old laws, if he only owed fifty pounds, he was shut within walls just as tightly as the greater debtor who owed fifty thousand; and he could no more get out without the payment or forgiveness of his smaller liability than the bigger debtor could. A bird held by a string is as much a prisoner as a bull that is tied by a rope.

Now, you good people who have always tried to do your duty, and are numbered with the fifty-pence debtors, you must confess that you have become somewhat indebted to God by committing a measure of sins. Take note that you cannot be saved except by the free forgiveness of God through the precious blood of Christ. The fifty-pence debtor must obtain his discharge by grace alone. It is also a most blessed thing to perceive that he forgave the five-hundred-pence debtor with equal freeness. Perhaps I have some here, men and women, who have never made any claim of being good, who from their childhood have gone from bad to worse. There is a possibility of free and instantaneous forgiveness for you at this moment. You who are over your head and ears in debt to God can be freely forgiven by the same Lord who forgives the smaller debtors.

When a man has his pen in his hand, and is writing receipts, it takes him no more trouble to write a receipt for five hundred pounds than it does for a bill of fifty – the same signature will suffice. And when the Lord has the pen of his Spirit in his hand, and he is about to write upon a conscience the peace that comes from reconciliation, he can write upon one as well as upon another. Ho! you with a little bill, bring it here so that infinite grace may write upon it "canceled!" Ho! you with a more weighty account, come and place it near that gracious right hand, for though your bill be never so long and heavy, the hand of infinite love can write "canceled" in a moment! My joy overflows at having such a gospel to preach to you: whatever your guilt, my gracious God is ready to forgive you for Jesus' sake, *because he delighteth in mercy* (Micah 7:18).

I now beg your very special attention to the last point, and that is the connection between this bankruptcy and this free discharge. It is said that when they had nothing to pay, he frankly forgave them both. There is a time when pardon comes, and that time is when self-sufficiency goes. If any person in this place has in his own conscience come to this point, that he feels he has nothing to pay, then he has come to the point at which God is ready to forgive him. He that will own his debt, and confess his own incapacity to meet it, shall find that God frankly blots it out. The Lord will never forgive us until we are brought to the starvation of pride and the death of boasting.

A sense of spiritual bankruptcy shows that a man has become *thoughtful;* and this is essential to salvation. How can we believe a thoughtless person to be a saved man? If we so think about our state as to mourn our sin and feel its wickedness, and if we have made a close search into our hearts and lives, and find that we have no merit and no might, then we are prepared in all thoughtfulness to say, *In the Lord have I righteousness and strength* (Isaiah 45:24). Must there not be serious thought before we can hope for mercy? Would you have God save us while we are asleep, while we are giddy, frivolous, trifling, and without concern about our sin? Surely that would be giving a premium to folly! God acts not so. He will have us know the seriousness of our danger, for otherwise we shall treat the whole matter with lightness, and *we* shall miss the moral effect of pardon, while *he* will be robbed of his glory.

Next, when we come to feel our bankruptcy, we then *make an honest confession,* and to that confession a promise is given – *Whoso confesseth and forsaketh [his sin] shall have mercy* (Proverbs 28:13). The two debtors had owned up to their debts, and they had also openly confessed, though it must have gone against the grain a bit, that they could not pay. They humbled themselves before their creditor, and then he said, "I frankly forgive you." If one of these debtors had bounced and bragged,

"Oh, we can pay," then in all probability he would have been sent to prison. As for you, poor trembling one, I do not know where you are this morning, but here is comfort for you: when you go unto God in your chamber and cry, "Lord, have mercy upon me, for I am guilty, and I cannot justify myself before you, nor offer any excuse to you," then it is that he will say, *Be of good cheer; [I have] put away thy sin; thou shalt not die* (Matthew 9:2; 2 Samuel 12:13). When you have nothing to pay and you confess your failure, the debt shall be wiped out. When you are brought to your worst, you shall see the Lord at his best.

It is in their utter destitution that *men value a discharge.* If God were to give his mercy to every man at once, without his ever having had any sense of sin at all, why, men would count it cheap and think nothing of it. "God is merciful" is a common saying everywhere; and it is such a bit of valueless talk with them, that they let it roll glibly out as if it were no matter. They do not worship him for his mercy or serve him for his grace. They say, "Oh, God is merciful," and then they go on to sin worse than ever; the idea has no effect upon their hearts or lives; they have no esteem for that mercy of which they speak so freely. So the Lord takes care that the sinner shall know his need of mercy by feeling the pinch of conscience and the terror of the law.

If I may so speak, he puts in the sheriff's officer, and puts a distress upon the soul by convincing the man of sin, of righteousness, and of judgment. The Lord puts an execution into the heart, and then it is, when the poor creature cries, "I have nothing to pay with," that free discharge is given by the Lord, and heartily prized by him to whom it comes. When our account is long and heavy, it is a blessed thing to see the Lord write "Canceled," and to behold the whole mountain of debt swallowed up in the sea of love. Christ is precious when sin is bitter. Is it not wise on God's part that the canceling of the debt shall come just when we have nothing to pay, and therefore are prepared to prize a free forgiveness?

Under conviction a poor soul *sees the reality of sin and of pardon.* My dear friend, you will never believe in the reality of forgiveness until you have felt the reality of sin. I remember when I felt the burden of sin, and though I was but a child, my heart failed me for anguish, and I was brought very low. Sin was no source of dread to scare me, it was a grim reality; as a lion it tore me in pieces. And now, today, I know the reality of pardon; it is no delusion, no dream, for my inmost soul feels its power. I know that my sins are forgiven, and I rejoice therein; but I would never have known the real truth of this happy condition if I had not felt the oppressive load of sin upon the conscience. I could not afford to play at conversion, for sin was an awful fact in my soul.

Our heavenly Father does not wish us to lack seriousness in a matter concerning which Jesus shed his blood, and so he brings us into trouble of soul, and afterwards into a vivid realization of free grace. He lets the whip fall on our shoulders until we bleed again, and this makes us weary of the slavery of sin. He sets conscience and the law upon us, and these two jailers thrust us into the inner dungeon and hold our feet firmly in the stocks. All this prepares us for the delivering power that shakes the prison walls and loosens our bonds, and for the tender love that washes our stripes and sets food before us.

I do believe that the Lord will give us our recompense when we have come to our last farthing, and not until then, because *only then do we look to the Lord Jesus Christ*. Ah, my dear friends, as long as we have anything else to look to, we never will look to Christ. That blessed port into which no ship did ever run in a storm without finding a sure haven is shunned by all your gallant vessels. They would rather put into any port along the coast of self-deceit than head for the harbor that is marked out by the two lighthouses of free grace and dying love. As long as a man can scrape the meal-barrel and find a little in it, as long as he can hold up the oil-jar, and it drips, if it only yields a drop in a week, he will never come to Christ for heavenly provision. As long as he has one rusty counterfeit farthing hidden away in the corner of a drawer, the sinner will never accept the riches of redeeming love; but when it is all over with him, when he has nothing in the parlor, nothing in the kitchen, nothing in the cellar, and when there is neither stick nor stock left, then he prizes Jesus and his salvation.

We break to make. We are emptied to be filled. When we cannot give, God can forgive. If any of you have any goodness of your own, you will perish forever. If you have anything you can trust in of your own, you will be lost as sure as you are living men and women. But if you are reduced to sore extremity, and God's fierce wrath seems to burn against you, then not only may you have mercy, but mercy is also yours already.

'Tis perfect poverty alone
    That sets the soul at large;
While we can call one mite our own
    We get no full discharge.

But let our debts be what they may,
    However great or small,
As soon as we have nought to pay
    Our Lord forgives us all.

Blessed are you poor, for you shall be rich! Blessed are you hungry, for you shall be fed! Blessed are you who are empty, for you shall be filled! But woe unto you that are rich and are increased in goods, and have need of nothing, and boast of your own goodness! Christ has nothing to do with you, and we have nothing to preach to you except this – *They that be whole need not a physician* (Matthew 9:12). The heavenly Surgeon did not come to save those who have no need of saving. Let those who are sick prick up their ears and hear with delight, for the Physician has come with a special eye to them. Are you a sinner? Then Christ is the Savior of sinners. Join hands with him by faith and trust him who died for sinners for salvation. God bless you, in the name of the Lord Jesus Christ. Amen.

Chapter 2

Love's Competition

Tell me therefore, which of them will love him most?
Simon answered and said, I suppose that he, to whom he
forgave most. And he said unto him, Thou hast rightly
judged. (Luke 7:42-43)

I remember seeing, somewhere or other, as a sign upon an inn, the words "The First and Last." I do not know what that may happen to mean among men, but I know that love is God's first and last. It is there that he begins with us in mercy – *We love him, because he first loved us* (1 John 4:19). His love at the first springs up like a fountain in the midst of a desert, and freely flows along the wilderness to the unworthy sons of men. In the end, the result of that love is that men love him: they cannot help it anymore than the rock can prevent the echo when the voice falls upon it.

Love is not a creature of law: it comes not on demand; it must be free or not at all. It has its reasons why it springs up in our hearts, but it is not a mercenary thing that can be procured at such and such a price. It is not a matter of argument: it is not to itself an act performed as a matter of duty. Love is a duty certainly, but it does not come to us that way: it comes to us like a doe or a young deer, over every mountain and hill, leaping and bounding; it comes not as a heavy burden dragged along an iron way. If a man should give all the substance of his house for love, it would utterly be scorned.

Men do not make themselves love by a course of calculation, but they are overtaken with it and carried away by its power. When godly men consider and enjoy the great love of God for them, they begin to love God in return, just as the bud, when it feels the sunshine, opens to it of its own accord. Love for God is a sort of natural consequence that follows from a sight and sense of the love of God for us. I think it is Aristotle who says that it is impossible for a person to know that he is loved without feeling some degree of love in return. I do not know how that may be, for I am no philosopher; but I am sure that it is so with those who taste of the love of God. As love is the first blessing coming from God to us, so it is the last return from us to God: he comes to us loving, we go home to him loving.

First notice that it is taken for granted that pardoned sinners will love. *Tell me therefore, which of them will love him most?* It is implied that the two debtors who had been frankly forgiven would both love their benefactor. The question was not, "Which of them will love him?" but "Which of them will love him *most?*" So then, I say, it is taken for granted in the text that those who are pardoned will love him who has so freely pardoned them.

And this, first, because *it seems most natural that where kindness is received, gratitude should be felt.* This is so generally admitted that gratitude is found among the lowest and worst of mankind. *If ye love them which love you, what thank have ye? for sinners also love those that love them* (Luke 6:32). It is manlike to return good for good, and ingratitude is looked upon most rightly as one of the vilest of the vices. Why, we find gratitude not only in men and women – intelligent creatures – but we also find it in the very beasts of the field! *The ox knoweth his owner, and the donkey his master's crib* (Isaiah 1:3). How a dog that has received benefits from you will be attached to you, and by every possible means will endeavor to show his affection!

The ancients had many rare stories of the gratitude of wild beasts. You remember that of Androcles and the lion. The man was condemned to be torn to pieces by beasts; but a lion, to which he was cast, instead of devouring him, licked his feet, because at some former time Androcles had extracted a thorn from the grateful creature's foot. We have heard of an eagle that so loved a boy whom he had played with, that when the child was sick, the eagle became sick too; and when the child slept, this wild, strange bird of the air would sleep, but only then; for when the child awoke, the eagle awoke. When the child died, the bird died too.

You remember that there is a picture in which Napoleon is represented as riding over the battlefield, and he stops his horse, as he sees a slain man with his favorite dog lying upon his bosom doing what he can to defend his poor dead master. Even the great manslayer paused at such a sight. There is gratitude among the beasts of the field, and the birds of the air. And, surely, if we receive favors from God, and do not feel love for him in return, we are worse than brute beasts; and so the Lord, in that pathetic verse in Isaiah, pleads against us: *The ox knoweth his owner, and the donkey his master's crib: but Israel doth not know, my people doth not consider* (Isaiah 1:3). If we receive favors from God, it is but natural that we should love him in return. Alas, that many should be so unnatural, so false to every noble instinct, so dead to the gratitude that goodness deserves!

But gratitude should surely arise when the benefit is surpassingly great. When favors are far above the common run of blessings – when these favors are not such as are confined to time and to the body, but when they reach to eternity and bless the soul; when favors are of such weight as the forgiveness of sin, the salvation of the soul from wrath to come – then surely here love must spring up with the greatest force and freedom. I would stand and sing to the fountain of the heart as Israel did in the wilderness, *Spring up, O well; sing ye unto it: The princes digged the well* (Numbers 21:17-18). And has not our great Prince, who has been struck upon the cheek, dug this well by giving us, through his free grace and dying love, to taste of full remission and complete pardon of our guilt?

Shall we not, must we not, love the Redeemer in return? To have sin forgiven and not to love God! I call common ingratitude worse than brutal; but in this case where shall I go for a word? I must call it devilish. It would be worse than damnable to receive a deliverance from guilt so great, and from punishment so justly terrible, and not to love the Lord through whom it is given to us. Oh, love the Lord, whose mercy endures forever! If, indeed, you have tasted of that mercy, you must love him. It cannot be otherwise – you are bound to God by bonds of love, and these draw you, by a secret but irresistible force, to love the Lord in return.

And moreover, not only is this natural and necessary, because of the greatness of the mercy, but also *the grace of God always takes care that wherever pardon is given love shall be guaranteed;* for the Holy Spirit cooperates with the work of Christ, and if we are cleansed from the stain of our former evil through the blood of Christ, we are renewed and changed in the spirit of our minds by the Holy Spirit. He does not take away our sin and then leave us with that old heart of stone, insensible, and ungrateful; but as he gives us a garment of righteousness, he gives us a heart of flesh. The Spirit works in us a degree of love at the same time that he creates the first look of faith. Immediately our faith increases by which we received remission, and then he works in us more and more that love for Christ by which we cling to him.

This love works in us a hatred of sin and a spirit of obedience, whereby we yield ourselves up to the service of him who has bought us with his precious blood. You know that it is so, brethren. Where pardon comes, delight in God comes with it. You know that God does not divide his gifts, and give justification to one and sanctification to another; but the covenant is one, and the blessings of the covenant are threaded on the one string of infinite wisdom, so that when there comes the washing in the blood, there comes also a cleansing with water by the Word. The Holy Spirit washes us from the power of sin, as the blood of Christ cleanses us from the guilt of sin. Where sin is forgiven, there must be love for the God who forgave it, because the Spirit of God makes sure work upon the heart of the believer, and one of his first works is love.

I need not argue this further, because all Christians know this as a matter of fact – *where there is no love there is no pardon.* You cannot be pardoned and not love God as a result of his loving forgiveness. What was the very first emotion that you and I felt when we had a sense of guilt removed? We felt joy for our own sake; but immediately after, or at the same moment, we felt such intense gratitude to God that we loved him beyond all expression. We have sometimes been half afraid that we do not love God as much now as we did at that moment, though I trust that that fear is groundless. But at that moment there was nothing too hot or too heavy for us to have attempted on behalf of him who had taken the burden from off our shoulder. We would have said at that moment, "Here am I; send me," if it had been to prison or to death.

Oh, the joy of those first days! They are rightly called the days of our betrothal. And what love we had then! We were willing to leave all for the Lord's sake. We snapped fond connections at his command. Truly, like Israel of old, we would have gone after our God into the wilderness – alas, after our Savior into the grave. Nothing could have kept us back or caused us to wander from him then. Do you not remember how you used to long for Sabbath days, to hear of Jesus, and praise his name with his people? If there was a weeknight service, you were always there, though no one persuaded you to go. Then, any corner in the meetinghouse was good enough for you.

Now, perhaps, you want a very soft cushion to sit upon. You sat then in a straight-backed pew and did not know it. Now, you want very tender interactions; and the preacher must take care that he interests you by illustrations and poetical allusions. But before then, the gospel itself interested you, and however dull the preacher might have been, you were so willing to hear about Jesus, and to know of his love, that there you were, eager to hear the humblest evangelist. Wisdom did not need to press you into her house, for you were earnestly waiting at the posts of her doors, glad to hear even the footfalls of those who came in and out. Oh, those were brave days! I hope that we have braver days now; but, for certain, as sure as we knew our pardon, we felt that we loved the Lord with all our heart.

Now I want to make a little practical use of this inference from the text. That pardoned souls love their pardoning God is a great truth, and a very solemn one in its bearings upon us at this time, for there are persons in this house of prayer who are not forgiven, and we are sure of that unhappy fact, since they do not love God. Their sins must be still upon them, because they have not the token of pardon, inasmuch as they have no love for Jesus Christ our Lord.

Oh, listen to me, you who do not love God, and yet, perhaps, dream that you are saved! Are there not some here that seldom think of God, who do not care if a day, a week, a month, a year should pass over their heads, and yet they have no thought of the almighty judge of all the earth? They receive his mercies, but they do not thank him. They feel his power, but they do not fear him. "God is not in all their thoughts." O my friend, if this be your situation, you do not love him; for if we love any person, we are sure to think of him. Thoughts fly that way in which the heart moves. I do not say that we are always thinking of those we love, but I do say that our thoughts will fly that way when they can.

You know at sunset where the crows live. Perhaps all day long you are unable to tell, for they may fly from one plowed field to another to find their meat. But watch when night comes on, and when they are free from other obligations, and wish to find rest, they fly straight to those tall trees on which they have built their nests. A man may, in the busy time of the day, think about fifty things; but let him be free from pressing labor and care, and he returns to his love as birds fly to their nests at night. His thought flies to Jesus, because Jesus is the home of his heart. If your hearts love God, your thoughts will run to him as the rivers run to the sea. Yes, and often in the very middle of business, the man who loves his God will be speaking with him. He may not interrupt the conversation, and those in the shop may not know what is on his mind; but his heart will be up above the mountains, where the angels dwell, communing with the great Father of lights. But where there is no thought of God, there is no love for him.

Are there not many who never *do* anything for God? He has made them, and he preserves them, and yet they never make him any return by way of willing action designed to give him pleasure. I may put it to some of you – did you ever do anything distinctly for God in all your lives? What! Not so much as once? Ah, me! a man so curiously made by the divine finger, displaying infinite skill in every blood vessel, and nerve, and muscle, that are necessary for his life and motion, and yet he has never thought of the Great One who has set all this machinery in motion, and keeps it in action! To live only by God, and yet to live without him! Strange! Can there exist a man who never does anything for his God who is constantly doing so much for him? If so, I would say to such a one, You have never been pardoned, for you do not love God, since you never think of him, and you do nothing for him.

Some men evidently do not love God, for they have *no care* about anything that concerns him. They do not refrain from sin because sin would grieve God. The idea of grieving God, perhaps, has not crossed their minds; so they vex the Holy Spirit most thoughtlessly. But, ah! if you love anyone, you will not like to cause him grief; you will not do the evil thing which he hates. He who loves God will often have a check put upon him, and will feel that he cannot do this great wickedness, and sin against God. To sin against God is the greatest of sins, and the essence of sin. The venom of sin lies there. This makes sin so exceedingly sinful, that it is against the God of love. But if you never felt that, then you do not love him, and, for certain, you are not forgiven.

Look at others: they do not love God, for they do not care *for his house* where his people meet. They seldom come to the meeting for worship; and if they come, it is from some other motive than to meet with God. They do not care for *his day.* Sundays are very dreary in London, so they say. There is nothing to interest them, for they have no interest in the great Father, or his incarnate Son; they do not care to hear of him, or to praise him, or to pray to him. They do not care for *his Book,* though it is a world of delights and comforts. The Bible is perfumed with the love of God, but they perceive not its fragrance. The Savior's face is to be seen reflected in almost every page, and yet some think that the Bible is more dull than an old almanac; and, though they must keep it in their house – for it is respectable to have a copy of it – yet to read it, and to read it with pleasure, why, that has never happened to them, nor is there any likelihood that it ever will unless they get made anew.

Nor do they care for *God's people.* In fact, they like a quiet joke against Christian people; and sometimes, if they can see faults in them – and, oh, how readily they may! – they report those faults with considerable exaggerations, and feel pleased to eat up the faults of God's people as they eat bread! Lack of love for the children indicates lack of love for their Father. *Every one that loveth him that begat loveth him also that is begotten of him* (1 John 5:1); and we know that we love God when we love his children. But if in your heart there is no such love for his children, for his Book, for his day, for his house, or for his service, you may rest quite certain, my friend, that your guilt clings to you still. You are unpardoned, and God will require that which is past, and call you to account. For every secret thing he will bring you into judgment, and for every idle word that you have spoken he will take a reckoning of you. Ah! how sad it is that when I am longing to speak joyously about the love that arises out of pardoned sin, I am compelled, for pity's sake, to turn aside to give a warning to many who, having no love for God, prove by that fact that they have never been forgiven!

So, I leave the first point. It is supposed in the text, and taken for granted, that all pardoned sinners will love him who has pardoned them.

But now, secondly, it is suggested in the text, that there are differences of degree in the matter of love for God. *Tell me therefore, which of them will love him most?* These words evidently show that some persons love God more than others, and that, albeit there must be a sincere love for God in all pardoned sinners, yet there is not the same degree of love. Love is evidently a grace that is not stereotyped and cast in a mold, so as to be the same in every case and at every time. *Love is a thing of life; it is, therefore, a thing of growth.* It is certainly so in our own selves.

There was a time when we did not love God as much as we do now; and I grieve to say that there are even now times when we do not love God as much as we once did, for we grow cold and backsliding. Love is not like a piece of cast iron, fixed and set; but it grows, and has its times of budding, flowering, and leaf shedding. It is like a fire; at one time it may burn low, and at another time it may be blown up to a very vehement heat. Love rises and falls: I speak not of God's love for us, but of our love for God. It has its ups and downs, its summers and its winters, its flood-tides and its ebbs; and if we find a change in love, in the same heart, we are not at all astonished that it should differ in different hearts.

Besides, we know that there are differences in love because *there are differences in all the other graces.* Faith – some men have much faith. God be thanked that there are men of strong faith still on the face of the earth! But there are others who have a faith which, though a true faith, is a very weak one. It is a trembling faith. It cannot walk the waves with Peter, but it can sink with him, and it can cry out for deliverance. Faith, in some Christians, seems to be a very feeble affair. As I said the other day, they hardly know whether it is faith or unbelief. Their cry is, *Lord, I believe; help thou mine unbelief* (Mark 9:24), as if they had made a mistake in calling it faith at all, for it was so mixed with unbelief.

It is not always such an infant grace, for there are strong believers who have put to flight the armies of the aliens – men who have borne their cross without impatience, and their testimony without cowardice; men who have conquered sin and lived in holiness, and brought glory to God. Faith, like a ladder, has its lower and its higher rungs. Faith has its dawning, its noon, its shade. We are sure that it is so, for we have observed it in ourselves and have seen it in others. We have seen it great, and we have seen it little.

The practical point I would reach is just this: *Let us look, first of all, to our love in its sincerity.* What if my love may not be compared with yours as to degree? Yet the Lord grant that I may truly love him. Peter could not say that he loved Christ more than others, but he did say, *Thou knowest all things; thou knowest that I love thee* (John 21:17). A little pearl is a pearl as much as a great one is, though every one of us would sooner have the greater pearl. There is the queen's image on a fourpenny piece as certainly as there is upon the gold coin, though we would all prefer the gold coin. There is the image of God on all his people's faith and love, whether great or little. The main thing with the coin is to be sure that it is genuine metal. So, if love be real love, that is the main point. Do you love the Lord with all your heart? If so, strive to have more love, but do not fling away what you have, for you would thus despise what the Spirit of God has effected in you.

Endeavor also, dear friends, to have growing love. Do not be satisfied to be today what you were twelve months ago. I am afraid that some Christians do not grow much. I am very glad when I see them grow downward, when they are rooted in humility, when they have truer views of themselves than they ever had before, and a deeper sense of their indebtedness to God. That is good growth. Try to have, however, a love that grows, so that you may more forcibly love Jesus Christ than you did in days that are past. Do say to yourself, "Well, if I have ever so little love, it shall be practical love, and I will show it. I will be doing something for my Lord."

The woman by whose means this parable was called forth loved Christ so much that she brought her alabaster box of ointment, and anointed his feet, and washed them with tears, and wiped them with the hair of her head. And one of the best ways to make love grow is to use all the love you have. Is it not so with merchants and their money? If they want to increase their capital, they trade with it. If you want to increase your love for Jesus, use it. Do not merely talk about it, but actually serve him under its sweet constraint. It is a very poor Christianity that consists in sitting still and dreaming, and never attempting any practical service for Jesus, our Lord. He that thinks that he will quietly enjoy religion all alone will soon find that he has very little of it to enjoy, for doubts and fears will breed in swarms in a stagnant atmosphere. Where there is none of the blessed wind of activity, there will soon be mists and dampness – perhaps foul gas and fevers.

And if you have but little love at present, *cry to God to give you a more intense love;* and, though I have said that to use your love is a good way to increase it, yet there is something still better, and that is to know more and feel more of the love of Christ for you. If you exercise, you will increase your sense of warmth; but it will be a far surer thing if you get where the sun shines with equatorial heat. So other means are good, but to get near to Jesus is best of all. In proportion as you live close to the glorious central sun of the love of Christ, you will yourself be warm. I was about to compare the heart of my Lord to a volcanic mountain constantly streaming with the burning lava of love. Oh, that my soul could but get that firestorm poured into it to set the whole of my nature on fire and consume me in the flaming torrent of love!

You see that it is suggested in the text that there are differences in the degrees of love; and there let us leave it, for we must come to the third point.

Thirdly, the text puts to us a question: *Which of them will love him most?*

I want to introduce the question to you by saying that it is a *very interesting one.* After what the Lord has done for us, one takes pleasure in thinking what will come of it. One likes to think of the farmer's harvest. After all that plowing and sowing, what will come of it? It is interesting to begin to calculate the crop, and to anticipate the shouts of harvest home. Now, what will come of infinite love, the supreme act of God's heart to men? What will come out of the gift of his only begotten Son, and the putting away of sin through the death of Jesus? What will men do for God after this? How much will they love him? It is an interesting question. What have you to say upon it?

And it is *a personal question,* which the Lord puts to each one of us. You know he put it to Simon. *Tell me therefore,* said he, *which of them will love him most?* And he puts it to us to consider it, to turn it over, and to give our own verdict, because there may be some blunder in our heart that this question is meant to set right; and the thoughts that the question will bring about in the spirit are meant to correct our judgments. Therefore, do not put it aside, but try now to answer it as the Lord puts it.

It is *a practical question – Which of them will love him most? –* for everything in conduct depends upon love. Where there is much love, there is sure to be much service in proportion to the strength. Give us a church that loves Christ Jesus much. You will have mighty prayer meetings; you will have a holy membership; you will have liberal giving to the cause of Christ; you will have hearty praising of his name; you will have careful walking before the world; you will have earnest endeavors for the conversion of sinners. Missions at home and abroad will be set on foot when love is fervent. When the heart is right, everything is likely to be right; but when the heart goes wrong, oh, what a fatal thing it is! A disease of the heart is looked upon as the worst of mischiefs that can happen to a man. One old doctor of my acquaintance used to say, "We can do nothing with the heart." God keep us from a diseased heart: a fatty degeneration of the heart, or a hardening of the heart towards the Lord Jesus Christ!

The question asked in the text is, however, *a somewhat limited one.* It is not, Who in all the world will love Christ most? but who out of two persons, in whom there is no particular difference of character, but only this one difference – that the one owes five hundred-pence, and the other fifty – which out of these two will love Christ most? We will suppose that they are equally tender of heart, and equally born again; and that they do know, each of them, certainly, that their debt has been discharged. The only difference between them is that one has been a grosser sinner than the other; and the question asked is: "Which of those two will love the Savior most?"

It is *a very simple question,* too, not at all hard to answer; for even this Simon, the Pharisee, who, like the rest of the Pharisees, was very badly instructed, yet, nevertheless, could see his way to answer the question correctly. So he answered, *I suppose that he, to whom he forgave most;* and the Lord replied, *Thou hast rightly judged.* Thus, I have set before you the question.

And so, lastly, it is expected that we give a reply; and I do wish for myself – and therefore wish the same for you – that each one of us may say, "I am the man that ought to love the Lord Jesus most; and by his grace I will surely do so."

The most indebted should love most. Have we not here many

five-hundred-pence debtors? Some of my dear brethren present here were among outward sinners the very chief – men who could drink, and swear, and lie, ringleaders in everything that was evil. Blessed be God that such have been here led to Jesus! We heard the other night a dear brother tell us of what he used to be. With modesty and shamefaced-ness, he mentioned how great his sin had been, but his sin was put away; he was pardoned, and he knew it, and rejoiced in it. Such a man must say, "I will love him most." Where there has been overt sin, noticeable, undeniable – where the outward character has been defiled and stained with it – forgiveness involves us in deep obligation to grateful love. You may stand in the front rank, and love Jesus most.

But I am not going to let you rise to that supremacy of obligation, or rather sink to that depth of indebtedness without having a struggle for it myself. Some of us take that place of distinguished obligation on another ground, and yet it is the same ground; for while some of us never were openly profane, or drunken, or immoral, we have to con-fess the equal greatness of our sin on account of our offending against light and knowledge, against early convictions, against a holy training, against a tender conscience, against unique favors received from God; and therefore with shame we begin to take the lowest room, acknowl-edging that to us belongs the greatest debt of grateful praise to God. When I was preaching once I said – and I meant it – that I should be the deepest debtor to divine grace that ever entered the gates of glory, and I ventured to say,

> Then loudest of the crowd I'll sing,
>   While heaven's resounding mansions ring,
> With shouts of sovereign grace.

It was in a country place, and as I came down the pulpit stairs many clustered around me to shake hands, and one old lady said to me, "You made one great blunder in your sermon." I said, "My dear soul, I dare say I made a score of them. I am a great blunderer." "No," said she, "but you said that you would sing the loudest when you get to heaven; but you shall not, for I owe more to divine grace than you can possibly owe. I was once a great sinner, and I have had much forgiven, and therefore

I shall praise God more than you." I did not yield the point, but I held my tongue. I could let her be first, and yet take the same place myself. As I went down the aisle, many friends declared that they would not give way to me in that point, and that they ought to praise God more than I, for they owed him more.

It was a happy controversy. It reminded me of Ralph Erskine's "Contention among the Birds of Paradise," where he represents the saints in glory, each saying that he shall lie the lowest, and shall praise the most sweetly the infinite love of God. I think that there are grounds upon which some here, who have been kept from everything that is out-wardly evil, may, nevertheless, feel that inwardly they are five-hundred-pence debtors; and so, when the question is asked, "Which will love him most?" they will say, "Why, I! I was not so honest as some of those wicked fellows; I did not dare to say all they said, nor to be as openly vile as they were; but I was quite as bad at heart, and if I dare have had my full swing, I should have been as vile as they were."

But I do not think that the spirit of the parable is exhausted by either of these cases. I think it includes more. There are some who evidently have not had more sins forgiven than others as to outward sin; on the contrary, they have been prudently brought up from their childhood, and yet for many a year they have been foremost in service, and have been special lovers of the Lord. Though by no means great offenders in their unconverted state, they are certainly great saints now – intense in their service, consistent in their character, fervent in their love. How is it that some who shout that they have been snatched from the burning, and according to their own statement were the very chief of sinners, and make a great trumpet-blowing over their own conversion, yet do not love the Lord Jesus one-half so much as these dear, quiet souls who never went into open sin?

I take it that the reason is this. Our estimate of sin is, after all, the thing that will create and inflame our love; for if a man thinks sin to be exceedingly sinful, and feels it to be so, he *has a deeper sense of his indebtedness* than the man who may have committed grosser sins, but has never seen them in their real wickedness, as they appear in the light of God's countenance. Too many believers know little of what it is to be amazed and astounded at the heinousness of their transgressions.

Why, time was with me – and is now – when, if I had inadvertently spoken a word that was not exactly true, it cost me more pain to think of what was only a hasty error than it has cost many men to repent of their cursing and swearing.

I am sorry to say it, but I believe that some make a glory of their shame and dare to brag about what they used to be. They stand up and make confession without a tear in their eye, or a blush on their cheek. Such testimony ought never to be heard, for it is a positive creator of evil in the minds of those that hear it. I am sorry to have to say it, but I know that it is so. Testimonies are published which are provocations to sin, and rather tend to make men immoral than make them turn to God. In certain circles he is treated as a hero who can prove that he has been a great rascal. It was not thus that the prodigal was received by his father: he never hung up his old rags as a trophy.

O brethren, when we talk about what we were, we had better veil our faces. Our former follies are things to be confessed to God in secret; and if they must be spoken in public, to the praise of divine grace, there must be a careful avoidance of anything like boasting, *for it is a shame even to speak of those things that [were] done of them in secret* (Ephesians 5:12). When there is really a deep sense of sin, there is a holy, delicate way of speaking of it. Old sins are not to be talked of as an old soldier shoulders his crutch and shows how fields were won. A crimson blush is the best color to wear when we speak of our lost estate. To talk smilingly of injuries done to the delicacy of our own conscience, of awful injuries done to others by a foul example, is not to glorify God but to enthrone sin.

And, dear friends, I believe that some, whom God has preserved by preventing grace from going into great sin, will, nevertheless, love him most because *they have a clearer view than others of what it cost in order that they might be pardoned.* Happy are they who remember well the griefs of our Lord in the garden of Gethsemane.

> There's ne'er a gift his hand bestows
> But cost his heart a groan.

Oh, if your heart dwells on Calvary, where falls the crimson shower of Christ's most precious blood – if you gaze intently upon the wounds of Jesus until you die into the death of the Crucified One, then do you love much. It is well to have the soul torn with anguish because

> It cost him cries and tears
>   To bring us near to God:
> Great was our debt, and he appears
>   To make the payment good.

For, in proportion as you estimate the sacrifice, you will love him whose own self was the sacrifice for sin. Brethren, I hope you all love Christ Jesus more than I do; for I would have him possess the highest love of every human heart, and yet I will not be willingly exceled by any one of you in a competition of love for Jesus. I will run my very best so that no man take my crown.

But supposing, dear friends, any of you do love him most, then *show it,* just as that woman did who brought the alabaster box of precious ointment. If you love him most, *do most.* Do everything that is possible to humanity, energized by the Spirit of God. If you have done much, do ten times more. Never talk of what you have done, but go on to something else. An officer rode up to his general and said, "Sir, we have taken two guns from the enemy." "It is well," said the general. "Take two more."

If you have the most love for Christ, then do the most spiritual good to men. Yet *do something distinctly for Jesus.* It is a blessed token for good when our work among men is not so much for the sake of sinners as for love of Jesus. When we love the brethren, it should be because they belong to Christ. It is sweet to serve the Lord Christ himself. See how the holy woman offered homage distinctly to her Lord: tears for his travel stains, hair to wipe his feet, ointment to anoint his flesh. Do your choicest and best for Jesus, for Jesus personally.

Try to do it most humbly. Stand behind him. Do not ask anybody to look at you. Do it very quietly. Do it, feeling that it is a great honor to be permitted to do the least service for Jesus. Do not dream of saying, "I am somebody. I am doing great things. I do more even than Simon, the Pharisee. Come see my zeal for the Lord of Hosts." Jehu talked in that fashion, but he was good for nothing. Do your personal part without seeking to be seen of men.

Do it self-sacrificingly. Bring your best ointment. Pinch yourself for Christ. Make sacrifices – go without this and that to have something with which you can do him honor.

Do it very repentantly. When you serve him best, still let the tears fall on his feet, mingling with the costly ointment. The tears and the ointment go well together. Mourn your guilt, while you rejoice in his grace.

Do it continuously. This woman, said Christ, *since the time I came in hath not ceased to kiss my feet* (Luke 7:45). Do not cease loving him and serving him. Do it on, and on, and on, however much the flesh may ask for respite from service.

Do it enthusiastically. See how she kissed his feet; nothing less than this would express her love. Stoop down, and kiss and kiss again those blessed feet that traveled so far in love for you. Throw your whole soul into your deed of love. "Why," they will say, "Mrs. So-and-so is enthusiastic. She is quite carried away by her zeal." Let it be true, more and more. Never mind what the coldhearted think, for they cannot understand you. They will say, "Ah! that young person is too fast by half." Never mind. Be faster still. Wise people cry out, "He has too many irons in the fire." But I say to you, blow up the fire; get all the irons red-hot; and hammer away with all your might. With all your strength and energy plunge into the service of your Master. If you love your Master, you can best show your love by passionate service. The Lord bless you with the utmost degree of love, in the Lord Jesus Christ's name. Amen.

Chapter 3

The Good Samaritan

*And, behold, a certain lawyer stood up, and tempted him, say-
ing, Master, what shall I do to inherit eternal life? He said unto
him, What is written in the law? how readest thou? And he
answering said, Thou shalt love the Lord thy God with all thy
heart, and with all thy soul, and with all thy strength, and with
all thy mind; and thy neighbour as thyself. And he said unto
him, Thou hast answered right: this do, and thou shalt live.
But he, willing to justify himself, said unto Jesus, And who is
my neighbour? And Jesus answering said, A certain man went
down from Jerusalem to Jericho, and fell among thieves, which
stripped him of his raiment, and wounded him, and departed,
leaving him half dead. And by chance there came down a
certain priest that way: and when he saw him, he passed by on
the other side. And likewise a Levite, when he was at the place,
came and looked on him, and passed by on the other side. But
a certain Samaritan, as he journeyed, came where he was: and
when he saw him, he had compassion on him, and went to
him, and bound up his wounds, pouring in oil and wine, and
set him on his own beast, and brought him to an inn, and took
care of him. And on the morrow when he departed, he took out
two pence, and gave them to the host, and said unto him, Take
care of him; and whatsoever thou spendest more, when I come
again, I will repay thee. Which now of these three, thinkest
thou, was neighbour unto him that fell among the thieves? And
he said, He that shewed mercy on him. Then said Jesus unto
him, Go, and do thou likewise. (Luke 10:25-37)*

Our text is the whole story of the Samaritan; but as that is very long, suppose, for our memories' sake, we consider the exhortation in the thirty-seventh verse to be our text. *Go, and do thou likewise.*

There are certain persons in the world who will not allow the preacher to speak upon anything but those doctrinal statements concerning the way of salvation that are known as "the gospel." If the preacher shall insist upon some virtue or practical grace, they immediately say that he was not preaching the gospel, that he became legal, and was a mere moral teacher. We do not stand in any awe of such criticism, for we clearly perceive that our Lord Jesus Christ himself would very frequently have come under it. Read the Sermon on the Mount and judge whether certain people would be content to hear the like of it preached to them on the Sabbath. They would condemn it as containing very little gospel and too much about good works.

Our Lord was a great practical preacher. He frequently delivered addresses in which he made an answer to questioners, or gave direction to seekers, or rebuked offenders, and he gave a prominence to practical truth such as some of his ministers dared not imitate. Jesus tells us over and over again the manner in which we are to live towards our fellow man, and he lays great stress upon the love which should shine throughout the Christian character. The story of the Good Samaritan, which is now before us, is a case in point, for our Lord is there explaining a point which arose out of the question, *What shall I do to inherit eternal life?* The question is legal, and the answer is to the point. But let it never be forgotten that what the law demands of us the gospel really produces in us.

The law tells us what we ought to be, and it is one object of the gospel to raise us to that condition. Therefore, our Savior's teaching, though it be very practical, is always evangelical, for even in expounding the law he always has a gospel design. Two ends are served by his setting up a high standard of duty: on the one hand, he slays the self-righteousness that claims to have kept the law by making men feel the impossibility of salvation by their own works; and, on the other hand, he calls believers away from all contentment with the mere decencies of life and the routine of outward religion, and stimulates them to seek after the highest degree of holiness – indeed, after that excellence of character which only his grace can give.

This morning I trust that though I keep very much to practical points, I shall be guided by the Spirit of holiness, and shall not really be guilty of legality, nor will any of you be led into it. I shall not hold up the love of our neighbor as a condition of salvation, but as a fruit of it. I shall not speak of obedience to the law as the road to heaven, but I shall show you the pathway that is to be followed by the faith that works by love.

Let us proceed to the parable at once.

Our first observation will be that the world is very full of affliction. This story is but one among a thousand based upon an unhappy occurrence. *A certain man went down from Jerusalem to Jericho, and fell among thieves.* He went upon a short journey, and almost lost his life on the road. We are never secure from trouble; it meets us around the family hearth, and causes us to suffer in our own persons or in those of the dearest relatives; it walks into our shops and countinghouses, and tests us; and when we leave home it becomes our fellow traveler, and communes with us on the road. *Although affliction cometh not forth of the dust, neither doth trouble spring out of the ground; yet man is born unto trouble, as the sparks fly upward* (Job 5:6-7).

Frequently, the greater afflictions *are not caused by the fault of the sufferer.* Nobody could blame the poor Jew that when he was going down to Jericho about his business the thieves surrounded him, and demanded his money, and that when he made some little resistance they wounded him, stripped him, and left him half dead. How could he be blamed? It was to him a pure misfortune.

Believe me, there is a great deal of sorrow in the world that does not arise out of the sin or folly of the persons enduring it; it comes from the hand of God upon the sufferer, not because he is a sinner above others, but for wise ends unknown to us. Now, this is the kind of distress which above all others demands Christian sympathy, and the very kind which abounds in our hospitals. The man is not to blame for lying there beaten and bruised: those gaping wounds from which his life is oozing are not of his own inflicting, nor were they received in a drunken brawl or through attempting a foolhardy feat; he suffers from no fault of his own, and therefore he has a pressing claim upon the benevolence of his fellow man.

Still, *very much distress is caused by the wickedness of others.* The poor Jew on the road to Jericho was the victim of the thieves who wounded him and left him half dead. Man is man's worst enemy. If man were but tamed to peace, the wildest beast in the world would be subdued; and if evil were purged from men's hearts, the major part of the ills of life would cease at once. The drunkard's wastefulness and brutality, the proud man's scorn, the oppressor's cruelty, the slanderer's lie, the trickster's cheat, the heartless man's grinding of the faces of the poor – these put together are the roots of almost all the poisonous weeds that multiply upon the face of the earth to our shame and sorrow.

If dominant sins could be taken away, as blessed be God they shall be when Christ has triumphed through the world, then much of human sorrow would be alleviated. When we see innocent persons suffering as the result of the sin of others, our pity should be provoked. How many there are of little children starving, and languishing in chronic disease through a father's drunkenness, which keeps the table bare! Wives, too, who work hard themselves are brought down to languishing sickness and painful disease by the laziness and cruelty of those who should have cherished them. Work-people, too, are often sorely oppressed in their wages, and have to work themselves to death's door to earn two cents. Those are the people who ought to have our sympathy when accident or disease brings them to the hospital gates "wounded and half dead."

The man in the parable was quite helpless; he could do nothing for himself. There he must lie and die; those huge wounds must bleed his very soul away unless a generous hand shall interfere. It is as much as he can do to groan; he cannot even dress his wounds, much less arise and seek a shelter. He is bleeding to death among the pitiless rocks of the descent to Jericho, and he must leave his body to be fed upon by hawks and crows unless some friend shall come to his aid. Now, when a man can help himself, and does not, he deserves to suffer; when a man flings away opportunities by his idleness or self-indulgence, a measure of suffering ought to be permitted to him as a cure for his sins. But when persons are sick or injured, and are unable to pay for the aid of the nurse and the physician, then is the time when truehearted philanthropy should promptly step in and do its best. So our Savior teaches us here.

Certain paths of life are peculiarly subject to affliction. The way that led from Jerusalem to Jericho was always infested by robbers. Jerome tells us that it was called "the bloody way," on account of the frequent highway robberies and murders which were committed there. And it is not so long ago as to be beyond the memory of man that an English traveler met his death on that road, while even very recent travelers tell us that they have been either threatened or actually attacked in that particularly gloomy region, the desert which goes down to the city of palm trees. So also, in the world around us there are paths of life which are highly dangerous and fearfully haunted by disease and accident.

Years ago, there were many trades in which from lack of precaution death slew its thousands. I thank God that sanitary and precautionary laws are better regarded, and men's lives are thought to be somewhat more precious. Yet still there are ways of life which may each be called "the bloody way": pursuits which are necessary to the community, but highly dangerous to those who follow them. Our mines, our railways, and our seas show a terrible list of suffering and death. Long hours in ill-ventilated workrooms are accountable for thousands of lives, and so are stinted wages, which prevent a sufficiency of food from being procured. Many a needlewoman's way of life is truly a path of blood.

When I think of the multitudes of our working people in this city who have to live in close, unhealthy rooms, crowded together in lanes and courts where the air is stagnant, I do not hesitate to say that much of the road which has to be trodden by the poor of London is as much deserving of the name of the way of blood as the road from Jerusalem to Jericho. If they do not lose their money, it is because they never have it; if they do not fall among thieves, they fall among diseases which practically wound them and leave them half dead.

Now, if you do not have to engage in such vocations, if your pathway does not lead you from Jerusalem to Jericho, but takes you, perhaps, very often from Jerusalem to Bethany, where you can enjoy the sweetnesses of domestic love and the delights of Christian fellowship, you ought to be very thankful, and be all the more ready to assist those who for your sakes, or for the benefit of society at large, have to follow the more dangerous roads of life. Do you not agree with me that such persons ought to be among the first to receive our Christian kindness? Such people abound in our hospitals and elsewhere.

Let that stand. It is clear that there is a great deal of affliction in the world, and much of it is of the sort which deserves to be helped at once.

Secondly, there are many who never relieve affliction. Our Savior tells us of two at least who *passed by on the other side,* and I suppose he might have prolonged the parable so as to have mentioned two dozen if he had chosen to do so, and even then he might have been content to mention but one good Samaritan, for I hardly think that there is one good Samaritan to two heartless persons. I wish there were, but I fear the good Samaritans are very few in proportion to the number who act the part of the priest and the Levite.

Now, notice who the persons were who refused to render aid to the man in distress.

First, they were *brought to the spot by God's providence on purpose to do so.* What better thing could the Lord himself do for the poor man half dead than to bring some man to help him? An angel could not well have met the condition. How would an angel, never wounded, understand binding up wounds and pouring on wine and oil? No, a man was needed who would know what was necessary, who would with brotherly sympathy cheer the mind while doctoring the body. In our English version we read: **By chance** *there came down a certain priest that way* (emphasis added), but learned Greek scholars read it: "By a coincidence." It was in the order of divine providence that a priest should come first to this afflicted person, so that he might go and examine the case as a man of education and skill, and then when the Levite came afterwards, he would be able to carry on what the priest began; and if one could not carry the poor man, the two might between them be able to bear him to the inn, or one might remain to guard him while the other ran for help.

God brought them to this position, but they willfully refused the sacred duty that providence and humanity demanded of them. Now, you who are wealthy are sent into our city on purpose so that you may have compassion upon the sick, the wounded, the poor, and the needy. God's intent in endowing any person with more substance than he needs is that he may have the pleasurable office, or rather let me say, the delightful privilege, of relieving need and woe. Alas, how many there are who consider that store which God has put into their hands on purpose for the poor and needy to be only so much provision for their excessive luxury, a luxury which pampers them but yields them neither benefit nor pleasure. Others dream that wealth is given them so that they may keep it under lock and key, corrupting and corroding, breeding covetousness and care.

Who dares roll a stone over the well's mouth when thirst is raging all around? Who dares keep the bread from the women and the children who are ready to gnaw their own arms from hunger? Above all, who dares allow the sufferer to writhe in agony uncared for, and the sick to languish into their graves unnursed? This is no small sin: it is a crime to be answered for to the judge when he shall come to judge the quick and dead. Those people who neglected the poor man were brought there on purpose to relieve him, even as you are, and yet they passed by on the other side.

They were both of them persons, too, who ought to have relieved him, because *they were very familiar with things which should have softened their hearts.* If I understand the passage, the priest was coming down from Jerusalem. I have often wondered which way he was going – whether he was going up to the temple, and was in a hurry to be on time for fear of keeping the congregation waiting, or whether he had fulfilled his duty, and had finished his month's course at the temple and was going home. I conclude that he was going from Jerusalem to Jericho, because it says, *By chance there came **down** a certain priest that way* (emphasis added).

Now to the metropolis it is always "going up": going *up* to London, or *up* to Jerusalem; and as this priest was coming *down,* he was going to Jericho. It was quite literally going down, for Jericho lies very low. I conclude that he was going home to Jericho, after having fulfilled his month's engagements in the temple, where he had been familiar with the worship of the Most High, as near to God as man could be, serving amidst sacrifices and holy psalms and solemn prayers, and yet he had not learned how to make a sacrifice himself. He had heard those prophetic words which say, *I will have mercy, and not sacrifice* (Matthew 9:13), but he was entirely forgetful of such teaching. He had often read that law: *Thou shalt love thy neighbour as thyself* (Leviticus 19:18), but he regarded it not.

The Levite had not been quite so closely engaged in the sanctuary as the priest, but he had taken his share in holy work, and yet he came away from it with a hard heart. This is a sad fact. They had been near to God,

41

but were not like him. Dear people, you may spend Sunday after Sunday in the worship of God, or what you think to be so, and you may behold Christ Jesus set forth visibly crucified among you, and themes which ought to turn a heart of stone to flesh may pass before your minds; and nevertheless you may return into the world to be as miserly as ever, and to have as little feeling towards your fellow man as before. It ought not to be so. I implore you permit it not to be so in any case again.

These two persons, moreover, were *bound by their profession to have helped this man,* for though it was originally said of the high priest – though I think it could be said of any priest – that he was taken from among men so that he might have compassion. If anywhere there should be compassion towards men, it should be in the heart of the priest who is chosen to speak for God to men and for men to God. No stone should ever be found in his bosom; he should be gentle, generous-hearted, kind, and full of sympathy and tenderness; but this priest was not so, nor was the Levite, who ought to have followed in his wake.

And oh, you Christian ministers, and all of you who teach in schools, or who undertake any service of Christian ministry – and you ought all to do so, for the Lord has made all his people to be priests unto him – there ought to be in you from your very profession a readiness of heart towards the kindest actions for those who need them.

And there is one thing to be mentioned also against this priest and Levite, and that is that *they were very well aware of the man's condition.* They came close to him and saw his state. It is a narrow trackway down to Jericho, and they were obliged to go almost over his wounded body. The firstcomer looked at him, but he hurried on; the second appears to have made a further investigation, to have had sufficient curiosity, at any rate, to begin to examine the state of the case; but his curiosity being satisfied, his compassion was not aroused, and he hurried away. Half the neglect of the sick and poor arises from not knowing that there are such cases, but many remain willfully in ignorance, and such ignorance is no available excuse.

In the case of the hospitals for which we plead today, you do know that there are persons in them at this moment suffering, persons suffering grievously, for no fault of their own, and you know that these need your aid. As I rode the other evening by that noble building on our side of the water, St. Thomas' Hospital, I could not help meditating upon what a mass of pain and suffering was gathered within those walls; but then I thanked God that it was within those walls where help would be most surely rendered to it to the best of human ability.

So you do know that there is poverty and sickness around you, and if you pass by on the other side, you will have looked at it, you will have known about it, and on your heads will be the criminality of having left the wounded man unhelped.

Yet the pair had important excuses: both the priest and the Levite had excellent reasons for neglecting the bleeding man. I never knew a man to refuse to help the poor who failed to give at least one admirable excuse. I believe that there is no man on earth who wickedly rejects the plea of need who is not furnished with arguments that he is right: arguments very satisfactory to himself, and such as he thinks should silence those who press the case. For instance, the priest and the Levite were both in a hurry. The priest had been a month away at Jerusalem from his wife and dear children, and he naturally wanted to get home; if he lingered, the sun might go down. It was an awkward place to be in after sundown, and you could not expect him to be so tactless as to stay in a lone place with darkness coming on.

He had spent a very laborious month in the temple. You do not know how exhausting he had found it to act as a priest for a whole month, and if you did, you would not blame him for wanting to get home to enjoy a little rest. Besides, he had promised to be home at a certain hour, and he was a man of punctuality, and would by no means cause anxiety to his wife and children who would be looking from the housetop for him. A very excellent excuse was this, but he also felt that he really could not do much good. He did not understand surgery, and could not bind up a wound to save his life; he shrank from it; the very sight of blood turned his stomach, and he could not bring himself to go near a person who was so frightfully mangled.

If he did try to bind up a wound, he felt he would be sure to make a mess of it. If his wife had been with him, she could have done it; or if he had brought some plaster, liniment, or strapping, he would have tried his best; but as it was, he could do nothing. The poor man, moreover, was evidently half dead, and would be quite dead in an hour or two, and therefore it was a pity to waste time on a hopeless case. Then the priest was only one person and could not be expected to carry a bleeding man, and yet it would be idle to begin with the case and leave him there all night. True, he could almost hear the sound of the Levite's feet, indeed he hoped he was coming up behind, for he felt very nervous at being alone with such a situation; but then that was all the more reason for leaving the matter, since the Levite would be sure to attend to it.

Better still was the following line of excuse – you would not have a person stop in a place where another man had been half killed by thieves. The thieves might be back again; they were scarcely out of hearing distance even then, and a priest after a month's service ought to have some fees in his purse, and it was important not to run the risk of losing the support of his family by stopping in a place that was evidently swarming with highwaymen. He might be wounded too, and then there would be two people half dead, and one of them a valuable clergyman.

Really, philanthropy would suggest that you take care of yourself, since you could not possibly do any good to the poor man. And then the man might die, and the person found near the body might be charged with the murder. It is always awkward to be found alone in a dark spot with the corpse of one who has evidently suffered from foul play. The priest might be taken up upon suspicion, and did not all the principles of prudence suggest that the very best thing that he could do was to get out of the way as quickly as possible?

Moreover, he could pray for the man, you know, and he was glad to find that he had a tract with him which he would leave near him, and what with the tract and the prayer, what more could a good man be expected to do? With this pious reflection he hastened on his way. It is just possible also that he did not wish to be defiled. A priest was too holy a person to meddle with wounds and bruises. Who would propose such a thing? He had come from Jerusalem in all the odor of sanctity; he felt himself to be as holy as he could conveniently be, and therefore he would not expose such rare excellence to worldly influences by touching a sinner. All these powerful reasons put together made him content to save trouble and leave the doing of kindness to others.

Now, this morning, I shall leave you to make all the excuses you like about not helping the poor and aiding the hospitals; and when you have made them, they will be as good as those which I have set before you. You have smiled over what the priest might have said, but if you make any excuses for yourselves whenever real need comes before you, and you are able to relieve it, you need not smile over your excuses, for the devil will do that; you had better cry over them, for there is the gravest reason for lamenting that your heart is hard toward your fellow creatures when they are sick, and perhaps sick unto death.

In the third place, the Samaritan is a model for those who do help the afflicted. He is a model, first, if we notice *who the person was whom he helped*. The parable does not *say* so, but it *implies* that the wounded man was a Jew, and, therefore, the Samaritan was not of the same faith or order. The apostle says, *As we have therefore opportunity, let us do good unto all men, especially unto them who are of the household of faith* (Galatians 6:10). This man was not of the household of faith, as far as the Samaritan's judgment went, but he was one of the *all men*. The Jew and he were as much apart in religious sympathy as they well could be. Alas, but he was a man. Whether he was a Jew or not, he was a man, a wounded, bleeding, dying man, and the Samaritan was another man, and so one man felt for another man and came to his aid.

Do not ask whether a sick man believes in the Thirty-nine Articles, or the Westminster Assembly's catechism. Let us hope that he is sound in the faith; but if he is not, his wounds need to be staunched just as much as if he held a perfect creed. You need not inquire whether he is a sound Calvinist, for an Arminian feels sharp pain when he is wounded, a churchman feels as much pain as a Dissenter when his leg is broken, and an infidel needs nursing when he is crushed in an accident. It is as bad for a man to die with an unorthodox creed as with the orthodox faith; indeed, in some respects it is far worse, and therefore we should be doubly anxious for his cure. We are to relieve real distress irrespective of creed, as the Samaritan did.

Moreover, the Jews were great haters of the Samaritans, and no doubt this Samaritan might have thought, "If I were in that man's situation, he would not help me. He would pass me by and say, 'It is a Samaritan dog, let him be accursed.'" The Jews were accustomed to cursing the Samaritans, but it did not occur to the good man to remember what the Jew would have said: he saw him bleeding and he bound up his wounds.

Our Savior has not given us for a golden rule: "Do you to others as others would do to you," but "as you would they should do to you." The Samaritan went by that rule, and though he knew of the enmity in the Jewish mind, he felt that he must heap coals of fire upon the wounded man by loving help; therefore, he went straightaway to his relief. Perhaps at another time the Jew would have put off the Samaritan and refused even to be touched by him; but the tenderhearted sympathizer does not think of that. The poor man is too sick to hold any quirks or prejudices, and when the Samaritan bends over him and pours on the oil and wine, he wins a grateful glance from the son of Abraham.

That poor, wounded man was one who *could not repay him.* He had been stripped of all that he had, even his garments were taken from him; but charity does not look for payment, or else it would be no charity at all. The man was *a total stranger* too. The Samaritan had not even seen him before. What did that matter? He was a man, and all men are kindred. God *hath made of one blood all nations of men for to dwell on all the face of the earth* (Acts 17:26). The Samaritan felt that touch of nature which makes all men kin, and he bent over the stranger and relieved his pains.

He might have said, "Why should *I* help? He has been rejected by his own people; the priest and the Levite have left him; his first claim is upon his own countrymen." So have I known some to say, "These persons have no claim; they ought to go to their own people." Well, suppose they have gone and failed, now comes your turn; and what the Jew would not do for the Jew, let the Samaritan do, and he shall be blessed in the deed. He had been neglected by the officials and neglected by the saints; the best, or those who ought to be the best, the priest and the Levite, had deserted him, and left him to die. The Samaritan is neither saint nor official, but yet he steps in to do the deed. Oh, Christian brethren, take care that you are not put to shame by this Samaritan.

He is a model to us next in *the spirit in which he did his work.* He did it without asking questions. The man was in need, he was sure of that, and he helped him at once; doing so without hesitation, and making no compact nor agreement with him, but at once proceeding to pour on the oil and wine. He did it without attempting to shift the labor from himself to others.

Charity nowadays means that A asks B to help him, and B, in his wonderful charity, does him the great favor of sending him on to C. That is to say, the common tendency of benevolent persons nowadays is to put their hands seldom into their own purses, but to send people on to a few individuals who find cash for all. It seems to me to be a very mean way of getting rid of a case by saving your own pocket and passing the applicant on to another who is no better off than yourself, but far more generous. The Samaritan was personally benevolent, and therein he is a mirror and model to us all.

He did it without any selfish fear. The thieves might have come upon him, but he cared nothing for thieves when a life was in danger. Here is a man in need, and the man must be relieved, thieves or no thieves, and he does it. He does it with self-denial, for he finds oil and wine, and money at the inn, and everything, though he was by no means a rich man, for he gave twopence, a larger sum than it looks, but still a small sum. He did not fling his charity about because he was rich: he is not said to have given a handful of pence, but two, for he had to count his pence as he spent them.

It was a poor Samaritan who did this rich and noble act. The poorest can help the poor; even those who feel distress themselves may manifest a generous Christian spirit and give their services. Let them do so as they have opportunity.

This man helped his poor neighbor with great tenderness and care. He was like a mother to him. Everything was done with loving thought and with whatever skill he possessed. He did the best he could.

Brethren, let what we do for others always be done in the noblest style. Let us not treat the poor like dogs to whom we fling a bone, nor visit the sick like superior beings who feel that they are stooping down to inferiors when they enter their rooms; but in the sweet tenderness of real love, learned at Jesus' feet, let us imitate this Good Samaritan.

But *what did he do?* Well, first he came to where the sufferer was, and put himself into his position. Then he put forth all his skill for him, and bound up his wounds, no doubt tearing his own garment to get the bands with which to bind up the wounds. He poured on oil and wine, the best healing mixture that he knew of, and one which he happened to have with him. He then set the sick man on his mule, and of course he had to walk himself, but this he did very cheerfully, supporting his poor patient as the mule proceeded. He took him to an inn, but he did not leave him at the inn and say, "Anybody will take care of him now," but he went to the manager of the establishment and gave him money, and he said, "Take care of him."

I admire that little sentence, because it is first written that he *took care of him,* and next he said, *Take care of him.* What you do yourself you may exhort other people to do. He said, "I leave this poor man with you, I pray do not neglect him. There are a great many people in the inn, but take care of him."

"Is he a brother of yours?"

"No, I never saw him before."

"Well, are you at all under obligation to him?"

"No! – yes, yes, I feel under obligation to everybody that is a man. If he wants help, I am obliged to help him."

"Is that all?"

"Yes, but do take care of him. I feel a great interest in him."

The Samaritan did not cease until he had gone through with his kindness. He said, "This money may not be sufficient, for it may be a long time before he is able to move. That leg may not soon heal, that broken rib may need long rest. Do not hurry him away, let him stay here, and if he incurs additional expense, I will be sure to pay it when I come back from Jerusalem again." There is nothing like the charity which endures even to the end. I wish I had time to enlarge on all these things, but I cannot do so; exhibit them in your lives, and you will best know what they mean. Go and do likewise, each one of you, and thus reproduce the Good Samaritan.

But now, fourthly, we have a higher model than even the Samaritan – our Lord Jesus Christ. I do not think that our divine Lord intended to teach anything about himself in this parable, except so far as he is himself the great example of all goodness. He was answering the question, *Who is my neighbour?* and he was not preaching about himself at all. There has been a great deal of straining at this parable to bring the Lord Jesus and everything about him into it, but this I dare not imitate.

Yet by analogy we may illustrate our Lord's goodness by it. This is a picture of a generous-hearted man who cares for the needy, but the most generous-hearted man that ever lived was the Man of Nazareth, and none ever cared for sick and suffering souls as he has done. Therefore, if we praise the Good Samaritan, we should much more extol the blessed Savior whom his enemies called a Samaritan, and who never denied the charge, for what did he care if all the prejudice and scorn of men should vent itself on him?

Now, brethren, our Lord Jesus Christ has done better than the Good Samaritan, because our case was worse. As I have already said, the wounded man could not blame himself for his sad state; it was his misfortune, not his fault; but you and I are not only half dead, but also altogether dead in trespasses and sins, and we have brought many of our ills upon ourselves. The thieves that have stripped us are our own iniquities, the wounds which we bear have been inflicted by our own suicidal hand. We are not in opposition to Jesus Christ as the poor Jew was to the Samaritan, from the mere force of prejudice, but we have been opposed to the blessed Redeemer by nature; we have from the first turned away from him. Alas, we have resisted and rejected him.

The poor man did not put his Samaritan friend away, but we have done so to our Lord. How many times have we refused almighty love! How often by unbelief have we pulled open the wounds that Christ has bound up! We have rejected the oil and wine which in the gospel he presents to us. We have spoken evil of him to his face, and have lived even for years in utter rejection of him; and yet in his infinite love he has not given us up, but he has brought some of us into his church, where we rest as in an inn, feeding on what his bounty has provided. It was wonderful love which moved the Savior's heart from where he found us in all our misery, and bent over us to lift us out of it, though he knew that we were his enemies.

The Samaritan was akin to the Jew because he was a man, but our Lord Jesus was not originally akin to us by nature. He is God, infinitely above us, and if he was *found in fashion as a man* (Philippians 2:8), it was because he chose to be so. If he journeyed this way, via Bethlehem's manger, down to the place of our sin and misery, it was because his infinite compassion brought him there. The Samaritan came to the wounded one because in the course of business he was led there, and, being there, he helped the man; but Jesus came to earth on no business but that of saving us, and he was found in our flesh that he might have sympathy with us. In the very existence of the man Christ Jesus you see the noblest form of pity manifested.

And being here, where we had fallen among robbers, he did not merely run risks of being attacked by thieves himself, but he also *was* attacked by them. He was wounded, he was stripped, and not half dead was he, but altogether dead, for he was laid in the grave. He was slain for our sakes, for it was not possible for him to deliver us from the mischief which the thieves of sin had effected upon us except by suffering that mischief in his own person; and he did suffer it so that he might deliver us.

What the Samaritan gave to the poor man was generous, but it is not comparable to what the Lord Jesus has given to us. He gave him wine and oil, but Jesus has given his heart's blood to heal our wounds: *[He] loved [us], and gave himself for [us]* (Galatians 2:20). The Samaritan *loaned* himself with all his care and thoughtfulness, but Christ *gave* himself even to death for us. The Samaritan gave twopence, a large amount out of his meager stock, and I do not depreciate the gift, but *though [Christ] was rich, yet for [our] sakes he became poor, that [we] through his poverty might be rich* (2 Corinthians 8:9). Oh, the marvelous gifts which Christ has bestowed upon us! Who is he that can count them! Heaven is among those blessings, but his own self is the chief favor.

The Samaritan's compassion did but show itself for a short time. If he had to walk by the side of his mule, it would not be for many miles; but Christ walked by the side of us, dismounted from his glory, all through his life. The Samaritan did not stop long at the inn, for he had his business to attend to, and he very rightly went about it; but our Lord remained with us for a lifetime, even until he rose to heaven: yes, he is with us even now, always blessing the sons of men.

When the Samaritan went away, he said, *Whatsoever thou spendest more, when I come again, I will repay thee* (Luke 10:35). Jesus has gone up to heaven, and he has left behind him blessed promises of something to be done when he shall come again. He never forgets us. The Good Samaritan, I dare say, thought very little of the Jew in later years; indeed, it is the mark of a generous spirit not to think much of what it has done. He went back to Samaria and minded his business, and never told anybody. "I helped a poor Jew on the road." Not he.

But of necessity our Lord Jesus acts differently. Because we have a constant need, he continues to care for us, and his deed of love is being done, and done, and done again upon multitudes of cases, and will always be repeated as long as there are men to be saved, a hell from which to escape, and a heaven to win.

I have thus set before you the highest example, and I shall conclude when I have said two things. *Judge yourselves,* all you my friends, if you are hoping for salvation by your own works. Look to what you must be throughout an entire life if your works are to save you. You must love God with all your heart and soul and strength, and your neighbor in this Samaritan's fashion, even as yourself, and both of these without a single failure. Have you done this? Can you hope to do it perfectly? If not, why do you risk your souls in this frail skiff, this leaky, sinking craft of your poor works, for you will never get to heaven in that way.

Lastly, you who are Christ's people are saved, and you are not going to do these things in order to save yourselves. The greater Samaritan has saved you. Jesus has redeemed you, brought you into his church, put you under the care of his ministers, bidden us to take care of you, and promised to reward us if we do so in the day when he comes. *Seek, then, to be true followers of your Lord* by practical deeds of kindness, and if you have been backward in your gifts to help either the physical or the spiritual needs of men, begin from this morning with generous hearts, and God will bless you. O divine Spirit, help us all to be like Jesus. Amen.

Chapter 4

Good News for You

But a certain Samaritan, as he jour-
neyed, came where he was. (Luke 10:33)

The Good Samaritan is a masterly picture of true benevolence. The Samaritan had no kinship with the Jew, he was purely of foreign origin; yet he pities his poor neighbor. The Jews cursed the Cushites, and would have no dealings with them, for they were intruders in their land. There was nothing, therefore, in the object of the Samaritan's pity that could excite his national sympathies, but everything to arouse his prejudices, thus the grandeur of his benevolence.

It is not my intention this morning to indicate the delightful points of excellence that Christ brings out in order to illustrate what true charity will perform. I want you only to notice this one fact, that the benevolence which the Samaritan exhibited towards this poor wounded and half-dead man was available benevolence. He did not say to him, "If you will walk to Jericho, then I will bind up your wounds, pouring on the oil and wine"; or "If you will journey with me as far as Jerusalem, I will then attend to your needs." Oh no, he came *where he was*, and finding that he could do nothing whatever for his own assistance, the Good Samaritan began with him there and then upon the spot, putting no impossible conditions upon him, proposing no stipulations which the man could not perform, but doing everything for the man, and doing it for him as he was and where he was.

Beloved, we are all quite aware that a charity of which a man cannot avail himself is no charity at all. Go among the agents of Lancashire, and tell them that there is no necessity for any of them to starve, for on the top of Mount St. Bernard there are hospitable monks who keep a dining hall, where they relieve all passersby; tell them they have nothing to do but to journey to the top of the Alps, and there they will find food enough. Poor souls! they feel that you mock them, for the distance is too great.

Penetrate one of our back streets, climb up three pairs of stairs into a wretched room, so dilapidated that the stars look between the tiles, see a poor young girl dying of tuberculosis and poverty, and tell her if you dare, "If you could get to the seaside, and if you could eat so much beefsteak, you would no doubt recover." You are shamefully laughing at her – she cannot get these things – they are beyond her reach. She cannot journey to the seaside – she would die before she reached it.

Like the wicked, your tender mercies are cruel. I have noticed this unhelpful charity in hard winters. People give away bread and soup tickets to poor people, who are to give sixpence and then receive soup and bread; and often I have had persons come to me saying, "Sir, I have a ticket; it would be worth a great deal to me if I had sixpence to go with it to get the relief, but I have not a farthing in all the world, and I cannot make out the good of giving me this ticket at all." This is hardly charity.

Think about seeing Jeremiah, down in the low dungeon. If Ebedmelech and Baruch had stood over the top of the dungeon and called out to him, "Jeremiah, if you will get halfway up, we will pull you out," when there was not a ladder, nor any means by which he could possibly get so far, how cruel would have been this charity. But instead, they took old rags from under the king's treasury, and put them on ropes, and bade him to put the rags under his armpits, and sling his arms through the ropes, and then they pulled him up all the way. This was available charity; the other would have been hypocritical pretense.

Brethren, if in the description of a good Samaritan, Christ hits him off to the life, as giving to this poor wounded man a charity of which he could avail himself, does it not seem to be strongly probable – no, even certain – that when Christ comes to deal with sinners, he gives them available mercy – grace which may be of real service to them?

Therefore, permit me to say, I do not believe in the way in which some people pretend to preach the gospel. They have no gospel for sinners as sinners, but only for those who are above the dead level of sinnership and are technically styled *sensible* sinners. Like the priest in this parable, they see the poor sinner, and they say, "He is not conscious of his need, we cannot invite him to Christ." "He is dead," they say. "It is of no use preaching to dead souls"; so they pass by on the other side, keeping close to the elect and the revived, but having nothing whatever to say to the dead, lest they should make Christ out to be too gracious, and his mercy to be too free.

The Levite was not in quite such a hurry as the priest. The priest had to preach, and might be too late for the service, and therefore he could not stop to relieve the man; besides, he might have soiled his garment, or made himself unclean; and then he would have been hardly fit for the dainty and respectable congregation over which he officiated. As for the Levite, he had to read the hymns; he was a clerk in the church, and he was somewhat in a hurry, but still he could get in after the opening prayer, so he indulged himself with the luxury of looking on. Just as I have known ministers to say, "Well, you know we ought to describe the sinner's state, and warn him, but we must not invite him to Christ."

Yes, gentlemen, you must pass by on the other side, after having looked at him, for on your own confession you have no good news for the poor wretch. I bless my Lord and Master that he has given to me a gospel which I can take to dead sinners, a gospel which is available for the vilest of the vile. I thank my Master that he does not say to the sinner, "Come halfway and meet me," but he comes *where he [is]*, and finding him ruined, lost, and callous, he meets him on his own ground, and gives him life and peace without asking or expecting him to prepare himself for grace. Here is, I think, set forth in my text, the available benevolence of the Samaritan; it is mine this morning, to show the available grace of Christ.

The sinner is without moral qualification for salvation, but Christ comes where he is.

I want, if I can, not to talk about this as a matter having to do with the multitude that are abroad, but with us in these pews. I speak not of *them* and *those*, but of *you* and *me*. I want to say to every sinner, "You are in a state in which there is nothing morally that can qualify you for being saved, but Jesus Christ meets you where you are now."

Remember first, that when the gospel was first sent into the world, *those to whom it was sent were clearly without any moral qualification.* Did you ever read the first chapter of Paul's epistle to the Romans? It is one of those awful passages in Scripture, not intended to be read in congregations, but to be read and studied in the secrecy of one's chamber. The apostle gives a portrait of the manners and customs of the heathen world, so awful, that unless our missionaries had informed us that it is exactly the photograph of life in Hindustan at the present moment, infidels might have declared that Paul had exaggerated.

Heathenism in the time of Paul was so desperately wicked that it would be utterly impossible to conceive of a sin into which men had not fallen, and yet, *We turn to the Gentiles* (Acts 13:46), said the apostle; and yet the Lord himself commanded, *Go ye into all the world, and preach the gospel to every creature.* What! To Sodomites, whose very smallest sin is adultery and fornication; to thieves and murderers, to murderers of fathers and mothers? Yes, go and preach the gospel *to them!*

Clearly, the fact that the world was steeped up to its very throat in the filth of abominable wickedness, and yet the gospel was sent to it, proves that Christ does not seek for any qualification of morality or righteousness in man, before the gospel is available to him. He sends the Word to the drunkard, to the swearer, the harlot, the vilest of the vile; for such is the gospel of Christ intended to save.

Recollect again *the biblical descriptions of those whom Christ came into the world to save, which prove to a demonstration that he comes to the sinner where he is.* How does the Bible describe those whom Christ came to save? As men? No, my brethren; Christ did not come to save men as men, but men as sinners. As sensible sinners? No, I declare not; they are described as **dead** *in trespasses and sins* (Ephesians 2:1, emphasis added). But to the law and to the testimony, let me read you one or two passages; and, while I read them, I hope you may be able to say, "There is hope for me." First, those whom Christ came to save are described in 1 Timothy 1:15 and in many other places as *sinners. This is a faithful saying, and worthy of all acceptation, that Christ Jesus came into the world to save sinners; of whom I am chief. Sinners,* without any adjective before the word; not awakened sinners, not repenting sinners, but sinners as sinners.

"Surely," says one, "I am not shut out." Another account is found in Romans 5:6: *For when we were yet without strength, in due time Christ died* – for whom? those who had some desires after God? some respect for his name? No, *for the ungodly*. Now, an ungodly man means a man without God, who cares not for God; God is not in all his thoughts, and therefore he is not what men call a sensible sinner. *The ungodly . . . are like the chaff which the wind driveth away* (Psalm 1:4): even these are the persons that Christ came to save.

In the same chapter, Romans 5, and the tenth verse, you find them mentioned as *enemies* – *When we were enemies, we were reconciled to God by the death of his Son.* What say you to this? They are not described as friends. Christ laid down his life for his friends in one sense; *but God commendeth his love toward us, in that, while we were yet sinners, Christ died for us* (Romans 5:8). Enemies to God were the objects of grace, so that in enmity Christ comes and meets man where he is.

In Ephesians 2:1, we read of them as **dead** *in trespasses and sins – and you hath he quickened, who were dead in trespasses and sins.* Christ, then, does not ask the sinner to make himself alive; the gospel is not only to be preached to those who have some good notions, some good desires, and some tremblings of the heavenly life within, but also to the dead as dead; for to the dead does Christ come and meet them in the grave of their sin.

Again (Ephesians 2:3), they are *children of wrath* – we *were by nature the children of wrath, even as others.* Yet the gospel came to such. Can you see anything hopeful in a child of wrath? I ask you to look him over from head to foot, if this be his name and character; can you see a spot of goodness as large as a pin's point in the man? And yet such as these Christ came to save.

Once again, they are mentioned as *accursed* (Galatians 1:8-9). "Ah," says one sinner, "I have often cursed myself before God, and asked him to curse me." Well, Christ died for the accursed; *Christ hath redeemed us from the curse of the law, being made a curse for us* (Galatians 3:13), that is, for us who were under the curse.

And, once more, they are described by the dreadful word *lost*. They are lost to all hope, to all consideration for themselves; even their own friends have given their case up as hopeless. *The Son of man is come to seek and to save that which was lost* (Luke 19:10). If I understand those passages which I have read in your hearing, they mean just this – that those whom Christ came to save have no good whatsoever in them to cooperate towards their salvation, and Christ does not look upon them in order to find anything that is good in them. I am bold to say that the only fittedness for cleansing is filthiness; the only fittedness for a Savior is being lost; and the only character under which we come to Jesus is as sinners, lost, dead, and accursed.

But thirdly, it is quite certain from *the work of grace itself,* that the Lord does not expect the sinner to do anything or to be anything in order to meet him, but that he comes to him where he is. See, sinner, Christ *dies* on Calvary, a weight of sin is on his shoulders, and on his heart; in the most awful agonies he shrieks under the desertion of his God. For whom did he die? For the innocent? Why for the innocent? What sacrifice did they need? For those who had some good thing in them? Why all these agonies for such? Surely a lesser price might do for them if they could eke it out themselves. But because Christ died on account of sin, I take it that those whom he died for must be viewed as sinners, and only as such. Inasmuch as he paid a dreadful price, I gather that they must be dreadfully in debt, and that he died for those who had nothing to pay with.

But Christ *rose again,* rose again for our justification. For whose justification? For the justification of those who were justified in themselves? Why, this would be to perform an unnecessary work. No, my brethren, but for those who had no justification of their own, not a shadow of any, who were condemned, utterly condemned on account of their own works.

Moreover, I hear him by the ear of faith *pleading* before the eternal throne. Who does he plead for? For those who have something to plead on their own account? That would be needless. Do men give their money to the rich? Do they spend their charity on those who do not need it? If men have something to plead for themselves, then why does Christ plead for them? No, brethren, he pleads for those who have nothing whatsoever that they can bring as an argument with which to enforce their prayers.

But Christ ascended and *received gifts.* Who for? For those who merited rewards? No, truly, let them get them for themselves. But he received gifts for men, yes, for the rebellious also, that the Lord God might dwell among them. But he *gives the Holy Spirit.* To whom does he give the Holy Spirit? To those that are strong, and good, and can do all themselves? O, my brethren, this would be a work of supererogation (an act of performing more than is required by duty, obligation, or need); but he gives the Holy Spirit to those that are powerless, weak, and dead; he gives the Holy Worker to those who are all unholy and full of sin; he puts the omnipotent influence into those who were slaves to the spirit of evil. Brethren, the work of Christ supposes a lost, ruined, and rebellious sinner, and so I say, Christ meets the man where he is.

Yet there is more, for I would clear up this point before I leave it: *the godlike character of the grace of God* proves that he meets the sinner where he is. If God forgives little sinners only, then he is little in his mercy. If the Lord does not do something more than men can think, then we have made too much noise about the gospel and have exalted the cross above measure.

Unless there be something extraordinary in divine grace, then I cannot understand such a passage as this: *As the heavens are higher than the earth, so are my ways higher than your ways, and my thoughts than your thoughts* (Isaiah 55:9). I venture to say, brethren, that many of us have thought of forgiving our enemies. It has sometimes been our happy portion to do good to them that hate us. Now, if God would be godlike in his grace – and I am sure he will – he must do something more than that; he must not only forgive his enemies, but they must also be enemies of such an atrocious character that no *man* would have forgiven them.

> Who is a pardoning God like thee?
> Or who hath grace so rich and free?

But where is the meaning of this boast if the Lord merely pardons sinners who are sensible of their sins and lament them? The marvel is in this, that while they are still enemies he calls them by his grace, and invites them to mercy; yes, even more, he blots out their sins and makes them friends, thus meeting the sinner where he is.

The spirit and genius of the gospel utterly forbid the supposition that God requires anything in any man in order to save him. If salvation be offered to man upon a condition, then they who fulfill the condition have a claim to the blessing. This is the old covenant of works. The substance of the legal covenant is: "Do this and I will reward you." When the man has done it, he deserves what has been promised. Yes, and if you make the condition never so easy, yet, mark you, so long as it be a condition, God is bound by his own Word, the condition being fulfilled, to give man what he has earned. This is works and not grace; it is debt and not free favor. But inasmuch as the gospel is free favor from beginning to end, I am absolutely sure that God asks nothing – neither good wishes, good desires, nor good feelings of a sinner – before he may come to Christ. But that he may know that everything is of grace, the rebel is commanded to come just as he is, bringing nothing, but taking everything from God, who is superabundant in mercy, and therefore meets the sinner just where he is.

I say to the sinner, wherever you may be today, if you be without any virtue, and if you be filled with all vice, if there be no good points in your character, but if there be everything that is bad against man and against God; if you have committed every crime in the catalog, if you have ruined your body and damned your soul, yet still Christ has said, *Him that cometh to me I will in no wise cast out.* And if you come to him, he can no more cast you out than if you had been the most virtuous, the most honorable, and the most devout of all living men.

Only choose you today to believe in the mercy of God, in Christ, and cast yourself on him, and you are saved to the praise and glory of that grace which meets you just where you are, and saves you from sin.

In the second place, there are very many of the lost race of Adam who say that they are without any mental qualification.

This is their excuse – "But sir, I never was a scholar. I was sent out as a boy to earn my own living, so that I never had a week's schooling; I am so ignorant that I cannot read my book, and if anybody were to ask me to say a prayer I could not, for I have not sense enough." Now, you see the Lord Jesus meets you just where you are. And how does he do this? Why, first, *the saving act is one that requires no mental power.* Faith lays hold on eternal life.

Now, a child whose faculties are never so little developed can believe what he is told. The child cannot reason, cannot argue, cannot dispute, cannot split hairs, cannot see a knotty point in theology, but he can believe what he is told. Faith requires so little mental vigor or intellectual clearness, that there have been many who were idiots in other things, who have been made wise unto salvation by the act of faith in Christ. You remember our Lord's own words: *I thank thee, O Father, Lord of heaven and earth, that thou hast hid these things from the wise and prudent, and hast revealed them unto babes* (Luke 10:21). But this never could have happened had not the act which brings us into communion with Christ been the lowest act of the human faculty, that of simply trusting in Christ, as the result of crediting that which is told us upon good testimony.

But then, again, to meet this defect of mental power, remember *the unique simplicity of that which is believed.* Is there anything more simple in the world than the doctrine of the atonement? We deserve to die, Christ dies for us; we are in debt, Christ pays for us. Is not this plain enough for a ragged school? It is so plain that many of our learned doctors of divinity try to get it out of the Bible; they think, "If this be the core of it all, then any fool can be a theologian"; so they kick against it.

What is Unitarianism but a stumbling over the simplicity of the cross. They were Unitarians who stood at the cross when Christ died; they said, *Let him now come down from the cross, and we will believe him* (Matthew 27:42). That has been the Unitarian character ever since; they will receive Jesus anywhere but on his cross; but up there, dying in man's place, he is so commonplace that these great gentlemen run to philosophy and vain deceit sooner than lay hold on that which the most common person may as fully understand as they.

Yet there is more. To meet any mental deficiency in man, while the truth itself is simple, it is *taught in the Bible under such simple metaphors* that none can say they cannot understand it. How simple is the metaphor of the brazen serpent, held up before the snake-bitten Israelites, while they are commanded to look at it and live. Who does not understand that a look at Christ who dies in the place of men will make them live? *If any man thirst, let him come unto me, and drink* (John 7:37). Who does not understand the figure of a fountain flowing in the streets, that every thirsty passerby may put his lips down and drink? *Behold the Lamb of God!* (John 1:36). Who does not understand the sacrifice? Here is a lamb killed for the sin of Israel, and so Christ dies for the sin of those who believe in him. The act of faith is simple; the object of faith is plain; the metaphors make it clear, and he is without excuse who does not understand the gospel of Christ.

To cap it off to you, my beloved friends, Christ *has given you an abundance of teachers.* There sits in your pew with you today a man of your own rank and calling who will explain to you the gospel if you do not understand it. Here are many of us who are but too glad if we can roll away the stone from the door of your sepulcher; here are children of God themselves saved by sovereign grace, and if you really do not know the way, do but touch your next neighbor, and say to him, "Can you explain to me yet more clearly what I must do to be saved?" Now, this is meeting you, let your brains be of the very smallest; this is coming down to you though you sit on the lowest step of human intellect. Jesus Christ meets you just where you are.

But yet again, I think I hear another say, "I am in despair, for I cannot find any reason in myself, or out of myself, why God should forgive such a person as I am."

So then, you are in a hopeless state, or at least you see no hope. The Lord meets you where you are by putting *the reason of your salvation altogether in himself.* Shall I remind you of one or two texts which will surely satisfy you? *I, even I, am he that blotteth out thy transgressions.* What for? *For mine own sake* (Isaiah 43:25). He cannot pardon you for your sake, you clearly see that; and you feel that he cannot pardon you for other people's sake; but *for mine own sake,* says he, that he may glorify himself. Not in you, but in his own mighty breast he finds the motive, so that he may make his own mercy illustrious; for his own sake he will do it.

Or take another – *For my name's sake will I defer mine anger, . . . that I cut thee not off* (Isaiah 48:9). Here it is again for his *name's sake,* as if he knew he could not find any other motive, so he puts it all on himself; he pardons so that he may honor and glorify his own name. Sinner, you cannot say that this does not suit your case: for if you be the most hellish good-for-nothing sinner that ever cursed God's earth, and polluted the air you breathe, yet he can save you, for his own sake. There still is room for you to hope; for the bigger the sinner you are, the more glory to him if he saves you; and if salvation is given for a reason only in himself, there is therefore yet a reason by which he can save you, even you.

Remember, that *he puts his own design* before your eyes to show you that if you have no reason in yourself, that is no hindrance to his saving you. What is God's design in saving men? When he brings them to heaven, what will be the result of it? Why, that they may love and praise his name forever, and sing, *Unto him that loved us, and washed us from our sins in his blood, . . . to him be glory* (Revelation 1:5-6). You are just the man; if you are ever saved and brought to heaven, oh, will not you praise his grace? "Yes," said one old man who had long lived in sin. "If he ever does bring me to heaven, he shall never hear the last of it, for I will praise him throughout eternity." Why, you are the man, do you not see, you are the very man that will answer God's design, for who shall love so much as he who has had much forgiven, and who shall praise so loudly as he whose mighty sins have been overcome by the mighty love and goodness and grace of God? You cannot say that it does not meet you, for here is a motive and a reason, though you can find none in yourself.

Here is another reason why God should save you: it is *his own Word,* the Word of him that cannot lie. I will bring up that text again; perhaps there is a heart here that will be able to cast anchor on it – *Him that cometh to me I will in no wise cast out.* You say, "But if I come, I can see no reason why he should save me." I answer, there is a reason in his own promise. God cannot lie. You come; he will not cast you out. He says, *I will in no wise cast out;* but you say, "He may for such and such a reason." Now, this is a flat contradiction; the two cannot stand. If there be anything that is necessary in order for a soul to come, and you come without it, still there is the promise, and since it has no limit in it, plead it, and the Lord will not refuse to honor his own Word.

If he can cast you out because you do not have some necessary qualification, then his Word is not true. Whoever you may be, whatever you may not be, and whatever you may be, if you believe in Jesus Christ, there is a reason in every attribute of God why you should be saved.

63

His truth cries, "Save him, for you have said, 'I will.'" His power says, "Save him, lest the Enemy deny your might." God's wisdom pleads, "Save him, lest men doubt your judgment." His love says, "Save him"; his every attribute says, "Save him"; and even Justice, with its hoarse voice, cries, "Save him, for God *is faithful and just to forgive us our sins, if we confess our sins*" (1 John 1:9).

I am trying to fish in deep waters after some of you that have long escaped the net. I know when I have given free and full invitations, you have said, "Ah! that cannot mean me." You are without faith in Christ because you think you are not fit. I will be clear of your blood this morning; I will show you that there is no fittedness needed, that you are commanded now to believe in the Lord Jesus Christ as you are, for Jesus Christ's gospel is an available gospel, and it comes to you just where you are. Without moral or mental qualification, and without any sort of reason why he should save you, he meets you as such, and bids you to trust him.

We proceed to our fourth point. "Oh," says one, "but I am without courage; I dare not believe on Christ. I am such a timid, trembling soul, that when I hear that others trust in Christ I think it must be presumption. I wish I could do the same, but I cannot; I am kept under by such a sense of sin that I dare not. O sir, I dare not, for it would look as if I were flying in the face of justice if I were to dare to trust Christ, and then to rejoice in the pardon of my sin." Very well. Christ comes to meet you where you are by very tender *invitations. Ho, every one that thirsteth, come ye to the waters, and he that hath no money; come ye, buy, and eat; yea, come, buy wine and milk without money and without price* (Isaiah 55:1). *Come unto me, all ye that labour and are heavy laden, and I will give you rest* (Matthew 11:28). *The Spirit and the bride say, Come. And let him that heareth say, Come. And let him that is athirst come. And whosoever will, let him take the water of life freely* (Revelation 22:17). How sweetly he puts it to you. I do not know where more wooing words could be found, than those the Savior uses. Will you not come when Christ beckons, when with his loving face streaming with tears he bids you to come to him? What! Is an invitation from him too little a thing for you? O sinner, trembling though you are, say in your soul,

I'll to the gracious king approach,
    Whose sceptre pardon gives;
Perhaps he may command my touch,
    And then the suppliant lives.

Knowing that you would neglect the invitation, he has put it to you in the light of a *command*. *This is the [commandment] of God, that ye believe on [Jesus Christ] whom he hath sent* (John 6:29). *Believe on the Lord Jesus Christ, and thou shalt be saved* (Acts 16:31). *He that believeth and is baptized shall be saved; but he that believeth not shall be damned* (Mark 16:16). He thought you would say, "Ah, but I am not fit to accept the invitation." "Well," says he, "I will command the man to do it." Like a poor hungry man with bread before him, who says, "Ah, it would be presumption on my part to eat"; but the king says, "Eat, sir, or I will punish you." What a generous and liberal command; even the threat itself has no anger in it.

Like the mother, who when the child is near to dying, and nothing will save him but the medicine, and the child will not drink, she threatens the child, but only out of love for him that he may be saved. So the Lord adds *threatenings* to commands; for sometimes a black word will drive a soul to Christ where a bright word would not draw it. Fears of hell sometimes make men flee to Jesus. The weary wing made the poor dove fly to the ark, and the thunderbolts of God's justice are only meant to make you fly to Christ the Lord.

Beloved, once more, my Master has sweetly met your lack of courage by bringing many others, so that you may follow their example. As waterfowl hunters sometimes have their decoy birds, so my Master has decoy birds that are to draw others to him. Other sinners have been saved, others he has cleansed who did but trust him. There was Lot. Ah, Lot! guilty of drunkenness and incest, and yet a saint of God. David the adulterer and murderer of Uriah, and yet washed *whiter than snow* (Psalm 51:7). Manasseh the bloody persecutor, who had Isaiah cut in two, sawing him in halves, and yet he was taken among the thorns, and God had mercy on him. What shall I say of Saul of Tarsus, the persecutor of God's people? and the robber dying on the cross for his crimes, and yet saved? Sinner, if these do not induce you to come, what can overcome your sinful distrustfulness?

"But," says one, "you have not hit my case yet; I am an outrageous sinner!" Well now, I will hit it this time. In 1 Corinthians 6:9-11, hear the word of the Lord: *Neither fornicators, nor idolaters, nor adulterers, nor effeminate, nor abusers of themselves with mankind, nor thieves, nor covetous, nor drunkards, nor revilers, nor extortioners, shall inherit the kingdom of God. And such were some of you: but ye are washed, but ye are sanctified, but ye are justified in the name of the Lord Jesus, and by the Spirit of our God.* Why, brethren, what horrible descriptions there are here; there are some of them so bad that when we have read the description, we wish to forget the sin; and yet, and yet, glory be to your almighty grace, O God! Such have you saved, and such you can save still. O, timid sinner, can you not trust in Jesus after this?

Hear you the word of the Lord again in Titus 3:3-5: *For we ourselves also were sometimes foolish, disobedient, deceived, serving divers lusts and pleasures, living in malice and envy, hateful, and hating one another. But after that the kindness and love of God our Saviour toward man appeared, not by works of righteousness which we have done, but according to his mercy he saved us.* Now, you hateful sinners, and you that hate others; you that are full of malice and envy, here is the gate open even for you, for the kindness and love of God towards man appears in the person of Christ.

Listen to another, for God's words are more than mine, and I do hope they will attract some of you. Ephesians 2:1-7 says, *Dead in trespasses and sins; wherein in time past ye walked according to the course of this world, according to the prince of the power of the air, the spirit that now worketh in the children of disobedience: Among whom also we all had our conversation in times past in the lusts of our flesh, fulfilling the desires of the flesh and of the mind; and were by nature the children of wrath, even as others. But God, who is rich in mercy, for his great love wherewith he loved us, even when we were dead in sins, hath quickened us together with Christ, (by grace ye are saved;) and hath raised us up together, and made us sit together in heavenly places in Christ Jesus.* What for? *That in the ages to come* – mark this – *he might shew the exceeding riches of his grace in his kindness toward us through Christ Jesus.*

One more passage, and I will not weary your attention. O that this last passage might comfort some of you. It is Paul who speaks in

1 Timothy 1:13-15: *[I] was before a blasphemer, and a persecutor, and injurious: but I obtained mercy, because I did it ignorantly in unbelief. And the grace of our Lord was exceeding abundant with faith and love, which is in Christ Jesus. This is a faithful saying;* see how he puts it from his own experience: *and worthy of all acceptation,* and therefore worthy of yours, poor sinner, *that Christ Jesus came into the world to save sinners; of whom I am chief.*

"Ah," says one, "but he would not save anymore." Let me go on – *Howbeit for this cause I obtained mercy, that in me first Jesus Christ might shew forth all longsuffering, for a pattern to them which should hereafter believe on him to life everlasting* (1 Timothy 1:16). So that if you trust as Paul did, you shall be saved as Paul was, for his conversion and salvation are a pattern to all those who would believe in the Lord Jesus Christ unto life everlasting. So, sinner, timid as you are, here Jesus meets you.

O, I wish I could say a word that would lead you poor tearful ones to look to Jesus. O, do not let the devil tempt you to believe that you are too sinful. *He is able also to save them to the uttermost that come unto God by him* (Hebrews 7:25).

> "Let not conscience make you linger, nor of fitness fondly dream."

Fittedness is not needed – do but come to him. You are wicked, and you do not feel your wickedness as you ought – that makes you all the more wicked. Come, then, and be clean. You are sinful, and this is your greatest sin, that you do not repent as you ought; but come to him and ask him to forgive your unrepentance. Come as you are. If he rejects one of you, I will bear the blame forever; if he casts one of you away who shall trust him, then call me a false prophet in the day of the resurrection. But I pledge my life upon it – I stake my own soul's interest on this – that whosoever comes to him, he *will in no wise cast out.*

I hear one more complaint. "I am without strength," says one. "Will Jesus come just where I am?" Yes, sinner, just where you are. You say you cannot believe, that is your difficulty. God meets you, then, in your inability. First, he meets you with *his promises.* Soul, you cannot believe; but when God, who cannot lie, promises, will you not believe, can you not believe then? I do think God's promise – so sure, so steadfast – must overcome this inability of yours. *Him that cometh to me I will in no wise cast out.* Can you not believe now? Why, that promise must be true!

But next, as if he knew that this would not be enough, he has taken *an oath* with it – and a more awful oath was never sworn – *As I live, saith the Lord God, I have no pleasure in the death of the wicked; but that the wicked turn from his way and live: turn ye, turn ye from your evil ways; for why will ye die, O house of Israel?* (Ezekiel 33:11). Can you not believe now? What, will you doubt God when he swears it, not only making God a liar but – let me shudder when I say it – will you think that God can perjure his own self? God forbid you should so blaspheme. Remember, *he that believeth not God hath made him a liar; because he believeth not the record that God gave of his Son* (1 John 5:10). Do not do this. Surely you can believe when the promise and the oath compel you to faith.

But still more, as if he knew that even this were not enough, he has given you of *his Spirit. If ye then, being evil, know how to give good gifts unto your children: how much more shall your heavenly Father give the Holy Spirit to them that ask him?* (Luke 11:13). Surely with this you can believe. "But," says one, "I will try." No, no, do not try; that is not what God commands you to do; no trying is needed; believe Christ now, sinner. "But," says one, "I will think about it." Do not think about it, do it now, do it at once, for this is God's gospel. There are some of you standing in these aisles and sitting in these pews whom I feel in my soul will never have another invitation, and if this be rejected today, I feel a solemn stirring in my soul – I think it is of the Holy Spirit – that you will never hear another faithful sermon, but you shall go down to hell unrepentant and unsaved, unless you trust in Jesus *now.*

I speak not as a man, but I speak as God's ambassador to your souls, and I command you, in God's name, trust Jesus, trust *now.* At your peril reject the voice that speaks from heaven, for *he that believeth not shall be damned* (Mark 16:16). *How shall [ye] escape, if [ye] neglect so great salvation* (Hebrews 2:3)? When it comes right home to you, when it thrusts itself in your way, oh, if you neglect it, how can you escape? With tears I would invite you, and, if I could, would compel you to come in. Why will you not? O souls, if you will be damned, if you make up your mind that no mercy shall ever woo you, and no warnings shall ever move you, then, sirs, what chains of vengeance must you feel that make light of these bonds of love. You have deserved the deepest hell, for you make light of the joys above. God save you. He will save you, if you trust in Jesus. God help you to trust him even now, for Jesus' sake. Amen.

Chapter 5

Judgment Threatening
but Mercy Sparing

Cut it down; why cumbereth it the ground? And he
answering said unto him, Lord, let it alone this year also.
(Luke 13:7-8)

The comparison of a man to a tree, and of human works to fruit, is exceedingly common in Scripture, because it is most suggestive, natural, and appropriate. As fruit is the production of the tree's life, and the end for which the tree exists, so obedience to the divine will, and holiness unto the Lord, should be the product of man's life, and for it he was at first created. When men plant trees in a vineyard, they very naturally expect to find fruit thereon; and if at the age and season of fruit bearing they find no produce, their natural and justifiable expectation is disappointed. Even thus, speaking after the manner of men, it is natural that the great Maker of all should look for the good fruit of obedience and love from the men who are the objects of his providential care, and be grieved when he meets with no return.

Man is very much more God's property than a tree can ever be the property of the man who plants a vineyard. As God has spent so much more skill and wisdom in the creation of a man than a husbandman can have spent in the mere planting of trees, it becomes the more natural that God should look for fruit from his creature, man; and the more reasonable that his most righteous requirements should not be refused. Trees that bring not forth fruit must be cut down; and sinners who bring not forth repentance, faith, and holiness must die. It is only a matter of time as to whether or not the vineyard shall be cleared of the burden of its barren trees; it is but a matter of time as to when the world shall be delivered from the burdensome presence of barren souls.

It stands to reason that barren trees which soon become the haunts of all sorts of mischief-doing creatures should be a nuisance to the vineyard; neither can sinners be permitted forever to become the dwelling places of evil spirits, and the dens of iniquity. A thorough riddance must be made of unrepentant sinners as well as of rotten trees. There is a time for felling fruitless trees, and there is an appointed season for hewing down and casting into the fire the useless sinner.

We shall not linger on the threshold of our solemn work this morning, for our burden is very heavy, and we would rather be rid of it speedily. We shall address ourselves at once to those persons who are living without God and without Christ, among whom many of you must be numbered. We shall speak to those who are not saved: there are such in the professing church everywhere. O may the Holy Spirit find them out by our word, and bring them in real earnest to consider their ways. To all unprofitable, unfruitful sinners we utter this hard but needful sentence: to cut you down would be most reasonable. It is right and reasonable to fell barren trees, and it is just as right and reasonable that *you* should be cut down.

This will appear, in the first place, if we reflect that *this is the shortest and the surest way to deal with you;* it will cost the least trouble, and be most certainly effective in removing you from the place to which you are an injury rather than a benefit. When the owner of the vineyard says to the gardener concerning the tree, *Cut it down,* the remedy is very sharp, but it is very simple; the felling is soon done, the clearance is thorough, and when another tree is planted, the benefit is evident. To dig around the tree, to trench it, to fertilize it, to prune it, and to water it – all this is a long affair, requiring care, and labor, and attention, while after all, the process may fail, and love's labor may be lost. To spare is difficult and involves trouble; to cut down is easy and effective.

Unconverted hearer, to preach the gospel to you, to call you to repentance, to beg, exhort, instruct, and warn you is a laborious process, and will probably be unsuccessful after all. The work will require much thought; providential agencies must be directed with wisdom, saints must pray with earnestness, ministers must plead with tears, the Scriptures must be written, and those Scriptures must be expounded and explained. All this is more than you have any natural right to expect that God should do with you, when he has in his hands a far simpler remedy by which he may at once ease himself of his adversary, and prevent your being any further offense. He has but to take away your breath and permit your body to descend into the grave and your soul into hell, and then the vineyard is clear, and there is room for another tree.

This sharp, short, and simple process is one which commends itself to men in the case of trees, and it is one which it is a thousand wonders that the Lord has not used with you. There will be no more blaspheming God, sinner, when the axe has laid you low! There will be no more rejecting the promise of his mercy, no more violating of Sabbath days, no more despising Scripture, when the day of doom arrives! Death shall end all these abominations forever. We shall no more have to agonize for you in vain, no more shall we weep bitterly because of your hardness of heart, no longer study to meet your objections, and sigh at your constant oppositions; the flames of hell will end all this, to your sad and awful cost.

No longer will a long-suffering God be wearied with your sins and pressed down under the load of your iniquities. He will make short work in righteousness, and a clean work too. He will sweep you away with the broom of destruction, and your rebellions will have an end, and your iniquities a reward most sure and terrible. Barren fig tree, you will draw the fatness from the ground no longer, and you will overshadow with evil influence your fellow trees no more. You have become a mere waste, and worse than a waste. Sinner, I ask you, is not the most ready plan to be rid of you suggested by the text, *Cut it down*? You yourself would do thus with a tree; what reason is there why the Lord should not deal thus with you?

Do you argue that you are of far greater importance than a tree? How do you make this appear? A tree is far more valuable to you than you can be supposed to be to the infinite God. The gardener would lose something possibly by cutting down his tree, but how can you suppose that your ruin would be any damage to the great God? The man who has many acres of vineyard is not much distressed if one barren vine be cut down, for there are so many more. If God had but one man in his dominions, it might seem to be of importance whether that man were saved or not; but there are so many of our race that your loss will be no more than the blowing of one atom of sand from the shore, or the removal of one drop from the sea.

You yourself could not well complain of being cut down, for you do not think much of your own soul; you are not concerned about its salvation; you trifle with its best interests. Why should you expect another to value you at a higher rate than you have set upon yourself? You fling away your soul for passing joys; you neglect the great salvation; you live in daily disobedience against God, who alone can do you good; even the preaching of the gospel, that all-powerful engine, seems to have no effect upon you, because you despise your own self. Well, man, if God despises you too, and commands his angels to cut you down, you cannot complain; it is but reasonable that God should estimate you at your own price, and weigh you in your own balances.

You have mischievously used the axe on yourself on many occasions, so why should not the proper executioner use it in earnest? Some men ruin their health by their sins; they wildly dash the axe against their own root and wound themselves terribly. On your soul you are using that axe continually, for you damage it by sin, and seek out folly, and choose the way to damnation, and labor to be lost. You cannot, therefore, complain. The crushing of you will be of no more consequence in this great universe than the killing of some ant upon the hill. You will never be missed. You may think greatly of yourself, but you are no more than a mere worm compared with the great universe of God. Beware, O rebellious, unrepentant sinner! My love yearns for your salvation, but my reason approves of your ruin, foresees it, and expects it speedily unless you turn unto the Lord and live.

Another reason makes the argument for judgment very powerful, namely, *that sufficient space for repentance has already been given.* If there had been any hope of your repentance, it seems to me that many of you would have repented long ago. I do not know what can be done for some of you more than has been done. You have been dug around – the digging,

I suppose, is to loosen the roots of their hold upon the earth – and you have had affliction, trial, and trouble, like the gardener's great spade, to wean you from earth, and loosen your hold of carnal things; you have had sickness – you have tossed to and fro upon the bed of pain; you have been in the jaws of death, and the horrid teeth seemed above and beneath you, as though they would enclose you forever; but all this has been of no avail.

Why should you be stricken anymore? You will revolt more and more. Already some of you have been struck until your whole head is sick, and your whole heart faint, but you will not hear the rod. By the blueness of the wound, says Solomon, the heart is made better (Proverbs 20:30), but in your case it has not been so. Those blue wounds of yours, those great and grievous afflictions, have not been sanctified to you, but rather you have gone on offending God, and provoking the Most High.

The gardener spoke of fertilizing as well as of digging, and some of you have had plentiful helps towards repentance. The gospel has been put close by your roots hundreds of times; you have a Bible in every house; you have had, some of you, the advantage of godly training from your youth up. You have been warned again, and again, and again, sometimes sternly, sometimes affectionately; you have heard the wooing voice of mercy, and the thundering notes of judgment; but yet, though Jesus Christ's own gospel has been laid close to your root, O barren tree, you are barren still. What is the use then of sparing you? Sparing has been tried, and it has had no effect; the other remedy is certain – *Cut it down.* O God, cut not down the sinner! And yet we dare not say it would be unreasonable, but on the contrary, it would be the most natural result of offended mercy. O sinner, you may well say,

> I have long withstood his grace,
>   Long provoked him to his face;
> Would not hearken to his calls;
>   Grieved him by a thousand falls.

> Depths of mercy! can there be
>   Mercy still reserved for me?
> Can my God his wrath forbear?
>   Me, the chief of sinners spare?

Sinner, I argue your case somewhat harshly, you think. Ah! man, would God I could make you think *me* harsh, if you would but have pity on your own soul, for my harshness is only apparent, not real, and your carelessness for your soul is real harshness, for you do not care for your own soul, but treat it as a thing to be cast away, and its ruin to be laughed at, as though it were contemptible. *All this while there has been no sign of improvement whatever in you.* If there had been some little fruit, if some tears of repentance had been flowing from your eyes, if there had been some seeking after Christ, if your heart had been a little softened, if you had but a little faith in Jesus, though it were but as a grain of mustard seed, then there would indeed be reasons for sparing you; but, sorrowful to add, *this sparing has had an ill effect upon you.*

Because God has not punished you, therefore you have become unruly and bold; you have said, *How doth God know? and is there knowledge in the most High?* (Psalm 73:11). You think that he is altogether such a one as you are, and that he will never bring you into judgment. You imagine that his sword is rusted into the scabbard, and his arm has grown short. Strange madness of evil, that you should pervert the long-suffering, which calls you to repentance, into a reason for running to greater lengths of sin! What, when the Lord spares you so that you may turn to him, shall that very sparing make you lift up the foot of your rebellion and reject him? It has done so. Up to this time you have grown hardened instead of softened. You have grown older, but you are no wiser, except it be with Satan's subtlety to be more wise in sin.

The gospel has not now the effect it had once on you. This voice could make your soul shiver and your very blood chill in its veins, but it cannot do so now. These eyes have sometimes looked on you and seemed as though they flashed with fire, but now they are as dull as lead to you. Once, when we spoke to you of the wrath to come, the tears would flow: there were some tears of gentle pity for your own soul; but ah! it is not so with you now. You will go your way, and our most earnest tones will seem but as the whistling wind, and our most urgent appeals as a child's playful song. O God, it is reasonable indeed that you should uplift that sharp axe of yours and say, *Cut it down.* I think I could abundantly justify the severity of God, if now he were to use it, when I thus perceive that all his sparing has had no effect but to make you worse, when I perceive that, notwithstanding these years of waiting, there are no tokens of improvement. If he says, *Cut it down,* then justice and reason say, "Alas, Lord, it is well it should be so."

But there are other reasons why *Cut it down* is most reasonable, *when we consider the owner and the other trees.* First of all, *here is a tree which brings forth no fruit whatever, and therefore is of no service.* It is like money badly invested, bringing in no interest; it is a dead loss to the owner. What is the use of keeping it? The dead tree is neither useful nor an ornament: it can yield no service and afford no pleasure. *Cut it down* by all manner of means. And even so with you, sinner; what is the use of you? You are of use to your children, to your family; in business you may be of some service to the world, but then the world did not make you; and your children, and your family – they did not create you. God has made you, God has planted you, God is your proprietor – you have done nothing for God.

Even in coming up to his house today, you did not come with any desire to honor God; and tomorrow, if you should chance to give something to the poor, it will not be because they are God's, nor out of love for *him.* You neither pray to God, nor praise God, nor live for God; you live for anything, for everything, for nothing, sooner than live for the God that made you. Then what is the good of you to God? All his other creatures praise him. There is not a spider spinning its web from leaf to leaf but does his bidding. *The ox knoweth his owner, and the donkey his master's crib,* but you do not know. Would you keep a horse that never did you service? Would you have a dog in your house that never licked your hand or fawned upon you, or did your will? You would say, "What is the good of this? A servant in my house to feed upon my bread, to be clothed with my bounty, and yet never to obey me, but to live in constant reckless disregard of my most reasonable commands?" You would say to such a servant, "Be gone; you are no servant of mine." Well might the Lord say this of you. All these years preserving goodness has winked at the past; long-suffering has borne with your follies and your faults, but it cannot be so forever, for reason demands that a useless thing should not always stand, and *Cut it down* is the natural inference from the uselessness of your life. Nor is this all. While you have been thus living without yielding anything, *you have been a very costly tree.*

The tree in the vineyard does not cost much except to dig around it, and to fertilize it, and to prune it. There is, of course, the expense of the gardener who has to watch over it, but this is very little. You may let the barren tree stand, for it is no great expense; but see what it costs to keep you! You have to be fed daily. The breath in your nostrils must come from God every moment. There has to be an exhaling from omnipotence at every single tick of that clock, or else you would not live. The complicated machinery of the human body needs to be tended and kept in order by the great Master Craftsman, or else before long the cogs would cease to act upon one another, and the wheels would be broken, and the whole machinery would be put out of gear.

Your body is a harp of a thousand strings, and it fails if one is gone. The good harpist must watch with diligent care to prevent the strings from snapping. You cost God much – much patience, much bounty, much skill, much power. Why should he spare you? What is there in you that he should go on with you in this manner? You would not spare the gnat that was always stinging you, buzzing in your face, and every moment insulting you. If it costs you much of your poor gold to spare that poor gnat's life, you would not be hesitant about it; you would crush it. And oh! it is a marvel that the Lord does not deal thus with you, for you are more brash than that gnat could be. Sinner, if you were in God's place, and were as ill-treated by your creature as the Lord is by you, would you lavish love and goodness upon him, to receive hardness of heart and rebellion in return? Assuredly not. Judge then whether it be not right that the Lord should say, *Cut it down.*

But there is a worse consideration, namely, that *all this is while you have been filling up a space which somebody might have been filling to the glory of God.* Where that barren tree stands there might have been a tree loaded with fruit. You are cluttering the ground, as the text says, that is, doing nothing but just being a troublesome nuisance. If another mother had those children, she would pray for them and weep over them, and teach them about Christ, but you do no such thing.

If another man had that money, it would be laid out for God's glory, and you lay it out for your own pleasure and forget the God who gave it to you. If another had sat in that seat which you occupy, it may be that he had long ago repented in sackcloth and ashes; but you, like the men of Capernaum, have been hardened instead of being softened under the gospel. It may be, man of influence, if another had stood where you have stood in the world's judgment, he would have led hundreds in the path of righteousness, but you, standing there, have done no such thing.

Oh! if another had your gifts, young man, he would not be making people laugh in the tavern, but would be pleading with all his might for Jesus. If another had but your gifts of utterance, he would be spending in prayer and teaching what you now spend in fun and frolic to make amusement for fools. Oh! if another had that time to live in, he would live in earnest for his Master.

If that young saint, just going through the flood, had your health and vigor, how would he spend and be spent! I recollect a minister of Christ who had but one talent, but much heart. I remember hearing him pray this prayer: "O God, I wish I had ten talents, that I might serve you better. When I think of some that have them, and do not serve you with them, I am inclined to pray, 'Lord take away their ten talents, and trust me with them if you will, for I do desire to have something more to lay out for you.'" Take heed, O my dear but sinful hearer, lest the Lord remove you suddenly, and fill up your place with one who will be obedient to his will.

Moreover, and to make bad worse even to the worst degree, *all this is while ungodly men are spreading an evil influence.* Thinking over the two lines of the verse we have been singing, I felt a horror of great darkness as I realized fully their solemn truthfulness with regard to some of you.

> I have shed his precious blood,
> Trampled on the Son of God;
> Filled with pains unspeakable
> *I who yet am not in hell.*

Well may the question arise –

"Whence to me this waste of love?"

It is so apparently a waste of long-suffering and mercy that some transgressors should be spared at all, that they may well marvel. Look at it, and I think you will see it very clearly so, *that the very fact that God does not punish sin on the spot is mischievously interpreted.* Men in all ages have drawn a wicked inference from the patience of the great judge. The preacher, in Ecclesiastes, says, *Because sentence against an evil work is not executed speedily, therefore the heart of the sons of men is fully set in them to do evil* (Ecclesiastes 8:11).

"Why," you say, "So-and-so drinks and swears, and he has lived to be a robust, hearty old man. Such a one has plunged into all sorts of folly and wickedness; he was a thief, and everything bad besides, and yet he prospers in the world and grows rich. Instead of God sinking him down at once to hell, he has favored him, and fattened him as a bullock in rich pasture." "Oh," the worldling says, "there is no justice in God. He does not punish sin." The very fact that you are spared, O sinner, is doing mischief in the world. Do you see that? Your mere existence in this world is to others an inducement to continue in sin; for while you are spared, others look at you and say, "God has not punished him." Therefore, they infer that he will not punish sin at all.

Moreover, how many there are of you *whose example is fearfully contagious;* whose lips and lives combine to lead your associates astray from God. In this dreadful plague which has ravaged our fields and destroyed the cattle, farmers have been advised, as soon as ever the cow is attacked with the disease, to kill it on the spot, and bury it five-feet-deep out of the way.

Let us reflect that the plague of sin is much more pestilential and more certain to kill than this plague among the cattle, and therefore stern justice cries, "Let the sinner be at once sent where he cannot increase the plague of iniquity. It is of no use sparing him; he grows no better; all the means used only make him worse, and meanwhile we must look to the welfare of others, lest he perish not alone in his iniquity. He teaches his children to swear; he makes others worldly; the whole current of his life is to incite men to rebel against God. Let his desperate course be stopped at once. The leprosy is upon him, and all that he touches he pollutes. For high sanitary reasons, therefore, he must be removed." It is better that one die than that many should be struck, and therefore, the highest consideration for the good of mankind in general renders it necessary that the mandate should go forth: *Cut it down.*

Our second most solemn work is to remind you, O unrepentant sinner, that for God to have spared you for so long is a very wonderful thing. That the infinitely just and holy God should have spared you, unconverted man, unconverted woman, up until now, is no small thing, but a matter for adoring wonder.

Let me show you this. Consider, *negatively, God is not sparing you because he is insensible towards your sins:* he is angry with the wicked every day (Psalm 7:11). If the Lord could be indifferent towards sin, and could bring his holy mind to treat it as a mere trifle, then it would be no wonder that he should let the transgressor live; but he cannot endure iniquity – all the day long his anger smokes and burns towards evil, and yet he holds back the thunderbolt, and does not strike the guilty. If *you* had been angry for half an hour, you would have come to hard words or blows; but here is the judge of all the earth angry every day for twenty, thirty, forty, fifty, sixty, seventy, or eighty years with some of you, and yet he has not struck. *It is not because the offense is at a distance,* and therefore far from his observant eye; no – your sins are like smoke in his nose; your iniquities provoke him to his face; you touch the apple of his eye, and yet, for all that, though this accursed thing called sin intrudes into his presence every instant, yet still he has spared you until now.

Observe, sinner, that he has spared you *not because he was unable to have destroyed you.* He might have bidden the tiles to fall from the roof, or the fever might have struck you in the street; the air might have refused to heave your lungs, or the blood might have ceased its circulation in your veins. The gates to death are many. The quiver of judgment is full of sharp arrows. The Lord has but to will it, and your soul is required of you. He said to the foolish rich man, *This night thy soul shall be required of thee,* and he never saw the morning; and he might as easily have sent the same sad message to you, *and what then?*

As I have said before, this great patience is not manifested towards your sinful soul because the Lord is at all dependent upon you; your living will not increase, and your dying will not diminish his glory. You will be no more missed than one withered leaf is missed in a forest, or one dewdrop in a thousand leagues of grass. Judgment needs but a word to work its utmost vengeance, and besides, you are so provoking that the marvel is that divine severity has spared you for so long. Admire and wonder at this long-suffering.

Remember that this wonder is increased when you *think of the fruit he deserved to have had from you.* A God so good and so gracious ought to have been loved by you. He has treated you so well, and given you such capacities for pleasure, that he ought to have had some service from you. You are not to God precisely what the ox is to its owner – you give to the ox only his grass or his straw, and you are done with him; but God gives to you not only your daily food, but also your very life – you are wholly dependent upon him.

Nothing can be so much yours as you are God's. You ought to have served him, to have delighted in that service, to spend and to have been spent for your Lord. He asks no more of you than he ought to have had, and yet he asks you to love the Lord your God with all your heart, your soul, and your strength – this was his first and great commandment, but this you have constantly, persistently broken. Oh, think then, when you have given to God such a bad return, when he ought to have received so much better – think, I pray you, how you must have provoked him.

And ah, my friends! I have to touch upon a very solemn part of the business now, when I notice again that some, perhaps present here, *have been guilty of very God-provoking sins.* Some offenses provoke God much more than others – I believe that *cursing* does, for it is malicious brashness, by which nothing can be gained. It is altogether a gratuitous piece of insult. To swear, to invoke the curse of God upon one's limbs and souls is an unnecessary, extra sin. There cannot be any pleasure in pronouncing oaths, anymore than in uttering any other form of words. It is just because man will hate his Maker, and will provoke him, that he does this.

O sinner, did you ever ask God to damn you, and are you not astonished that he has not done it? Did you ever desire that the blast should come upon you, and do you not marvel that he has not long ago swept you where his wrath would wither you forever? Swearing is a sin that provokes the Most High. O sinner, abhor this most detestable of vices.

There is also the sin of *infidelity,* and how many are guilty of that? How provoking to God for a man to deny his very existence; standing up and breathing God's air and living upon God's life, and yet saying that there is no God. An insignificant worm dares to challenge the Almighty to prove his deity and existence by a tremendous act of justice. This is a God-provoking sin.

So again is the sin of *persecution*. There may be some present here who have persecuted wife and child because of their following Christ. *He that toucheth you toucheth the apple of his eye* (Zechariah 2:8), says God. Beware, sinner, for you will not touch the Lord's eye for long without feeling his heavy hand. If any man injures your children, the blood is in your cheek at once, if you are a father, and you feel that you will show yourself strong in their defense; even so the heavenly Father will avenge his own elect. Therefore, take heed lest you persevere in this heaven-provoking sin.

And *slander,* too – lying against God's servants, inventing and spreading wicked tales against those who walk in the fear of God – is another evil which awakens the anger of God, and stirs up righteous fury against the man who is guilty of it. Beware! Beware!

Filthiness, filthiness of body and of life, will also provoke the Most Holy One. This once brought hell out of heaven upon Sodom; God sent down fire and brimstone because of the lusts of the flesh that made Sodom to stink in his nostrils; the harlot, and the adulterer, and the fornicator shall know that they sin not without provoking God very terribly.

And let me add here among these God-provoking sins, there is that *quenching of conscience* of which some of you have been guilty. Ah, my dear friends, there are not many of you to whom I spoke under these first topics, for I know that very few of you would indulge in these grosser sins; but there are some of you quite as bad in another sense, for you know the right and choose the wrong; you hear of Christ and do not give your hearts to him. We had hoped of some of you that long before this we would have seen you walking in the Lord's fear, but you are still strangers to Christ. You must have had hard work to do this. You must have had a terrible tug with conscience, some of you; I know you have been stifling many a holy desire, and when the Spirit of God has been striving with you, you have been so desperately set on mischief that still you have gone on in the error of your ways.

Now these sins provoke God. I do not believe that I stand in this pulpit and plead with you in God's name, and then go back and tell my

Master that you have rejected his warnings, without God's being angry with your hardness of heart and stiff-neckedness. I know if we send an ambassador to a foreign court to try and make peace, and he honestly and earnestly lays down proper stipulations for peace, if they are rejected, you will soon find the newspapers and public opinion ringing with indignation. "Why," they say, "will not the men have peace when the terms are so reasonable? Get out the ironclads and let them have war – a fight to the bitter end. If they will not yield to what is reasonable, then let us dress ourselves in thunder, and go forth across the sea."

And what do you think? Shall God be always provoked? Shall mercy be preached to you forever in vain? Shall Christ be presented and always rejected, and will you continue to be his enemies, and shall he never proclaim war against your souls? It is a marvel, it is a wonder that these God-provoking sins have so long been indulged in, and that you are not yet cut down.

And now, what is the reason for all this long-suffering? Why is it that this hindrance-ground tree has not been cut down? The answer is, because *there is one who pleads for sinners.* I have shown you, and some of you will think I have shown you with very great severity too, how reasonable it is that you should be cut down. I wish you felt it, for if you felt how reasonable it was that God should send you to hell, then you would begin to tremble, and there would be some hope for you. I can assure you I have trembled for you when I have thought how rational, how just, no, it would seem to me, how necessary it was that some of you should be lost. It has made me tremble for you, and I would to God you would tremble for yourselves.

But what has been the secret cause that you have been kept alive? The answer is, *Jesus Christ has pleaded for you; the crucified Savior has interfered for you.* And you ask me, "Why?" I answer, because *Jesus Christ has an interest in you all.* We do not believe in general redemption, but we believe in every word of this precious Bible, and there are many passages in the Scripture which seem to show that Christ's death had a universal bearing upon the sons of men. We are told that he tasted death for every man. What does that mean? Does it mean that Jesus Christ died to save every man? I do not believe it does, for it seems to me that everything that Christ intended to accomplish by the act of his death he must accomplish, or else he will be disappointed, which is not conceivable.

Those whom Christ died to save I believe he will save effectively, through his substitutionary sacrifice. But did he in any other sense die for the rest of mankind? He did. Nothing can be much more plain in Scripture, it seems to me, than that all sinners are spared as the result of Jesus Christ's death, and this is the sense in which men are said to trample on the blood of Jesus Christ. We read of some who denied the Lord who bought them. No one who is bought with blood for eternal salvation ever tramples on that blood; but Jesus Christ has shed his blood for the reprieve of men so that they may be spared, and those who turn God's sparing mercy into an occasion for fresh sin, do trample on the blood of Jesus Christ.

You can hold that doctrine without holding to universal redemption, or without at all contradicting that undoubted truth, that Jesus laid down his life for his sheep, and that where he suffered, he suffered not in vain. Now, sinner, whether you know it or not, you are indebted to him who did hang upon the tree for the breath that is now in you. You would not have been on praying ground and pleading terms with God this morning if it had not been for that dear suffering One. Our text represents the gardener as only *asking* to have it spared; but Jesus Christ did something more than ask – he pleaded, not with his mouth only, but also with pierced hands, and pierced feet, and pierced side; and those prevailing pleas have moved the heart of God, and you are yet spared.

May I speak to you then? If your life had been spared, when you were condemned to die, by my intervention – suppose such a case – would you despise *me*? If I had power at the court, and when you were condemned to die, I had gone in and pleaded for you, and you had been reprieved, year after year, would you hate me? Would you speak against me? Would you rail against my character? Would you find fault with my friends? I know you better. You would love me; you would be grateful for the sparing of your life.

O sinner, I wish you would treat the Lord Jesus as you would treat man. I wish you would think of the Lord Jesus Christ as you would think of your fellow man who had delivered you from death. You are not in hell, where you would have been if he had not come in and pleaded for you. I do implore you, think of the misery of lost souls, and recollect that *you* would have been in such a woeful condition yourself this morning if he had not lifted up that hand once pierced for human sin. There, there, where the flames can no abatement know, where a drop of water is a blessing too great to be received – there, where hope is excluded, and despair sits upon a throne of iron, binding captive souls in everlasting bands – where "Forever!" is written on the fire, and "Forever!" is printed on the chain, and "Forever! Forever! Forever!" rings out as the awful death knell of everything like hope, and rest – there you would have been this morning, this morning, if sparing grace had not prevented it.

Where are your companions, your old companions? You sat in the tavern with them; they are in hell, but you are not. When you were younger you sinned with them, and they are lost, but you are not. Why this difference made? Why are they cast away and you spared? I can only ascribe it to the gracious long-suffering of the Lord.

O, I pray you look at him who spared you, and weep and mourn for your sin. May the Spirit of God come down on you this morning and draw you to the foot of his dear cross; and as you see the blood which has spared your blood, and the death which has made you live until now, I do trust that the divine Spirit may make you fall down and say, "O Jesus, how can I offend you? How can I stand out against you? Accept me and save me for your mercy's sake."

For while I have thus spoken of the general interest which Christ has in you all, I have good hope that Christ has *a special interest in some of you.* I hope that he has specially redeemed you from among men, and bought you not with silver and gold, but with his own precious blood, having loved you with an everlasting love. I trust he intends with the bands of his kindness to draw you this morning. "Oh," says one, "I cannot think that such can be the case." But suppose you were to find out before long that you were chosen of God and dear to Christ, and were to be a jewel in his crown forever; what would you say then of yourself? "I would mourn that I could ever have hated him who loved me so well. Oh! that I could ever have stood out against him who was determined to save me! What a fool I was to quarrel with him who had paid my price, and chosen me by his grace, and taken me to be married unto himself forever!" I tell you that God will forgive you, but you will never forgive yourselves for having stood out and resisted so long.

Oh! may eternal mercy, which has not yet said, *Cut it down,* now dig around you and fertilize you, that you may bring forth fruit, and then it shall be all to the praise of him whose precious blood has saved us from eternal wrath. May God bless these feeble words of mine. He knows how I meant them – how I meant to speak them, how I meant to have wept over you, how I wanted that my soul should heave with passionate desire for your conversion. But if there have been no such outward manifestations, yet I pray God that the truth itself may be irresistible, and may he get to himself the victory, and his shall be the praise, evermore.

Chapter 6

This Year Too

This year also. (Luke 13:8)

W e earnestly desire to utter the word of exhortation; but alas, at this present time, the preacher is a prisoner, and he must speak from his pillow instead of his pulpit. Let not the few words which we can put together come with diminished power from a sick man, for the musket fired by a wounded soldier sends forth the bullet with none the less force. Our desire is to speak with living words, or not at all. He who enables us to sit up and compose these trembling sentences is implored to clothe them with his Spirit, that they may be according to his own mind.

The interceding vinedresser pleaded for the fruitless fig tree, *Let it alone this year also,* dating as it were a year from the time during which he spoke. Trees and fruit-bearing plants have a natural measurement for their lives: evidently a year came to its close when it was time to seek fruit on the fig tree, and another year commenced when the vinedresser began again his digging and pruning work. Men are such barren things that their fruit marks no certain periods, and it becomes needful to make artificial divisions of time for them; likewise there seems to be no set period for man's spiritual harvest or crop, or if there be, the sheaves and the clusters come not in their season, and therefore we have to say one to another, "This shall be the beginning of a new year." Be it so, then. Let us congratulate each other upon seeing the dawn of *this year also,* and let us unitedly pray that we may enter upon it, continue in it, and come to its close under the unfailing blessing of the Lord to whom all years belong.

The beginning of a new year suggests a retrospect. Let us take it, deliberately and honestly. *This year also* – then there had been former years of grace. The dresser of the vineyard was not for the first time aware of the fig tree's failure, neither had the owner come for the first time seeking figs in vain. God, who gives us *this year also,* has given us others before it; his sparing mercy is no novelty, his patience has already been stretched by our provocations. First came our *youthful* years, when even a little fruit unto God was peculiarly sweet to him. How did we spend them? Did our strength run all into wild wood and unruly branch? If so, we may well mourn that wasted vigor, that life misspent, that sin exceedingly multiplied.

He who saw us misuse those golden months of youth nevertheless affords us *this year also,* and we should enter upon it with a holy jealousy, lest what strength and ardor may be left to us should be allowed to run away into the same wasteful courses as formerly. Upon the heels of our youthful years came those of *early manhood,* when we began to muster a household, and to become as a tree fixed in its place; then also fruit would have been precious. Did we bear any? Did we present unto the Lord a basket of summer fruit? Did we offer him the firstling of our strength? If we did so, we may well adore the grace which so early saved us; but if not, the past chides us, and, lifting an admonishing finger, it warns us not to let *this year also* follow the way of the rest of our lives.

He who has wasted youth and the morning of manhood has surely had enough of fooling. The time past may well suffice him to have worked the will of the flesh; it will be an excess of naughtiness to suffer *this year also* to be trodden down in the service of sin. Many of us are now in the prime of life, and our years already spent are not few. Have we still need to confess that our years are eaten up by the grasshopper and the cankerworm? Have we reached the halfway house, and still know not where we are going? Are we fools at forty? Are we half a century old by the calendar and yet far off from years of discretion?

Alas, great God, that there should be men past this age who are still without knowledge! Unsaved at sixty, unconverted at seventy, unawakened at eighty, unrenewed at ninety! These are each and all startling. Yet, perhaps, they will each one fall upon ears which they should make to tingle, but they will hear them as though they heard them not. Continuance in evil breeds callousness of heart, and when the soul has long been sleeping in indifference, it is hard to arouse it from the deadly slumber.

The sound of the words *this year also* makes some of us remember *years of great mercy,* sparkling and flashing with delight. Were those years laid at the Lord's feet? They were comparable to the silver bells upon the horses – were they *holiness unto the Lord* (Zechariah 14:20)? If not, how shall we answer for it if *this year also* should be musical with merry mercy and yet be spent in the ways of carelessness?

The same words recall to some of us our *years of sharp affliction* when we were, indeed, dug around and fertilized. How did those years go? God was doing great things for us, exercising careful and expensive husbandry, caring for us with exceedingly great and wise care – did we render according to the benefit received? Did we rise from the bed more patient and gentle, weaned from the world, and welded to Christ? Did we bring forth clusters to reward the dresser of the vineyard? Let us not refuse these questions of self-examination, for it may be that this is to be another of these years of captivity, another season of the furnace and the refining-pot. The Lord grant that the coming tribulation may take more chaff out of us than any of its predecessors, and leave the wheat cleaner and better.

The new year also reminds us of *opportunities for usefulness* which have come and gone, and of *unfulfilled resolutions* which have blossomed only to fade; shall *this year also* be as those which have gone before? May we not hope for grace to advance upon grace already gained, and should we not seek for power to turn our poor sickly promises into robust action?

Looking back on the past we lament the follies by which we would not willingly be held captive *this year also,* and we adore the forgiving mercy, the preserving providence, the boundless liberality, and the divine love of which we hope to be partakers *this year also.*

If the preacher could think freely, he could row the text at his pleasure in many directions, but he is feeble, and so he must let it drive with the current which bears it on to a second consideration: the text mentions a mercy. It was in great goodness that the tree that cluttered the soil was allowed to stand for another year, and prolonged life should always be regarded as a blessing of mercy. We must view *this year also* as a grant from infinite grace. It is wrong to speak as if we cared nothing for life, and looked upon our being here as an evil or a punishment; we are here *this year also* as the result of love's pleadings, and in pursuance of love's designs.

The wicked man should reckon that the Lord's long-suffering points to his salvation, and he should permit the cords of love to draw him to it. O that the Holy Spirit would make the blasphemer, the Sabbath breaker, and the openly vicious to feel what a wonder it is that their lives are prolonged *this year also*! Are they spared to curse, and riot, and defy their Maker? Shall this be the only fruit of patient mercy?

The procrastinator who has put off the messenger of heaven with his delays and half promises, ought he not to wonder that he is allowed to see *this year also*? How is it that the Lord has borne with him and put up with his vacillations and hesitations? Is this year of grace to be spent in the same manner? Transient impressions, hasty resolves, and speedy apostasies – are these to be the weary story over and over again?

The startled conscience, the tyrannical passion, the smothered emotion! Are these to be the tokens of yet another year? May God forbid that any one of us should hesitate and delay through *this year also*. Infinite pity holds back the axe of justice; shall it be insulted by the repetition of the sins which caused the uplifting of the instrument of wrath? What can be more tantalizing to the heart of goodness than indecision? Well might the Lord's prophet become impatient and cry, *How long halt ye between two opinions?* (1 Kings 18:21). Well may God himself push for a decision and demand an immediate reply.

O undecided soul, will you swing much longer between heaven and hell, and act as if it were hard to choose between the slavery of Satan and the liberty of the Great Father's home of love? *This year also* will you sport in defiance of justice, and pervert the generosity of mercy into a license for still further rebellion? *This year also* must divine love be made an occasion for continued sin? O do not act so wretchedly, so contrary to every noble instinct, so injuriously to your own best interests.

The believer is kept out of heaven *this year also* in love, and not in anger. There are some for whose sake it is needful that he should abide in the flesh, some to be helped by him on their heavenward way, and others to be led to the Redeemer's feet by his instruction. The heaven of many saints is not yet prepared for them, because their nearest companions have not yet arrived, and their spiritual children have not yet gathered in glory in sufficient number to give them a thoroughly heavenly welcome. They must wait *this year also* so that their rest may be the more glorious, and that the sheaves which they will bring with them may afford them greater joy.

Surely, for the sake of souls, for the delight of glorifying our Lord, and for the increase of the jewels of our crown, we may be glad to wait here below *this year also*. This is a wide field, but we may not linger in it, for our space is little, and our strength is even less.

Our last feeble utterance shall remind you that the expression, *this year also,* implies a limit. The vinedresser asked for no longer a reprieve than one year. If his digging and manuring should not then prove successful, he would plead no more, but the tree would fall. Even when Jesus is the pleader, the request of mercy has its bounds and times. It is not forever that we shall be let alone and allowed to clutter the ground; if we will not repent we must perish, if we will not be benefited by the spade we must fall by the axe.

There will come a last year to each one of us; therefore, let each one say to himself, Is this my last? If it should be the last with the preacher, he would gird up his loins to deliver the Lord's message with all his soul and bid his fellow man to be reconciled to God. Dear friend, is *this year also* to be *your* last? Are you ready to see the curtain rise upon eternity? Are you now prepared to hear the midnight cry, and to enter into the marriage supper? The judgment and all that will follow upon it are most surely the heritage of every living man; blessed are they who by faith in Jesus are able to face the bar of God without a thought of terror.

If we live to be counted among the oldest inhabitants, we must depart at last; there must be an end, and the voice must be heard – *Thus saith the Lord; . . . this year thou shalt die* (Jeremiah 28:16). So many have gone before us, and are going every hour, that no man should need any other *memento mori* (reminder of mortality), and yet man is so eager to forget his own mortality, and thereby to forfeit his hopes of bliss, that we cannot too often bring it before the mind's eye. O mortal man, remind yourself! Prepare to meet your God, for you must meet him. Seek the Savior, yes, seek him before another sun sinks to his rest.

Once more *this year also,* and it may be for this year only, the cross is uplifted as the Pharos lighthouse of the world, the one light to which no eye can look in vain. Oh, that millions would look that way and live. Soon the Lord Jesus will come a second time, and then the blaze of his throne will supplant the mild radiance of his cross: the judge will be seen rather than the Redeemer. Now he saves, but then he will destroy. Let us hear his voice at this moment. He has prescribed a day; let us be eager to avail ourselves of the gracious season. Let us believe in Jesus this day, seeing it may be our last. These are the pleadings of one who now falls back on his pillow in utter weakness. Hear them for your souls' sakes and live.

Chapter 7

All Things Are Ready. Come.

Come; for all things are now ready. (Luke 14:17)

This invitation was first of all made to the Jews, but it seems to me
to have a peculiar appropriateness to ourselves. It is later in the
day than when first the Lord was here, and therefore the suppertime is
evidently closer at hand. The shadows lengthen, the sun of the present
dispensation is nearing its setting; by nearly nineteen hundred years
has its day been shortened since first the Lord sent forth his servants at
suppertime. The fullness of time for the marriage supper of the Lamb
must speedily arrive, and therefore it is necessary for us to be more than
ever earnest in delivering the message to the invited guests.

And if all things could be said to be ready even in our Savior's day, we
may say it with still greater emphasis now; for when he delivered this parable the Holy Spirit was not yet given, but Pentecost has now passed, and the
Spirit of God abides with us to accompany the Word, to fill it with power,
and to bless our souls as we feed upon the truth. Very emphatically, then, at
this time all things are now ready, and the supper awaits the guests. I pray
you do not begin to make excuses, but be prepared to follow us when we bid
you to come, to go with us when we seek to bring you in, or at least to yield
to our pleadings when with all the sacred violence of love we would compel
you to come in. We will not grudge the use of all the three increasing modes
of persuasion so long as you are but led to *come; for all things are now ready.*

There are two things clearly in the text, and these have a close relationship to one another. There is a plain invitation – *Come,* and then a forcible argument – *for all things are ready.* The argument is fetched from the divine preparations, gathered from among the dainty provisions of the royal feast. *My oxen and my fatlings are killed, and all things are ready: come unto the marriage* (Matthew 22:4). The readiness of everything on God's part is the argument for why men should come and partake of his grace, and that is the point upon which we will dwell at this time. The readiness of the feast of mercy is the reason why men should come to it at once.

We will begin our meditation by laying down the first statement which shall make our first division of discourse, namely, that it is God's habit to have all things ready, whether for his guests or his creatures. You never discover him to be late in anything. When the guests come, there is not a scramble to get the table arranged and the food prepared, but the Lord has great forethought, and every little point of detail is well arranged. *All things are now ready.*

It was so in creation. He did not create a single blade of grass upon the face of the earth until the soil and the atmosphere had been prepared for it, and until the kindly sun had learned to look down upon the earth. Imagine vegetation without a sun, or without the succession of day and night. But the air was full of light, the firmament upheld the clouds, and the dry land had appeared from out of the sea, and then all things were ready for herb, and plant, and tree. Nor did God prepare one single creature that has life, nor any bird that flies in the midst of heaven, nor fish that swims the seas, nor beast that moves on the dry land, until he had prepared its *habitat,* and made ready its appointed food. There were no cattle before there were meadows for their grazing; no birds until there were trees for their nests; no, nor even a creeping insect until its portion of meat had been provided. No creature had to wait in a hungry mood while its food was growing; all things were ready: ready first for vegetation, and then afterwards for animal life.

As for Adam, when God came to make him as his last and noblest work of creation, all things were ready. The garden was laid out upon the banks of flowing streams and planted with all kinds of trees, the fruits were ripe for his diet, and the flowers were in bloom for his delight. He did not come to an unfurnished house, but he entered upon a home which his Father had made pleasant and agreeable for his dwelling. The world was first fitted up, and then the man who was to govern that world was placed in it. *All things are now ready,* the Lord seems to say, "Spring up, O herb-yielding seed"; and then, "All things are ready, come forth you deers of the field!" and then, "All things are ready; stand forth, O man, made in my own image!"

In after times we may gather illustrations of the same truth from the ways of God with men. The ark was first of all built, and the various creatures were gathered into it, with all their necessary provisions, for that strange voyage which they were about to take. And then the Lord said to Noah, *Come thou and all thy house into the ark* (Genesis 7:1). "All things are ready, come," was his voice to the chosen eight as they entered into the ark. There was no need to wait any longer; every preparation was made, and therefore God shut them in. Everything is done with punctuality and exactness by the only wise God. The selfsame day that a thing is needed it is prepared.

Take another event in Providence, such as the going down of Israel into Egypt. God had determined that Jacob and his seed should sojourn awhile in the land of Ham, but how wisely he prepared for the whole matter. He sent a man before them, even Joseph, and Joseph was there upon the throne clothed with power to nourish them through the famine. He had been there years before, all in good time to store the wheat while the seven years of plenty lasted, that they might be well fed during the seven years of famine. Goshen also was at the disposal of Joseph, so that the flocks and herds of Israel might dwell in that fat land. Not into Egypt shall God's Israel go until all things are ready; and when all things are ready, they will come out again with a high hand and an outstretched arm.

So it was when the tribes migrated into Canaan itself. God took them not to the promised land until all things were ready. They were made to wait for the proper time, for the Lord said, *The iniquity of the Amorites is not yet full* (Genesis 15:16). Not until the inhabitants of the land had passed the bounds of mercy, and were condemned to die, were the Israelites brought upon the scene to be at once their executioners and successors; and when the tribes came to the river Jordan, God had prepared everything for them, for he had sent the hornet before them to drive out the people, and a pestilence also, for the spies said, *It is a land that eateth up the inhabitants thereof* (Numbers 13:32).

The Lord God had gone before them to fight their battles before they came, and to prepare a place for them, so that when they entered, they dwelt in houses which they had not built, and they gathered the fruit of olives which they had not planted. They came to a land that flowed with milk and honey, a land in a fine cultivated condition, and not a wilderness which with hard labor must be reclaimed. Israel came to a country that was as the garden of the Lord, whose fruit might at once be enjoyed, for they ate of the old corn of the land almost as soon as they passed the Jordan. So you see, *All things are ready* is a proclamation which the Lord has often in spirit made to those whom he chooses to bless.

Now the fact that in the great gospel supper all things are ready teaches us, first, that *God's thoughts go before men's comings. Come; for all things are now ready* (emphasis added). Not "If you come, all things will be ready," but "they are ready, and therefore come." Grace is first, and man at his best follows its footsteps. Long before we ever thought of God, he thought of us; yes, before we had a being and before time itself began, in the bosom of the Eternal there were thoughts of love towards those for whom the table of his mercy is now spread. He had planned and arranged everything in his dignified mind from of old, he had indeed foreknown and predestinated all the provisions and all the guests of his supper; all things were settled in his eternal covenant and purpose before ever the earth was.

Never think, oh sinner, that you can outstrip the love of God; it is at the end of the race before you are at the beginning. God has completed before you have begun. His thoughts are before ours, and *so are his acts,* for he does not say, "All things are planned and arranged," but *All things are now ready.* Jesus, the great sacrifice, is slain, and the fountain for our cleansing is filled with blood; the Holy Spirit has been given; the Word by which we are to be instructed is in our hands; and the light which will illuminate that sacred page is promised to us through the Holy Spirit.

Things promised ought to encourage us to come to Christ, but things already given ought to be irresistible attractions. All things necessary are already completed by the Lord before we come to cry for mercy; this should make us very hopeful and eager in our approaches to the Lord. Come, sinner, come at once: this ought to encourage you, since all that God has to do in your salvation is done before you have a thought of him or turn one foot towards his abode. All things are ready. Come!

This also proves how welcome those are who come. If you are invited to see a friend, and when you reach the place you find the door tightly shut, and after knocking many times no one answers, for there is no one at home, you reckon that there is some mistake, or that the invitation was not a sincere one. Even if your host should come to the door and admit you, but should evidently be embarrassed, for there is no meal provided, and he has made no arrangements for your rest at night, you soon detect it, and like a wise man you quickly move off somewhere else, for if you had been welcome, things would have been prepared for you. But oh, poor soul, if you come to God all things are ready for your entertainment.

> Spread for thee the festal board,
> With his richest dainties stored.

The couch of rest and quietness is prepared for you. All things are ready. How freely does the Lord welcome you, how genuine is the invitation, how sincere the desire that you should come to feast with him.

So much upon our first remark; it is the habit of the Lord to have all things ready for his guests.

Our second statement is that this readiness should be an argument that his saints should come continually to him and find grace to help in every time of need. O children of God, I will lift the parable away from the immediate use which the Savior made of it to employ it for your good. You know, beloved, that whenever the Lord Jesus Christ invites his people to come to him, and to taste of his bounty, all things are ready. It was a beautiful scene by the sea of Tiberias when the Lord spoke to those who had been toiling on the lake at fishing, and said to them, *Come and dine.* They were willing enough to dine, but they were busy dragging to the shore those great fishes.

Remember, when they did land, they found the invitation to be no vain one, for it is written, *They saw a fire of coals there, and fish laid thereon, and bread* (John 21:9). How the coals came there, and the fish, and the bread, the Gospel writer does not tell us, but our Lord would not have asked them to dinner if he had not been able to give them a warm reception; there was the fire of coals, and the fish laid thereon, and bread. Whenever therefore your Lord and Master, by his blessed Spirit, calls you to come near to him, you may be quite sure that all things are ready for your immediate enjoyment; you need never pause or hesitate, but approach him without delay.

I want to caution you against replying, "But Lord, I do not feel ready." That is most true, but that is not an argument that you should use to excuse yourself in holding back. It is *his* readiness that is the main thing, not yours, and as all things are ready, do come whether you feel ready or not. I have heard of some Christians who have said, "I do not feel in a proper frame of mind to pray." My brother, pray until you do. Some have said, "I do not think I shall go up to the house of God today; I feel so unhappy, so cast down." When should you go so much as then, in order that you may find comfort? "Still," says one, "you would not have me sing a hymn when I am of heavy heart." Alas, would I not? I would indeed. I would have you sing yourself up from the depths of the sea where all God's billows have gone over you.

David utterly often did so, when he began a psalm, in the deeps, and then gradually rose, and rose, and rose, until he was in a perfect rapture of delight before the psalm was over. All things are ready with your Lord; therefore, do come whether you happen to be ready or not.

Note the times when this truth ought to have power with you. All things are ready; therefore, come to *the storehouse of divine promise.* Are you in spiritual poverty? Come and take what God has provided for you, for all things are yours, and all the blessings of the everlasting hills belong to all the people of God. Are you needing strength? There is a promise: *As thy days, so shall thy strength be* (Deuteronomy 33:25). It is ready; come and take it.

Are you needing consolation? Do you not know that all things are ready for your comfort, that two unchangeable things, wherein it is impossible for God to lie, are already set before you? Come and take your solace. Alas, remember that all that God has promised belongs to all those who believe the promise, and that you may therefore come at all times, however deep your need, and if you only have faith, you shall find the special supply for the special need. All things are ready; therefore, come with holy confidence, and take what is ripe enough to gather, ripe for you.

Come next to *the mercy seat* in prayer; all things are ready there. The mercy seat is sprinkled with the precious blood of Christ. The veil also is torn in two, and from between the cherubim the Lord's glory now shines forth with gentlest radiance. Let us therefore come with boldness unto the throne of the heavenly grace, because everything there is ready for the pleading petitioner. You have no need to bring anything with you there. You have no need of making preparations other than what the Holy Spirit waits to give you in the form of groanings which cannot be uttered.

Come, child of God, notwithstanding your carelessness and indifference, or whatever it may be that you have to complain about, for though you be unready, the throne of grace is ready, and therefore do you draw near to it and find the grace you need.

If at this time we feel strong promptings towards *communion* with Christ, what a blessing it is that Christ is always ready to commune with his people. *Behold*, says he, *I stand at the door, and knock* (Revelation 3:20). We think that *we* stand at the door and knock, but it is scarcely so; the greater truth with regard to his people is that Jesus asks for fellowship with us, and tells us that if we open the door – and that is all he bids his people to do – he will enter in and dine with them, and they with him. Suppose there is no supper, he will provide it – he has all things ready. The Master says, *Where is the guestchamber?* (Luke 22:11). He does not say, "Where is the feast?" If your heart will be the guestchamber, he will provide the supper, and you shall dine with him and he with you.

At whose door did Christ knock according to the Scriptures? It was at the door of the Laodicean church, at the door of the very church concerning which he had said, *Because thou art lukewarm, and neither cold nor hot, I will spue thee out of my mouth* (Revelation 3:16). Therefore, you poor Laodicean believer that is here this morning, if you have any promptings towards Christ, arise, for all things are ready, and forevermore you are aware that your soul shall be as *the chariots of Amminadab* (Song of Solomon 6:12). He is ready to receive us to his heart of hearts. How sweetly this ought to constrain us to fly into the arms of Jesus.

I think the same thought ought to cross our minds with regard to *every daily duty.* We wake up in the morning, but we do not know exactly what lies before us, for God's providence has constantly new revelations. But I like to think in the morning that all things are ready for my pathway through the day, that if I will go out to serve God in my ministry, he has prepared some ear into which I am to drop a gracious word, and some heart in the furrows of which I shall sow some blessed seed effectively. Behold all providence with its mighty wheels is coworking with the servant of the living God; only go forward in zeal and confidence, my brother, and you shall find that every step of your way is ready for you. Thy Master has walked the road and marked out for you the houses of refreshment where you are to wait until you shall come to the Celestial City itself, and the holy spots where you shall bring glory to his blessed name. For a useful life, all things are ready for us.

Yes, and if beyond the daily service of life we should feel a prompting to aspire to *a higher degree of holiness,* if we want to grow in grace and reach the fullness of the stature of a man in Christ Jesus, all things are ready for us. No Christian can have a sacred ambition for holiness which the Lord is not prepared to fulfill. You that purpose to be like your Master, you that desire to make a self-sacrifice that will show the power of his grace in you, the Holy Spirit waits to help you; all things shall work for you, for all things are ready. Come therefore without fear.

One of these days it may be that you and I shall either have grown very old, or else disease will lay hold upon us, and we shall lie upon the sickbed watching and waiting for our Master's coming. Then there shall suddenly appear a messenger from him, who will bring us this word: *All things are ready: come unto the marriage* (Matthew 22:4), and closing our eyes on earth we shall open them in heaven and see what he has done who so sweetly said, *I go to prepare a place for you. And if I go and prepare a place for you, I will come again, and receive you unto myself; that where I am, there ye may be also* (John 14:2-3).

Oh, it will be a joyous moment when we shall hear the summons, "All things are ready, leave your house of clay, your farm, your merchandise, and even her who lies in your bosom, for the marriage of the Lamb has come, and you must be there; therefore, rise up, my love, my fair one, and come away. The winter is over and past, the time of the singing of birds has come for you; all things are ready, come!" I feel tempted to linger here, but I must tear myself away from that point to pass on to the next.

The perfect readiness of the feast of divine mercy is evidently intended to be a strong argument with sinners as to why they should come at once. To the sinner, then, do I address myself.

Soul, do you desire eternal life? Is there within your spirit a hungering and a thirsting after such things as may satisfy your spirit and make you live forever? Then listen while the Master's servant gives you the invitation. *Come, for **all things** are now ready* (emphasis added) – *all*, not some, but all. There is nothing that you can need between here and heaven but what is provided in Jesus Christ, in his person and in his work. All things are ready, life for your death, forgiveness for your sin, cleansing for your filthiness, clothing for your nakedness, joy for your sorrow, strength for your weakness, yes, more than all that ever you can want is stored up in the boundless nature and work of Christ. You must not say, "I cannot come because I have not this, or have not that." Are you to prepare the feast? Are you to provide anything? Are you the purveyor of even so much as the salt or the water?

You know not your true condition, or you would not dream of such a thing. The great Householder himself has provided the whole of the feast; you have nothing to do with the provision but to partake of it. If you lack, come and take what you lack; the greater your need, the greater reason why you should come where all things that your need can possibly want, will be at once supplied. If you be so needy that you have nothing good at all about you, all things are ready. What would you provide more when God has provided all things? Excess of naughtiness would it be if you were to think of adding to his *all things;* it would be but a presumptuous competing with the provisions of the great King, and this he will not endure. All that you need – I can but repeat the words – between the gates of hell, where you now lie, and the gates of heaven, to which grace will bring you if you believe – all is provided and prepared in Jesus Christ the Savior.

And all things are *ready* – dwell on that word. The oxen and the fatlings were killed; what is more, they were prepared to be eaten, they were ready to be feasted on, they smoked on the table. It is something when the king gives orders for the slaughter of so many bullocks for the feast, but the feast is not ready then; and when beneath the battle-axe the victims fall, and they are stripped and hung up ready for the fire, there is something done, but they are not ready. It is when the joints are served hot and steaming upon the table, and all that is needed is brought forth and laid in proper order for the banquet, it is then that all things are ready, and this is the case now.

At this very moment you will find the feast to be in the best possible condition; it was never better and never can be better than it is now. All things are ready, just in the exact condition that you need them to be, just in such condition as shall be best for your soul's comfort and enjoyment. All things are ready; nothing needs to be further mellowed or sweetened; everything is at the best that eternal love can make it.

But notice the word *now*. *All things are **now** ready* (emphasis added) – just now, at this moment. At feasts, you know, the good housewife is often troubled if the guests come late. She would be sorry if they came half an hour too soon, but half an hour too late spoils everything, and in what a state of fret and worry she is if when all things are *now* ready, her friends still delay. Leave food at the fire a while, and it does not seem to be *now ready*, but something more than ready, and even spoiled. So does the great Householder lay stress upon this; all things are *now* ready, therefore come at once. He does not say that if you will delay for another seven years, all things will then be ready. God grant that long before that space of time you may have gotten beyond the needs of persuasion by having become a taster of the feast, but he does say that they are all ready now, just now.

Just now that your heart is so heavy and your mind is so careless, that your spirit is so wandering – all things are ready now. Just now, though you have never thought of these things before, but dropped in this morning to see this large assembly with no motive whatever as to your own salvation, yet all things are ready *now*. Though your sins are as the stars of heaven, and your soul trembles under an awful foreboding of coming judgment, yet *all things are now ready*. After all your rejections of Christ, after the many invitations that have been thrown away upon you, come to the supper.

And if they are ready *now*, the argument is, come *now*, while still all things are ready. While the Spirit lingers and still does strive with men, while mercy's gates still stand wide open, that whosoever will, may come, while life and health and reason still are spared to you and the ministering voice that bids you to come can still be heard, come now, come at once – all things are ready – come! Delay is as unreasonable as it is wicked, now that all things are ready.

Notice that all things were ready for those who were bidden. They did not come, but they were not mocked when they were bidden to come. The fact of all things being ready proved that the invitation was a sincere one, although it was a rejected one. There are some who will not have us give an invitation to any but to those whom we believe are sure to come, no, in a measure, *have* come; that is to say, they make a minister to be a mere luxury. Why does he need to come and invite those who have already begun to come? But we believe it to be our duty and our privilege to invite the whole mass of mankind, and even those who will not come. If we knew they would not come, we should not therefore exempt them from the bidding, for the servant was sent to bid them to the wedding who nevertheless all with one consent began to make excuses. They were invited, and earnestly invited, and all things were ready, though they came not.

O my dear friends, if you do not come to Christ you will perish, but you will never be able to say you were not bidden, and that there was nothing ready for you. No, there stands the feast all spread, and you are sincerely and honestly bidden to come. God grant that you may come, and come at once.

Now I am going to pass on to my fourth and last point, which may God bless to the comfort of some seeking soul. This text disposes of a great deal of talk about the sinner's readiness or unreadiness because, if the reason why a sinner is to come is because all things are ready, then it is idle for him to say, "But I am not ready." It is clear that all the readiness required on man's part is a willingness to come and receive the blessing which God has provided. There is nothing else necessary; if men are willing to come, they may come, they will come. Where the Lord has been pleased to touch the will so that man has a desire towards Christ, where the heart really hungers and thirsts after righteousness, that is all the readiness that is needed. All the fittedness he requires is that first you feel your need of him (and that he gives you), and that secondly, in feeling your need of him you are willing to come to him.

Willingness to come is everything. A readiness to believe in Jesus, a willingness to cast the soul on him, a preparedness to accept him just as he is, because you feel that he is just the Savior that you need – that is all. There was no other readiness, there could have been none, in the case of those who were poor and blind, and lame, and maimed, yet came to the feast. The text does not say, "You are ready, therefore come"; that is a legal way of putting the gospel; but it says, "All things are ready, the gospel is ready, therefore you are to come." As for *your* readiness, all the readiness that is possibly needed is a readiness which the Spirit gives us, namely, a willingness to come to Jesus.

Now notice that the unreadiness of those who were bidden arose out of their possessions and out of their abilities. One would not come because he had bought a piece of land. What a great heap Satan casts up between the soul and the Savior! With what worldly possessions and good deeds he builds an earthwork of huge dimensions between the sinner and his Lord. Some gentlemen have too many acres ever to come to Christ: they think too much of the world to think much of him. Many have too many fields of good works in which there are growing crops in which they pride themselves, and these cause them to feel that they are persons of great importance. Many a man cannot come to Christ for all things because he has so much already.

Others of them could not come because they had so much to do, and could do it well. One had bought five yoke of oxen, and he was going to prove them. He was a strong man quite able for plowing, so the reason why he did not come was because he had so much ability.

Thousands are kept away from grace by what they have and by what they can do. Emptiness is more preparatory to a feast than fullness. How often does it happen that poverty and inability even help to lead the soul to Christ? When a man thinks himself to be rich, he will not come to the Savior. When a man dreams that he is able at any time to repent and believe, and to do everything for himself that is needed, he is not likely to come, and by a simple faith will rest in Christ. It is not what you don't have, but what you do have that keeps many of you from Christ. Sinful self is a devil, but righteous self is seven devils. The man who feels himself guilty may for a while be kept away by his guilt, but the man who is self-righteous will never come; until the Lord has taken his pride away from him, he will still refuse the feast of free grace. The possession of abilities and honors and riches keep men from coming to the Redeemer.

But on the other hand, personal condition does not constitute an unfittedness for coming to Christ, for the sad condition of those who became guests did not exclude them from the supper. Some were *poor,* and doubtless wretched and ragged; they had not a penny to bless themselves with, as we say. Their garments were tattered; perhaps worse, they were filthy; they were not fit to be near respectable people; they would certainly be no credit to my Lord's Table. But those who went to bring them in did not search their pockets, nor look at their coats, but they fetched them in. They were poor, but the messengers were told to bring in the poor, and therefore they brought them. Their poverty did not prevent their being ready; and oh, poor soul, if you be poor literally, or poor spiritually, neither sort of poverty can constitute an unfittedness for divine mercy.

The poorer the wretch the welcomer here.

If you are brought to your last penny; yes, if that is spent, and if you have pledged all, and you are left in debt over head and ears, and think that there is nothing for you but to be laid by the heels in prison forever, nevertheless you may come, poverty and all.

Another class of them were *maimed,* and so were not very comely in appearance. An arm had been lopped off, or an eye had been gouged out. One had lost a nose, and another a leg. They were in all stages and shapes of dismemberment. Sometimes we turn our heads away and feel that we would rather give anything than look upon beggars who show their wounds, and describe how they were maimed. But it did not matter how badly they were disfigured; they were brought in, and not one of them was disgusted because of the ugly cuts he had received.

So, poor soul, however Satan may have torn and lopped you, and into whatsoever condition he may have brought you, so that you feel ashamed to live, nevertheless this is no unfittedness for coming; just as you are, you may come to his table of grace. Moral disfigurements are soon rectified when Jesus takes the character in hand. Come to him, however sadly you are injured by sin.

There were others who were *lame;* that is to say, they had lost a leg, or it was of no use to them, and they could not come unless they had a crutch and crawled or hopped on it. But nevertheless that was no reason why they were not welcome. Ah, if you find it difficult to believe, it is no reason why you should not come and receive the grand pardon that Jesus Christ is ready to bestow upon you. Lame with doubting and distrusting, nevertheless come to the supper and say, *Lord, I believe; help thou mine unbelief* (Mark 9:24).

Others were *blind* people, and when they were told to come, they could not see the way; but in that case the messenger was not told to tell them to come – he was commanded to bring them, and a blind man can come if he is brought. All that was needed was a willingness to be led by the hand in the right direction. Now you who cannot fully understand the gospel as you desire to do, who are puzzled and perplexed, give your hand into the hand of Jesus, and be willing to be led, be willing to believe what you cannot comprehend, and to grasp in confidence that which you are not able yet to measure with your understanding. The blind, however ignorant or uninstructed they are, shall not be kept away because of that.

Then there were the men in the *highways* – I suppose they were beggars; and the men in the *hedges* – I suppose they were hiding, and were probably thieves. But nevertheless they were told to come, and though they were highwaymen and hedge birds, even that did not prevent their coming and finding welcome. Though outcasts, castoffs, spiritual gypsies, and people that nobody cared for, yet, whatever they might be, that was not the question. They were to come because all things were ready: come in rags, come in filth, come maimed, come covered with sores, come in all sorts of filthiness and abomination, yet because all things are ready, they were to be brought or to be compelled to come in.

Now, lastly, I think it was the very thing, which in any one of these people looked like unfittedness, that was a help to them. It is a great truth that what we regard as unfittedness is often our truest fittedness. I want you to notice these poor, blind, and lame people. Some of those who were invited would not come because they had bought some land, or five yoke of oxen. But when the messenger went up to the poor man in rags and said, "Come to the supper," it is quite clear he would not say he had bought a field, or oxen, for he could not do it; he had not a penny to do the thing with, so that he was completely delivered from that temptation. And when a man is invited to come to Christ and he says, "I do not want him; I have a righteousness of my own," he will stay away. But when the Lord Jesus came along to me, I never was tempted in that way, because I had no righteousness of my own, and I could not have made one if I had tried.

I know some here who could not patch up a garment of righteousness if they were to put all their rags together, and this is a great help to their receiving the Lord Jesus. What a blessedness it is to have such a sense of soul poverty that you will never stay away from Christ because of what you possess.

Then, next, some could not come because they had married a wife. Now, I think it is very likely that these people who were maimed and cut about were so injured that they had no wife, and perhaps could not get anybody to have them. Well then, they had not that temptation to stay away. They were too maimed to attract the eye of anybody who was looking for beauty, and therefore they were not tempted that way. But they found at the ever-blessed supper of the Lamb an everlasting wedlock, which was infinitely better. Thus do souls lose earthly joys and comforts, and by the loss they gain supremely: they are thus made willing to close in with Christ and find a higher comfort and a higher joy. That maiming which looked like unfittedness turned out to be fittedness.

One excuse made was, *I have bought five yoke of oxen, and I go to prove them* (Luke 14:19). The lame could not do that. When the messenger touched the lame man on the shoulder and said, "Come," he could not say, "I am going out tonight to plow with my new teams." He had never been over the soil ever since he had lost his leg, poor soul, so that he could not make such an excuse. The blind man could not say, "I have bought a piece of land and I must go to see it"; he was free from all the lusts of the eyes, and so far was all the more ready to be led to the supper. When a soul feels its own sinfulness, and wretchedness, and lost estate, it thinks itself unfit to come to Christ; but this is an assistance to it, since it prevents its looking to anything else but Christ, it kills its excuses, and it makes it free to accept salvation by grace.

But how about the men that were in the highways? Well, it seems to me that they were already on the road, and at least out of their houses, if they had any. If they were out there begging, they were all the more ready to accept an invitation to a meal of provisions, for it was *that* they were singing for. A man who is out of the house of his own self-righteousness, though he be a great sinner, is in a more favorable position and more likely to come to Christ than he who prides himself in his supposed self-righteousness.

As for those who were under the hedges, well, they had no house of their own, and so they were all the more likely to come and fill God's house. Men do not take to hedges to sleep under them as long as they have even a hut where they may rest their head; but oh, poor soul, when you are driven to such distress that you would rather hide under any hedge, when you have nothing left to you but a fearful anticipation of judgment, when you think yourself to be an outlaw and an outcast before God, left to wander like Cain, a homeless one and a stray, lost to all good, then you are the very man to come to Christ. Come out of your hedges, then. I am looking for you. Though you hide yourselves away, yet God's own Spirit will discover you, and bring you, I trust this very morning, to feed on love divine.

Trust Jesus Christ, that is all, just as you are, with all your unfittedness and unreadiness. Take what God has made ready for you – the precious blood to cleanse you, a robe of righteousness to cover you, eternal joy to be your portion. Receive the grace of God in Christ Jesus; oh, receive it now. God grant you may, for Jesus Christ's sake. Amen.

Chapter 8

A Bad Excuse Is Worse Than None

And they all with one consent began to make excuse. (Luke 14:18)

The provisions of the gospel of Christ may well be compared to a *supper*, provided, as they were, in the evening of the world – *in these last days* (Hebrews 1:2). The description, *a great supper* (Luke 14:16), is well borne out if we consider the greatness of the provision, how much love and mercy God has displayed towards the sons of men in the person of Christ Jesus, and how much power and gracious working he has shown by his Holy Spirit. A great supper it is if we think of the richness and sweetness of the provision – it is a feast worthy of the great King. The flesh of Jesus is our spiritual meat, and his blood our choicest wine. Our souls are satisfied with covenant mercies, most properly set forth as *a feast of fat things, a feast of wines on the lees, of fat things full of marrow, of wines on the lees well refined* (Isaiah 25:6). A great supper it is, moreover, when we consider the number of guests invited. *Go ye into all the world, and preach the gospel to every creature.* The call of the gospel comes to every man and woman born of Adam, within hearing of the ministers of God.

> None are excluded thence, but those
>   Who do themselves exclude;
> Welcome the learned and polite,
>   The ignorant and rude.

No other king ever sent out an invitation so broad as this. But wisdom *crieth at the gates, at the entry of the city, at the coming in at the doors. Unto you, O men, I call; and my voice is to the sons of man* (Proverbs 8:3-4). Is it not strange that when the householder made so great a supper, when he offered it without money and without price, that all his neighbors should with one consent begin to make excuses? He did not call them to prison or to misery; how then did they come to be so unwilling to obey the summons? From where came this unanimity in the rejection? We find good men differing; how is it that evil men can hold together so well? What! Not one who has respect enough to his generous friend to sit at his table and receive his bounty? Not one.

Truly, here, brethren, we have a picture of the universal depravity of man. All men are thus vile, and refuse the mercy of God. We never know how bad man is until the gospel is preached to him. The gospel acts as a white background to set forth the blackness of man's heart. Here human nature reaches to the greatest height of sin's enormity. Spitting forth his venom against the Lord of infinite love, man proves himself truly to be of the serpent's brood.

The gospel is preached to thousands, and do all make excuses? So the parable has it, and truly so the fact proves it. What! Is there not one whose free will is inclined towards Christ? Is there not one of so good a natural disposition that he will come to Jesus? No, the text says, not one: *They **all** with one consent began to make excuse* (Luke 14:18, emphasis added).

How thoroughly has father Adam ruined our understandings! What fools as well as rebels we are to refuse to partake of the banquet of love. *[We] are together become unprofitable; there is none that seeketh after God* (Romans 3:11-12). You will, perhaps, remind me that there were other men besides those who made excuses. That is most true; but these were in the highways and hedges, or in the streets and lanes of the city; and so those who do not hear the gospel, and therefore are not guilty of rejecting it, are nevertheless far off from God by wicked works, and *aliens from the commonwealth of Israel* (Ephesians 2:12). Thus, taking the two characters to represent all mankind, we find all to be enemies of God. Those in the highways need to be "compelled" to come in; they had a natural reluctance to feast at the good man's table; and so all sorts of men are averse to the gospel. They are perfectly willing to sin – content even to perish in sin; but to come to Christ, to accept the great atonement, to put their trust in Jesus, this is a thing they care not for, and with one consent, when they hear the gospel they begin to make excuses.

We fear that there are many in this meetinghouse this morning who have been blessed with hearing the gospel for years, but yet the only treatment they have given to the gracious message is to make excuses about it. I hope to deal with such ones very simply and very affectionately, earnestly desiring that they make their last excuse this morning, and that it may meet with its death blow. O that they may come to the feast which they have long rejected and rejoice in the mercy of God in Christ Jesus.

Why did they make an excuse? Let us, first, try to *account* for their conduct; secondly, *what excuses do they make?* – let us recount them; and thirdly, *how foolish thus to make excuses!* – here let us *encounter* them.

Let us try to account *for the fact, the sad fact, that men are so ready to make excuses rather than to receive the Word of God.*

We account for it in the first place by the fact that *they had no heart at all to accept the feast.* Had they spoken the truth plainly, they would have said, "We do not wish to come, nor do we intend to do so." If man's heart were not so deceitful, it would not make excuses, but it would say, outright, "We will not have this man to reign over us. We do not feel our sinfulness, and we will not therefore accept pardon. We believe that we can work out our own salvation with our own doings; or, if not, we are content to take our chances. If it shall go ill with us, it will go ill with a great many people. We will run all risks. We do not want salvation; we choose rather to have our full swing of carnal delights. Your religion involves too much self-sacrifice; it is altogether contrary to the lusts of our minds, and therefore we decline it."

This is at the bottom of it. Some of you have often been impressed, and partially convinced of sin, but you have put off Christ with excuses. Will you bear with me while I solemnly assure you that at its core your heart is at enmity against God? Your excuse may look very pretty, but it is as flimsy as it is fair. If you were honest with your own soul, you would say at once, "I do not love Christ; I do not want his salvation." Your put-offs, your false promises, your excuses are worthless; anyone with half an eye can see through them – they are so transparent. You are an enemy to God; you are unreconciled, and you are content to be so. This truth may be unpalatable, but it is nevertheless most certain. May God help you to feel this, and may it humble you before his presence.

Still, if they would not come to the good man's feast, why did not they say so? If the real secret of it was that they hated him and despised his provisions, is it not sad that *they were not honest enough to give him a "no" at once?* Well, they certainly were not, and one reason might be because *they wished to be upon good terms with their conscience.* They felt they ought to go. He was one who had a claim upon their courtesy, if not their gratitude, and therefore feeling that they ought to go, and yet not intending to go, they sought to compromise by an excuse. Conscience is a very unfriendly neighbor to men who live in sin.

It is said of David, *David's heart smote him* (1 Samuel 24:5), and it is a very hard blow which the heart is able to give. In order to ward off the blow, men hold up a shield of excuses. You cannot quite extinguish your conscience, which is the candle of the Lord, and therefore you put it under the bushel of an excuse. The thief fears the watchdog, and therefore throws him a piece of food to keep him quiet – that "piece of food" is made of excuses.

John Bunyan tells us that Mr. Recorder Conscience, when the town of Mansoul was in the keeping of Diabolus, sometimes used to cry out at such a rate that he made all the inhabitants afraid, and so they put him in a very dark place, and tried to put a gag into his mouth to keep him quiet; but for all that, sometimes when his fits came on, he made the town feel very uneasy. I know what conscience tells some of you: it says to you, "How is it that you can forget divine things? How can you trifle with the world to come? How can you live as if you never meant to die? What will you do when you come to die, without an interest in the Lord Jesus Christ?" So, that conscience may be quiet for a while, you make an excuse, and you persevere in refusing to come to the feast.

It may be that you make this excuse *to satisfy custom.* It is not the custom of this present age to fly immediately in the face of Christ? There are not many men of your acquaintance or mine, who seemingly oppose religion. Your father fears God; your mother is a woman of great devotion; your friends go to the house of God and speak experimentally of divine things. You do not like therefore to say to them, "I will never be a Christian; I dislike the ways of God; I do not choose the plan of sovereign grace"; and therefore to spare their feelings you make an excuse.

You do not want to grieve dear friends; you are afraid if you spoke out honestly what your soul feels, that it might bring your mother with gray hairs to the grave, or make your father's heart to break, and so you make the excuse, so that they may entertain a comfortable hope, whereas, while you make excuses, there is no hope for you at all.

For my part, I would rather you would speak outright and say what you mean. I wish that you would say, "I am an enemy of Christ; I do not believe his gospel; I will not serve him." This might sound very bad, but it would show, at least, that there was some sincerity in you, and we would hope that, before long, you might be bowed to the will of Christ. Excuses are curses, and when you have no excuses left, there will be hope for you.

It may be you make these excuses because *you have had convictions* which so haunt you at times that you dare not oppose Christ to his face. You have gone home from the services to weep. That little chamber of yours is a witness that you cannot live altogether without prayer. The other day when you went to a funeral, you came home with your mind very solemn, and you thought then that certainly you would yield to the commands of Jesus. When you were sick, and had that week or two upstairs alone, then you vowed and resolved; but your resolves melted into thin air.

The tear starts in your eye, and you are almost persuaded to be a Christian; you breathe a prayer, but ah! some ill companion tempts you the next morning, and according to the old proverb: *The dog is turned to his own vomit again; and the sow that was washed to her wallowing in the mire* (2 Peter 2:22). Ah! how many times did I have convictions of sin, and terrible ones too, and yet I said, like Felix to Paul, *Go thy way for this time; when I have a convenient season, I will call for thee* (Acts 24:25); but I could not quench these convictions by downright opposition to Christ. I knew too much, and felt too much that I needed to do that, and so I tried to patch up a truce between my soul and my convictions.

Satan is always ready to help men with excuses. This is a trade of which there is no end. It certainly commenced very early, for after our first parents had sinned, one of the first occupations upon which they entered was to make themselves aprons of fig leaves to hide their nakedness. Read the Scriptures through, and you will find that excuse-making has been a habit in all ages and among all classes of people; and until the last sinner shall be saved by sovereign grace, I suppose men will still be setting up their vain excuses in the temple of God.

If you will fire the gun, Satan will always keep you supplied with ammunition. When he thinks that a truth is about to come home to you, if you cannot frame an excuse, he will do it for you; he will run between you and the cannon-shot of God's Word to prevent your being wounded by it. If the preacher's sword should be too sharp for you, and should make your conscience bleed, the Evil One has a satanic plaster with which he very soon binds up the wound.

The natural self-righteousness of man prompts him to frame apologies. We are all the best men in the world according to our own gauge and measure. If we could sit as judges upon ourselves, the verdict would always be "Not guilty." Sin, which would be very shocking in another person, is very forgivable in us; no, what would be abominable in other men becomes almost commendable in ourselves, so partially do we judge our own case. Since the sinner cannot think it quite right for himself to be an unbeliever in Christ, since his enlightened conscience will not let him say that he is quite safe while he refuses to fly to the wounds of Jesus, he runs to excuses in order that he may still say, *I am rich, and increased in goods,* and not be driven to the unhappy necessity of crying, I am *wretched, and miserable, and poor, and blind, and naked.*

Sinful self is hard to conquer, but righteous self is the worst enemy of the two. When we can make men plead guilty, then God pronounces pardon upon them; but while men will mediate their partial excuses, there is little or no hope for them. O great God, our Master, tear away the excuses from every sinner here, and make him stand guilty before your bar in his own consciousness, that he may cry, *God be merciful to me a sinner* (Luke 18:13), and find pardon through the blood of Jesus Christ. Take heed, O you ungodly ones, lest you go on excusing, and excusing, and excusing, until you excuse yourselves down to the pit of hell; for know this, that you will never be able to excuse yourselves out again.

We come now to recount *these excuses.*

Many will not come to the great supper – will not be Christians on the same ground as those in the parable – *because they are too busy.* They have a large family, and it takes all their time to earn bread and cheese for those little mouths. They have a very large business – many servants in their employ, and from the first thing in the morning to the last thing at night, if they do not see after their business, their affairs will go wrong.

Or else, if they have no business, yet they have so many pleasures, and these require so much time – their butterfly visits during the morning take up so many hours, the dropping of their small pieces of pasteboard at other people's doors occupy all their leisure, and they really have no opportunity to think about matters so unpleasant as death and eternity. This excuse scarcely needs a word from me to answer it, because every man knows that it is grossly false.

Nobody starves because he does not have time to eat. Now, if God has given time for us to support our natural frame, much more has he given us time for the soul to feed. I do not find my friends in the street half dressed; but I find some of them spending many a half hour over that other pin, and that other ribbon. Now, surely if they have time to dress the body, they must have had time given them in which to put on the robe of righteousness and array the soul. If you have not the time, God gave it to you, and you must have misspent it. God gives you time as a steward, and if you say to your Master, "I have it not," he will reply to you, "I entrusted it to you; you must have spent it on yourself; you have robbed God." A little earlier rising, a little less time at the table – either of these might give you time enough. You know you have the time, and when you say you do not have it, the lie is too thin; you can see through it.

O soul! O soul! when holy men can find hours for prayer; when such a man as Martin Luther, when he was very busy, used to say, "I must have three hours prayer today at least, or else I cannot get through my business," do not tell me that you have not time to seek the Lord. Besides, it is not an affair of time. Salvation may be effected in an instant. There is life in a look at the Crucified One; there is life at this moment for you; and between now and the time when this service shall be done, there is time enough for you to have laid hold upon eternal life, and to have received Christ Jesus for your soul's salvation. That excuse will not do.

But then they fly to another. *They are too good.* When I have preached free grace and a full Christ, I have heard some say, "That is a good sermon for the crowd in a theater, for ignorant, low-lived people; but we respectable people do not require such salvation. To offer a free salvation to men who are neither drunkards nor swearers, why, the thing is ridiculous. The sermon was very good for Magdalenes, for thieves, and suchlike, but not for us." No, you are *too good* to be saved. You need not a physician, because you are whole. Your own table has enough upon it, you do not need to come to this feast. But cause yourself to consider, I pray you, whether this be not all a mistake.

In what are you better than other men, after all? What if you do not indulge in open sins; does not your heart often go lusting towards evil? Does your tongue always speak that which is right and true? If you cannot remember sins of commission, what about the sins of omission? Have you fed the hungry? Have you clothed the naked? Have you taught the ignorant? Have you loved God with all your heart, and soul, and strength? Have you given him all that he demands of you? Why, you cannot say this. Now the perfection, the holiness, which God demands in order for salvation must be like a perfect alabaster vase: if there be a single crack or spot on it, all is spoiled. You may say, "Well, it is not much broken; we have not seriously damaged it"; no, but God requires it to be perfect, and no matter how slight the damage it may have sustained, you cannot enter heaven upon the footing of your good works – you are cast out forever. Hear these words: *By the deeds of the law there shall no flesh be justified in his sight* (Romans 3:20). *As many as are of the works of the law are under the curse: for it is written, Cursed is every one that continueth not in all things which are written in the book of the law to do them* (Galatians 3:10). God save you from that false excuse.

Another class says, "*We are too bad to be saved.* The gospel cries, 'Believe in Jesus Christ and live,' but it cannot mean me; I have been too gross an offender. When I was but young, I went into evil, and since then I have gone from bad to worse. O sir, I have cursed God to his face; I have sinned against light and knowledge, against a mother's prayers and tears. I have spoken evil of God's Word; I have laughed at the very name of his Son Jesus Christ. I am too evil to be saved." Here is another bad excuse. You *know,* sinner, if you have been a hearer of the gospel, that this is not true, for as bad as you are, no man is excluded from Christ on account of his vileness. *All manner of sin and of blasphemy shall be forgiven unto men* (Matthew 12:31).

The invitations of the gospel do not stop at a certain point of sin; but on the contrary, they seem to select the worst sinners first. What did the Savior say? *[Begin] at Jerusalem* (Luke 24:47). "But Lord, the men live there who crucified you." *[Begin] at Jerusalem.* "But Lord, it was in Jerusalem that they shed your blood, and thrust out the tongue and laughed at you, and made a mockery of your prayers." *[Begin] at Jerusalem* – the worst first, just as the surgeon in a battle is accustomed to looking to the worst cases first. Here is a man who has lost his finger. Ah! well, let him wait awhile, we will see to that.

But here is another who has lost a limb, and he is bleeding fast, and if the blood be not stopped, his life will ooze out. The surgeon gives him the first turn. O you great sinners, you who feel yourselves to have been notorious offenders, I pray you be not so guilty as to make this an excuse for not coming to Christ; on the contrary, use it as a reason why you should fly to him at once. The more filth, the more need of washing; the more sick, the more need of a physician; the more hungry, the more welcome to the table.

Come to Jesus just as you are, with all your sins. *Though your sins be as scarlet, they shall be as white as snow; though they be red like crimson, they shall be as wool* (Isaiah 1:18). No form of sin, imaginable or unimaginable, can by any possibility be an impediment to any man's salvation, if he will but believe on the Lord Jesus Christ.

Then comes another excuse. "Sir, I would trust Christ with my soul this morning, but *I do not feel in a fit state to trust Christ.* I do not have that sense of sin which I think to be a fit preparation for coming to Christ.

> "'If aught is felt, 'tis only pain
> To find I cannot feel.'"

Ah! my dear friend, this is an excuse which looks like a very good one, but it has no truth in it. There is no fittedness needed before you may trust in Christ. Whatever may be your present condition, if you trust Jesus Christ with your soul, you are saved on the spot; your sins are forgiven you; you are made a child of God; you are accepted in the beloved. Where do you read of fittedness for Christ in the Scriptures? Were the dead whom Jesus restored fit to be raised, do you think? Why, Martha said of her brother, *Lord, by this time he stinketh: for he hath been dead four days* (John 11:39); was there any fittedness in Lazarus for a resurrection? And yet Jesus said, *Lazarus, come forth* (John 11:43). Does the gospel say, "He who is in a certain state, and then believeth, shall be saved"? No, but *he that believeth and is baptized shall be saved* (Mark 16:16).

How am I bidden to preach to you? Am I to say, "Whosoever feels this is to come"? No, but, *Whosoever will, let him take the water of life freely* (Revelation 22:17). Are you willing to have Christ? Then you may have him, for Christ is as free to every needy sinner as the drinking fountain in the street is free to every thirsty passerby. Trust Jesus, even if your heart be as hard as granite – he can soften it. Trust him, though conscience be asleep; though all the mental faculties be perverted – trust him. It is his business to make you holy, not your business – trust him to do it all. He is called *Jesus* because he saves his people from their sins. Trust him to overcome your corruptions, to kill your evil temper, to subdue your will, to soften your heart, to enlighten your conscience, to inflame your love – trust him to do it all.

O, be not so foolish as to say, "I am too ill to send for a doctor. When I get better, when I feel better, then I will send for him." Do not say, "I am so wicked; if I felt more clean, I would wash." No, but wash *because* you are wicked; wash *because* you have nothing but filth around you; send for the Great Physician *because* there is no health in you. There is nothing in you but wounds, bruises, and putrefying sores; therefore, let your faith entrust your healing entirely to him.

Here comes another, saying, "O sir, I would trust Christ with my soul, but *it seems too good to be true,* that God should save me on the spot, this morning. You little know where I was last night, or what I did yesterday; you cannot tell who I am, nor how bad I have been, and you tell me that if I trust Jesus Christ, I shall be saved. Sir, it is too good to be true; I cannot imagine it." My dear friend, do you measure God's wheat with your bushel? Because the thing seems an amazing thing to you, should it therefore be amazing unto him? What if his thoughts should be as high above your thoughts as the heavens are above the earth? Is not this just what he has said in Scripture? I know you find it hard to forgive your fellow man, but my Father, my God, can readily forgive you.

> Crimes of such horror to forgive,
>   Such guilty daring worms to spare:
> This is thy grand prerogative,
>   And none shall in the honour share.

He *creates* like a God; he does not make a few insects, or here and there a star, but this great world he fashioned, and he scattered the starry orbs with both his hands. So when the Lord comes to pardon, he does not pardon some small offenses and wink at trifles, but the whole mass of sin he cleanses away in a moment, and all manner of sin and blasphemy, in an instant, he casts behind his back. Believe that God is God and not such a one as you are; think that he is capable of doing greater things than you can dream of. Trust him, trust him now, and however good the things are, you shall find them true; however great, they shall be yours.

I think I hear one say, "*It is too soon for me to come.* Let me have a little look at the world first. I am scarcely fifteen or sixteen. There is plenty of time for me." You have been to the graveyard. Are there not there the records of those who have found fifteen or sixteen none too soon, for lo, at that age, they were taken away to their last account? Too soon! Is it ever too soon to be happy?

If religion made you miserable, I might advise you to put it off to the last, but inasmuch as to be in Christ is to be happy, you cannot be in him too soon. I have sat by many deathbeds, and heard many regrets, but never did I hear a Christian regret that he was converted too soon. I have received many young converts into church fellowship, but I never heard any one of them say they were sorry to be called by grace so early. If I were condemned to die, and anyone should bring me a pardon, I would not think I received it too soon. The wrath of God abides on you – can it be too soon to escape from it? You are the subject of daily temptations, and daily you add to your sins – can it be too soon to have a new heart and a right spirit?

Others will row in the opposite direction, pleading, "*Alas! it is too late.*" The devil first puts the clock back and tells you it is too soon, and when this does not serve his special purpose, he puts it on and says, "The hour is past, the day of grace is over; mercy's gate is bolted, you can never enter it." Let us answer this at once. It is never too late for a man to believe in Jesus while he is out of his grave. While the lamp of life continues to burn, the vilest sinner who returns shall find Christ ready to receive him. There have been men converted at a hundred years of age; we have instances on record of persons who have even passed the century mark and have become children of Christ Jesus. How old are you? Are you in the withered and yellow leaf of eighty?

Ah! you have many sins, but what a triumph of grace it will be when eighty years of sin shall all be washed away in a moment! I tell you, that if you were as old as Methuselah, and in every year of that long life you had as many sins as you have already committed in the whole eighty years, still the grace of Jesus Christ is sufficient to put all this away. Your sins may mount up like mountains, but the love of Christ, like Noah's flood, can go twenty cubits upwards, and the tops of the mountains shall be covered. It is not too soon; it is not too late; neither of these reasons are of any value though they delude many.

"Well," says another, "I would believe in Christ, but I do not know whether I am one of God's elect or not. Sir, that doctrine of election troubles me and staggers me. If I knew I was one of the elect, I would trust Christ." That is – if God will show you his secrets, then you will do God's will, and so the Almighty is to bend to your conditions, and then you will do as he bids you! You will come to feast at the man's table, if he will take you into his secret closet and show you all his treasure! He will do nothing of the kind. How foolish this talk is about election! The doctrine of election is a great and precious truth, but it never can be a valid reason for a man's not believing in Christ.

You are ill today, and the doctor comes. "There," says he, "there is the medicine. I will guarantee if you take it, it will heal you." You say, "Sir, I would take it at once, but I do not know whether I am predestinated to get over this fever. If I am predestinated to live, why then, sir, I will take the medicine, but I must know first." "Ah!" says the doctor, "I tell you what. If you do not take it, you are predestinated to die." And I will tell you this: if you will not believe in Jesus Christ, you will be damned, be you who you may, but you will not be able to lay it at pre-destination's door; it will lie at your own. A man has fallen overboard; a rope is thrown to him, but he says, "I would like to grasp that rope, only I do not know whether I am predestinated to be drowned." Fool! he will go down to the bottom with a lie in his mouth.

We do not say, "I would sit down to dinner today, but I will not eat, because I do not know whether I am predestinated to have any dinner today." We do not talk so foolishly in common things, so why then do we talk so in religion? When men are hard up for an excuse, they are glad to run to the mysteries of God to use them as a veil to cover their faces. O my dear friends, you must know that though God has a chosen people, yet when he commands you to believe in Christ, then his having a chosen people, or not having a chosen people cannot excuse you from obedience to the divine command: *Believe on the Lord Jesus Christ, and thou shalt be saved.* I could not attempt to go through all these excuses, and therefore after handling two more, I will be done.

"Well," says one, "if I were to believe in Christ, *I should be as bad after a short time as I used to be.* I might be a little better for a time, but I would go back again; so it is of no use trusting Christ." That is to say, dear friend, *Jesus Christ* says if you trust him, he will save you; *you* say if you trust him, he will not save you. That is what it comes to. Jesus Christ promises that if you trust him, he will save you from your sins; but you say, "No, I would go back to my sins and be as bad as before." Which am I to believe – your excuse, or his promise? Why, Christ's promise, surely! "But I tried once before," says one. Very likely *you* did, but *Christ* never tried, for if *he* had tried, *he* would have succeeded. "Well, but I did hold on for a certain length of time." I dare say you did – *you* held on; but if *Christ* had hold of you, he would never have let you go.

When *you* get hold of Christ you may soon drop him, but when *Jesus* gets hold of you, he says, *I give unto [my sheep] eternal life; and they shall never perish, neither shall any man pluck them out of my hand* (John 10:28). If you had greatly trusted Christ, he would not have suffered you to become what you used to be.

"Well," says one, *"I cannot trust Christ, I cannot believe him."* You talk Latin, brother; you talk Latin. "No," you say, "I do not talk Latin." Yes, you do. I will translate that word into the English for you. It means

"I will not." When you say, "I cannot," it means "I will not"; and understand, whenever the minister says "You cannot," he means "You will not"; for he does not mean that you have any natural inability, but that you have a moral inability caused by your love of sin – a willful inability. "I cannot" is the Latin, but "I will not" is the English of it.

A man once sent his servant to a certain town to fetch some goods, and he came back without them. "Well, sir, why did you not go there?" "Well, when I got to a certain place, I came to a river, sir, a very deep river. I cannot swim, and I had no boat, so I could not get over." A good excuse, was it not? It looked so, but it happened to be a very bad one, for the master said, "Is there not a ferry there?" "Yes sir." "Did you ask the man to take you over?" "No sir." Surely the excuse was a mere fiction! So there are many things with regard to our salvation which we cannot do. Granted, but then there is a ferry there!

There is the Holy Spirit who is able to do all things, and you remember the text: *If ye then, being evil, know how to give good gifts unto your children, how much more shall your Father which is in heaven give good things to them that ask him?* (Matthew 7:11). It is true you cannot make yourself a new heart, but did you ask for a new heart with sincerity and truth? Did you seek Christ? If you say, "Yes, I did sincerely seek Christ, and Christ would not save me," why then you are excused, but there never was a soul who could in truth say that. There never was a sinner yet who perished seeking Christ, and there never will be; and if your heart's sincere desire is for the salvation which is treasured in Christ Jesus, then heaven and earth may pass away, but Christ will never cast you out while his own word stands: *Him that cometh to me I will in no wise cast out.* "Still," you say, "I cannot trust Christ."

Now, I am at issue with you here – I am at issue with every awakened sinner. I agree with you, if you will let me give my own translation of the word *cannot* – that you *will not,* but if it is to stand as the word is generally used, I am at issue with you.

Suppose that you believe me to be an honest man; would it be fair after that to say, "Sir, I cannot believe you"? Now, if you believe me to be a liar, I can very well understand that you cannot trust me; but if you take it for granted that I am incapable of telling a falsehood, and yet do not believe what I tell you, *you* are a liar. Now, you believe that

Christ is incapable of falsehood; you are not like those who are ignorant of the character of Christ, and therefore you know him to be incapable of untruthfulness – and then you say you cannot believe him.

Seeing that Jesus Christ cannot but speak truth, it cannot be a difficult thing for any man to believe what he speaks. If you have sufficient light given to you by the Holy Spirit, to know that Christ is the truth, I believe you have sufficient power from the same source to believe what Christ says. I trace this to God's gift, but I do pray you to exercise the power which you certainly have. Tell Christ you cannot believe him? Will you tell him that to his face, when he sits upon the judgment seat at last? Will you dare to say this when his eyes of fire shall look you through and through? "Most holy Christ, I could not trust you! Most truthful Savior, I could not believe you! I distrusted you, I doubted you!"

"Why did you doubt me then? What cause had I ever given you? Why did you think me a liar? In what had I ever broken my promises, or when did I err from the truth?" *He that believeth not God,* says John, *hath made him a liar; because he believeth not the record that God gave of his Son.* O, do think of this, and never make that excuse again. Instead of saying, "I cannot believe," say, "I cannot make God a liar; I must therefore believe, for I know God is no liar – I must therefore trust his Son Jesus Christ."

I have recounted a few of these excuses; perhaps you will make another batch before the evening comes on – you who determine not to be saved. It is only the mighty Spirit of God who can sweetly constrain your will to yield to Christ, and so I close with these two or three words, upon the third point.

How foolish thus to make excuses. For first *remember with whom it is you are dealing.* You are not making excuses before a man who may be duped by them, but you make these excuses before the heart-searching God. My dear friends, let me speak very solemnly, and push this point closely home. You know that God can see through all of this – why then do you hang up such thin veils? Confess before him now your folly: "Lord, I have been an enemy to you; Lord, I have been averse to your Son Jesus Christ, and therefore have I patched up these excuses. Forgive me. I see how foolish I have been; grant that I may do so no more."

Remember again *what it is you are trifling with.* It is your own soul, the soul that can never die. You are trifling with a heaven that you will never see if you keep on with these excuses. You are trifling, sinner, with that hell which must be your never-ending portion if you continue as you are. Can you play with hellfire? O, can you make sport of heaven? Can you laugh at the blood of Jesus? You are really doing so while you are thus faltering between two opinions. Now, if you must play the fool, find something cheaper to play with than this.

O sirs, if you must have cheerfulness, I pray you have it out of something else than this. To be saved! listen to heaven's music! To be lost! listen to hell's groans! Neither of these things are matters for you to play with. Say, as now you are sitting here – I pray God help you to say it before you leave this house – "Lord, I have been trifling with eternity; I have been making frivolous excuses rather than accepting your love in Christ; I have trifled with heaven and hell. Grant, Lord, that this may be brought to an end, that I may love and trust you this day."

Remember, again, that these excuses will look very different soon.

How will you make excuses when you come to die, as die you must? When death gets the grip of you, and the strong man fails, and they wipe the death-sweat from your fevered brow; when the glaze of death's night is coming over your eyeballs, what will you think of these excuses then? It may be, you will rave with utter fury at yourselves, that you could have played with your souls to such an extent. What will you do with your excuses when you stand at the bar of judgment? The trumpet rings, you have awakened from your grave, you stand amidst the myriads to be judged. The books are opened, and Christ proclaims your doom – *Depart from me, ye cursed, into everlasting fire.*

Will excuses comfort you then? Will you be able to say then, "Lord, it was too soon; Lord, it was too late; Lord, I was too great a sinner to believe in Jesus, or I did not need a Savior." No, when the trumpet peals, and the heavens are in a blaze; when the sun is turned into sackcloth, and the moon into blood, and the stars fall like fig leaves from the tree, you will find other work to do than excuse-making; you will weep and wail because of sin, and when you are cast into hell, what will you make then of your excuses?

Written in letters of fire, you shall see in one tremendous arch above your heads: "You knew your duty, but you did it not; you heard the gospel, but you made excuses." Thundering more tremendously than the trump of resurrection, shall come these words to you: *Because I have called, and ye refused; I have stretched out my hand, and no man regarded; I also will laugh at your calamity; I will mock when your fear cometh; when your fear cometh as desolation, and your destruction cometh as a whirlwind; when distress and anguish cometh upon you* (Proverbs 1:24, 26-27).

O, the Lord have mercy upon you, excuse makers, and bring you to look to Jesus now. *Now,* I say, for the Scripture says, ***Now*** *is the accepted time; behold,* ***now*** *is the day of salvation* (2 Corinthians 6:2, emphasis added). The only way to end your excuses is not by praying nor resolving, but by looking to Christ. There hangs the bleeding Savior on the cross; he dies as the just for the unjust to bring us to God; he suffers there that sin may be forgiven. Look to him, trust yourself to him, and you shall be saved.

My friend, I give you now in God's name this invitation, this command: trust your soul to Jesus, the Son of God, who suffered for sin, and you shall be saved. But mind you this. I may never meet you all this side of the grave, but I will meet you all at God's great day, and if you do not receive Christ and trust in him, I am clear of your blood. Upon my skirts your doom cannot fall.

You have heard the gospel, you have been told to trust Jesus as you are, you have been assured that he is able to save to the uttermost them that come to him. You have been bidden to come, and now on your own heads be your soul's ruin if you come not. But may the Spirit of God take these things and apply them to your souls. May he be as a fire and as a hammer in your souls: as a fire to melt, and as a hammer to break; and may you today with brokenness of heart take Christ to be your Savior both now and forever. Amen.

Chapter 9

A Straight Talk

I cannot come. (Luke 14:20)

There are different ways of replying to the invitation of the gospel when you mean to refuse it. They are all, at bottom, bad, and they may all be classed under one heading; for *they all with one consent began to make excuse* (Luke 14:18); but yet some are more decently worded than others, and have a greater show of reason about them. The first two sets of people who were invited to the supper said to the servant, apologetically, with some appearance of courtesy, *I pray thee have me excused* (Luke 14:18). But the third man did not beat around the bush at all or pray to be excused; but he said tersely, bluntly, sharply, *I cannot come* (Luke 14:20). This was a final reply; he did not intend, nor wish to come to the supper. *I cannot come* was a snappy reply; but as he had married a wife, he thought the idea of his coming was utterly unreasonable, and he needed no sort of excuse.

Now, what did that mean? Well, it meant that he thought very lightly of the giver of the feast. He had no respect for this *certain man* who had made a great supper. He had an opportunity of offending him by refusing his invitation, and he did so outspokenly, saying, *I cannot come.*

It also showed that he had a very low opinion of the supper itself. It might be a respectable meal, but he did not want it; he could have quite as good a supper at home. He was better off than those people in the streets. Those vagrants might be glad enough for a supper for nothing, but he was not dependent upon anybody, and he could do very well for himself. Do you not know many in this world who have no opinion of Christ, no love for God?

Religion is to them mere nonsense – an unpractical, dreamy matter, about which they have no time to concern themselves. It is a pitiful thing that the God whom angels worship they will not even think of; and the Christ who is the loveliest of the lovely – in him they see no beauty; and the priceless provisions of mercy, the pardon of sin, the salvation of the soul, the heaven of God – they neglect these things as if they did not need them, or could get them whenever they please.

Thousands are proudly independent of the free grace of God; they are good enough, and virtuous enough, and need not cry for mercy, like the wicked and profane. In their own judgment, they are quite able to fight their own way to heaven. They do not want the charities of the gospel. Contempt of the great Feast-maker, and contempt of the feast itself – these two pieces of proud disdain induce a man to say, *I cannot come.*

But there was more than common pride in this brief, abrupt speech, for this man had, at the first, made a promise to come. He had been bidden, and it is implied in the parable that he had at that time accepted the invitation. He had accepted the cards of invitation to the supper; and though he had done so, he now flies in the face of his own self, and says, *I cannot come.*

I think that I am addressing some here who have pledged themselves many a time to come to Christ. If I remember rightly, you asked for the prayers of friends, and promised that you would be in real earnest. You looked your wife in the face, and said, "I hope that it will not be long before I am with you in the church of God, and shall no longer have to go away and leave you alone at the Lord's Table." You asked some of your Christian friends to make a point of praying for you, but still you have never carried out your intention of becoming a true Christian.

Your resolutions may be still read in God's eternal book of record; but they are there as witnesses to your falseness and changeableness. The counterfoils are there; but there is no fulfillment of any of the resolutions. God remembers them, although you have forgotten to carry them out. You accepted the invitation on the spur of the moment, but when worldliness had gotten the upper hand with you, you went back to your own obstinacy, and said, *I cannot come.*

Perhaps you have not said it in quite as sharp a tone as I used just now; but it has come to the same thing, for you have not come to the gospel supper. It matters little whether you say it angrily or quietly; for if you do not come, the practical result is the same. I think I hear some of you, even now, say, "Do not ask me so often. I cannot come. It is of no use to worry me about it. I do not wish to be uncivil or unkind. Though I said I would come, I retract my words: I cannot come."

In saying, *I cannot come,* the man intended, as it were, to dismiss the matter. He wished to be understood as having made up his mind, and he was no longer open to argument. He did not discuss; he did not talk; but he just said, off-the-cuff, "I want no more persuading; I cannot come, and that settles it." Certain of you have come to such a condition of heart that you would gladly silence our gospel challenges: with a kindly but determined tone you would say, "*I cannot come.* Do not trouble me anymore."

I suppose that this man, after he had made that positive declaration, felt that there was truth in what he had stated. He said, **Therefore I cannot come** (emphasis added). He had reason to support himself in what he said, and he went home, sat down, and enjoyed himself, and felt that he was a righteous man, quite as good as those who had gone to the supper, and perhaps rather better. He could not blame himself, for when a man cannot do it, why, of course, he cannot do it; and why should he be censured for an impossibility? *I cannot come;* how can I help that?

So, he sat down with a cool indifference to eat his own supper. It was nothing to him whether the great giver of the feast was grieved or not; whether his oxen and fatlings were wasted or not. He had said it to his conscience very often, until he half believed it – "*I cannot come,* and there is no disputing it."

I have no doubt that many who have never come to Christ have made themselves content to be without him by the belief that they cannot come. Although the impossibility, if it did exist, would involve the greatest of all calamities, yet they speak of it with very little concern. Practically, they say, "I cannot be saved. I must remain an unbeliever." What an awful thing for any mortal to say! Yet you have said it until you almost believe it; and you wish us now to leave you quite alone for this dreadful reason. You do not want to be troubled .

The text already begins to startle you a little, and you do not like it. You are almost sorry that you are here. If the Lord helps me, I will trouble you far more before you get out of this place. I have heavy news from the Lord for you. I shall endeavor, if I can, to pull away those downy pillows from your sleepy head, and wake you up to immediate anxiety, lest you perish in your sins. With kindly compulsion I would plead with you and try to show you that this little speech of yours, *I cannot come,* is a wretched speech. You must throw it to the winds and prove that you can come by coming at once, and receiving the great feast of love, and honoring him that spreads it for hungry souls.

Two or three things I would like to say about this case, for *it is very serious.* It was bad enough for this man to say, *I cannot come,* but it is far worse for you to say, "I cannot come to Christ." Remember, if the invited guests did not come, and come at once, they could never come, for there was only that one supper, and not a series of banquets. The great man who made the feast did not intend to prepare another. A very grave offense would be committed by their not coming to the one supper.

My dear friends, there is only one time of grace for you, and if that be ended, you will not have a second opportunity. There is only one Christ Jesus; there is no more sacrifice for sin. There is only one way of eternal love and mercy; do not forsake it. I pray you, do not turn away from the one door of life, the one way of salvation. If it is made light of now, and the feast is over, as it will be when you die, then you have lost the great privilege, and you have been guilty of a gross neglect, from the consequences of which you never will be able to escape. Note this and beware.

Besides, it is not merely a supper that you will lose when you say, *I cannot come.* To lose a supper would be little and might soon be set right when breakfast-time came around. But you also lose eternal life, and that lost in time can never be found in eternity. You lose the pardon of sin, reconciliation to God, adoption into the family of love – these are heavy losses. You lose the joy of faith for life, and you lose comfort in death – who can estimate this damage? Lose not your immortal soul! Oh, lose not *that*! For if you gain the whole world, it will not recompense you for such a loss. Lose what you will, but lose not your soul, I pray you! Seek that salvation without which it would have been better for you that you had never been born.

Besides, once more, if you do not come to Christ, it will imply the greatest insult that you can put upon your Maker. You have already grieved him by breaking his laws, but what will be his indignation when you refuse his mercy? when you turn your back on his Son? when you refuse not only your God, but also your crucified Savior, hanging there with outstretched arms, bleeding his life away, that he may save you? Do not turn your back on your own redemption. No blood was ever sprinkled on the threshold of an Israelite's house, for he must not trample on it: that would be ruinous indeed. The blood was on the lintel and on the two side posts, but never underfoot. Trample not upon the blood of Christ; but you will do so if you refuse his great salvation.

If you will not come to him to be saved, you have as good as said that you will be damned rather than be loved by God – that you will be damned rather than be saved through Jesus Christ his Son. It will prove a costly insult to you, as well as a grievous affront to your Lord.

Having said so much by way of preface, I am now going to take these words, *I cannot come,* and handle them a little with the hope that you may grow ashamed of them.

First, this man declared, *I cannot come,* because he said, *I have married a wife* (Luke 14:20). He had promised to come to the supper, and he was bound to fulfill his promise. Why did he want to get married just then? Surely, he had not been compelled to marry in a hurry, so that he could not keep engagements already made. He was bound to keep his promise to the maker of the feast; and that promise was claimed of him by the messenger. He could not say that his wife would not let him come. Such a declaration might be true in England; but in the East the men are always masters of the situation, and women seldom bear rule in the family. No Oriental would say that his wife would not let him come. Nor in these Western regions, where the woman more nearly gains her rights, can any man truthfully say that his wife will not allow him to be a Christian.

I do not believe that any of you will be able to say, when you come to die, that your wife was responsible for your not being a Christian. Most men would be angry if we told them that they were henpecked and could not call their souls their own. He must be a fool, indeed, who would let a woman lead him down to hell against his will. The fact is a man is a mean creature when he tries to throw the blame of his sin upon his wife.

I know that father Adam set us a bad example in that respect, but the fact that this was a part of the sin which caused the ruin of our race should act as a beacon to us. You certainly, as a man, ought not to demean yourself so much as to say, "I cannot come, for my wife will not let me." If one of you, however, continues to whine, "My wife is my ruin. I am unable to be a Christian because of my wife," I must ask you a question or two before I believe your pitiful story. Do you let her rule you in everything else? Does she keep you at home in an evening? Does she pick all your companions for you?

Why, my dear man, if I am not much mistaken, you are a self-willed, cross-grained, pigheaded animal about everything else; and then, when it comes to the matter of religion, you turn around and whine about being governed by your wife! I have no patience with you. It is more than probable that the very best thing that could happen to you would be to have your wife on the throne for the next few years. Upon such a solemn matter as this do not talk nonsense. You know that the blame lies with yourself alone: if you wished to seek the best things, the little woman at home would be no hindrance to you.

This man said, *I cannot come.* Why? Because he had a wife! Strange plea! For surely that was a reason why he should come and bring her with him. If any man, unhappily, has a wife opposed to the things of God, instead of saying, "I cannot be a Christian, for I have an unconverted wife," he should seek for double grace that he may win his wife to Christ. If a woman laments that she has an unconverted husband, let her live the nearer to God so that she may save her husband. If a servant has an unconverted master, let him labor with double diligence to glorify God, so that he may win his master. Thus you see there are two reasons why you should come to the gospel banquet – not only for your own sake, but also for the sake of your unconverted relatives.

My neighbor's candle is blown out; and is that a reason why I must not light mine? No, but that is a reason why I should be all the more careful to keep mine burning, that I may light my neighbor's candle too. It is a pity that my wife should be lost, but I cannot help her by being lost myself. No, but I may help her if I take my stand, and follow Christ the more resolutely because my wife opposes me. Good man, do not allow your wife to draw you aside! Good woman, do not let your husband hinder you! Do not say, "I cannot attend the house of God, nor be a Christian while I have such a husband as I have." No, that is the reason why you should take your stand the more bravely in the name of God that, by your example, those whom you love may be rescued from destruction.

How know you, O wife, but that you may save your unbelieving husband? How know, you, O servant, but that you may save your unbelieving master? I remember hearing Mr. Jay tell a story about a Nonconformist servant girl who went to live in a family of worldly people who attended the Church of England, although they were not real believers. They were outside buttresses of the church, and they had very little to do with the inside of it; and outsiders are generally the most bigoted. They were very angry with their servant for going to the little meetinghouse and threatened to discharge her if she went again. But she went all the same, and very kindly but firmly assured them that she must continue to do so.

At last she received a notice to go: they could not, as good church people, have a Dissenter living with them. She took their rough dismission very patiently; and it came to pass that the day before she was to leave her position, a conversation took place somewhat of this sort: The master said, "It is a pity, after all, that Jane should go. We never had such a good girl. She is very industrious, truthful, and attentive." The wife said, "Well, I have thought that it is hardly the thing to send her away for going to her chapel. You always speak up for religious liberty, and it does not look quite like religious liberty to turn our girl away for worshipping God according to her conscience. I am sure she is a deal more careful about her religion than we are about ours." So they talked it over, and they said, "She has never answered us snappily, nor found fault with us about our going to church. Her religion is a greater comfort to her than ours is to us. We had better let her stay with us, and let her go where she likes." "Yes," said the husband, "and I think we had better go and hear the minister that she goes to hear. Evidently, she has got something that we have not got. Instead of sending her away for going to chapel, we will go with her next Sunday, and judge the matter for ourselves." And they did, and it was not long before the master and mistress became members of that same church. Do not say, therefore, "I cannot come, because my master and mistress object to it."

Do not make idle excuses out of painful facts, which are reasons why you should be more determined than ever, even if you have to go to heaven alone, that you will be a follower of Christ. Keep to your resolve, and you may entertain the hope and belief that you will lead others to the Savior's feet.

A second reason is even more common. It is not everybody who can say, "I have married a wife"; but everywhere you can meet with a person who pleads, "I have no time." You say, "Sir, I cannot attend to religion, for I have no time." I remember hearing an old lady say to a man who said that he had no time, "Well, you have got all the time there is." I thought that it was a very conclusive answer. You have had the time, and you still have all the time there is – why do you not use it? Nobody has more than twenty-four hours in a day, and you have no less. You have no time? That is very unusual! What have you done with it? You certainly have had it.

Time flies with you, I know, but so it does with me, and with everybody. What do you do with it? "Oh, I have no time," says one. I say again, you have had the time, and that time was due, in part, to a solemn consideration of the things of God. You have robbed God of that part of time which was due to him, and you have given up to some inferior thing what your great Lord and Master could rightly claim for the highest purposes.

You have time enough for common things. See here, I never meet any of you, in the middle of the day, in the street in your shirtsleeves. I do not find you going up and down Cheapside half-dressed. "Oh no, of course not; we have time to put on our clothes." You have time to dress your bodies, and no time to dress your souls with the robe of Christ's righteousness? Do not tell me that! I do not meet any one of our friends saying, towards evening, "I am ready to faint, for I have had nothing to eat since I got up. I have had no time to get a morsel of meat." No, no; they have had their breakfast, and they have had their dinner, and so on.

"Oh yes, we have time to eat," says one. Do you tell me that you have time to feed your bodies, and that God has not given you time in which to feed your souls? Why, it is not common sense! Such statements will not hold water for a moment. You must have time to feed your souls, if you have time to feed your bodies.

People find time to look in the glass, and wash their faces, and brush their hair. Have you no time whatever to look at yourself, to see your spiritual spots, and to wash in the fountain that is open for sin and for uncleanness? O dear sirs, you have time for common things, and you must certainly have time for those much more serious and important matters which concern your souls and immortality!

You have no time? How is this, when you waste a good deal of it? How much do many of us spend in silly talk? How much time do certain persons spend in frivolous amusements? I have heard people say that they have no time, when I am sure I do not know what they can have to occupy them. Are there not many people about who, if they were tied in a knot, and thrown into the Bay of Biscay, would be missed by nobody; for they do no good to any mortal being? They are living without an object – purposeless, aimless lives; and yet they talk about not having time! Such claims will not do. When you plead with God, say something that looks like common sense.

You have no time, and yet you undertake more secular work. You keep a shop, do you not? "Yes, I have a large shop." You are going to enlarge it, are you not? Will you have time, do you think, to attend to it when the business grows? "Oh yes, I dare say that I shall find time, or at any rate, I must make time, somehow or other." You are going to take a second shop, are you not? How will you manage it? "Oh, I shall find time."

Yes, my dear sirs, you can find time for all those enlargements, and speculations, and engagements. Let me be plain with you, and say that you could find time for thought about your soul if you had a mind to do so. To plead that you have no time for religion is a fraud. It will not do! It is lying unto God to say that you have no time. When a man wants to do a thing, if he has no time, he makes time.

I beg the idle man not to go on to deceive himself with the notion that he has no time. "Where there's a will there's a way." Where there is a heart to religion there is plenty of time for it. Blame your unwilling minds, and not your scanty hours. You will have time enough when your hearts are once turned in the right direction.

Besides, time is not the great matter. Did the Lord demand of you a month's retirement from business? Did we command you to spend two days in a week in prayer? Did we tell you that you could not be saved unless you shut yourself up for an hour every morning for meditation? I would to God you could have an hour for meditation! But, if you cannot, who has demanded it of you? The command is that you believe on the Lord Jesus Christ and forsake your sin; and this is a matter which will not interfere with your daily work. A man can turn the potter's wheel and pray. A man can lay bricks and pray. A man can run machinery and pray. A man can walk behind a plow, and yet he can be walking with God.

A woman can scrub a floor, and commune with God. A man can be riding on horseback, and yet he can still be in communion with the Most High. A woman can be making the beds and growing in grace. It is not a matter in which time comes in so much as to interfere with any of the ordinary duties of life. Therefore throw away that excuse, and do not say any longer, "I cannot come because I have no time." At once repent of sin, and believe in the Lord Jesus; and then all your time will be free for the service of the Lord, and yet you will have not a moment the less for the necessary duties of your calling.

There is a third form of this excuse and a very common one: "I have more important things to do." Now, come! I will have you by the throat over that. I shall contradict you flatly. *You have nothing more important to do.* That would be utterly impossible. Nothing under heaven can be of one-hundredth part of the importance of your being reconciled to God and saved through Jesus Christ. What is that more important business? To make money? Where is the importance of that? You may get a pile of it, and the net result will be greater care, and the more to leave when you die.

You tell me you must have an opportunity for study. Well, that is better; but what are you going to study? Science? Art? Politics? Are these important as compared with the saving of your soul? Why, if you have an educated mind, and it is lost, it will be as bad to lose it in culture and learning as to lose it in ignorance. Your first duty is to be right with your God who made you. Put nothing before your God. Has Christ redeemed you? Rest not until you know the truth of that redemption by being reconciled to God through the death of his Son. Nothing can be so important to a man as to be obedient to his Maker and enjoy his Maker's love. Nothing, therefore, can be so important to a man as to be pardoned through the Savior, and changed by the power of the Holy Spirit from an enemy of God into a friend of God.

"Oh!" say you, "but my business occupies so much of my time." Yes; but do you not know that very likely your business would go on better if you were right with God? Many a time a business goes wrong because the man is wrong; and sometimes it is even burdensome upon God to be at cross-purposes with a man because a man is at cross-purposes with him. If you walk adversely towards him, he will walk adversely towards you; but when you are obedient to him, he can make other things subservient to you.

In a little church on the Italian mountains I saw, among many absurd paintings, one picture which struck me. There was a plowman who had turned aside at a certain hour to pray. The rustic artist drew him upon his knees before the opened heavens; and, lest there should be any waste of time occasioned by his devotion, an angel was going on with the plowing for him. I like the idea. I do not think an angel ever did go on with a man's plowing while he was praying, but I think that the same result often comes to pass, and that when we give our hearts to God, and seek first the kingdom of God and his righteousness, all these things are added unto us.

If religion does not make you richer, which it may not do, it will make you more contented with what you have. The blessing of God, with a dinner of herbs, will make it better than well-prepared meat without that benediction. He that would make the best of this world, and have the greatest enjoyment here of the truest and best kind, will do well to give his first attention to his Savior, and his whole heart to faith in him, and diligence in his service. You have no more important business, I am quite sure, than the business which concerns God and eternity.

I have heard some use the excuse, "I cannot afford to be a Christian." Well, my friend, let us have a talk about that. Cost you more than you can afford? What do you mean? What cost? Cost you money? It need not. It will cost you no more than you like to spend upon it with a glad heart. God will give you a generous spirit, which will make you love to support his cause, and to help the poor, and contribute your share to all Christian mission work. But in the kingdom of Christ there is no taxation. Giving becomes a gratification, liberality a luxury. Nothing will be dragged from you by force. Surely, our God abhors money that comes into his resources by anything but the freewill offerings of loving hearts. It will not cost you much in that way, I am sure, for you are only to give as God has prospered you.

Suppose man should say, "Well, I must take a seat in the chapel if I would comfortably hear the gospel." Very well. Will it be unjust that you bear your proportion of necessary expenses in supporting the man who gives all his time, thought, and ability to you? Will you pay as much in a year to hear the gospel as many pay for one night at the play? Alas, and do not many at a horse race spend a hundred times more than they ever gave throughout their whole existence either to the poor or to the church of God? What you will save by holy, gracious, thrifty habits will render this as no loss to you, but a gain.

"Oh, but I meant that I could not afford it, for I would have to lose several friends." Is that friend worth keeping who is an enemy to God? The woman who would lead you away from God, or the man who would keep you out of heaven – are friends of that sort worth having? Be brave, and end a connection which will otherwise endlessly connect you with the bottomless pit.

"Oh," says one, "but I mean that I would lose so much in trade." Ah, well! I will not ask you to explain what you mean by that, for there is an ugly look about that statement. You know more about your trade than I do. No doubt there are trades which pander to the vices of men and become all the more profitable in proportion to the growth of drunkenness and impurity. These must be given up. Moreover, there are traders who live by hype, and lying, and cheating; and I do not recommend you to profess to be a Christian if that is your line of things. It is better to give up all profession of religion when you go in for unrighteous gain. What? Did I hear a hint about adulteration? Did I also hear that you do not give full weight and true measure?

Ah, my dear fellow! give up that game at once, whether you become a

Christian or not; but certainly, if that is what you mean, then the loss of dishonest profits will be a great gain to you, both for this life and the next.

"Well," says one, "I would have to give up a good many pleasures." Pleasures which block the road to heaven ought to be given up at once. You may think me a very melancholy sort of person; but I imagine that I am about as happy as any man in England. I appreciate a merry thought and a cheerful speech as much as anybody. I can laugh, and I can enjoy good, clean, humorous remarks as well as most people; and, having now served the Lord for nearly forty years, I bear my witness that I have never had to relinquish a single pleasure for which I have felt a deliberate desire. As soon as you are renewed in heart, you are changed in your pleasures; and that which might have been a pleasure once to you would then be a misery. If I had to sit in some people's company, and hear what some people talk about, it would be hell to me.

One night, having to preach up in the north of England, this unfortunate circumstance occurred to me. When I got down to the railway, I was put into a first-class carriage with five racing gentlemen who were going to the Doncaster races. Happily, they did not know me, but from the beginning to the end the conversation of these gentlemen was garnished with expressions which tortured me, and at last they fell upon a subject that was unutterably loathsome. I pray God that I may not be condemned to dwell with such people forever, for it would be hell to me.

Ladies and gentlemen, you need not think that I rob myself of any pleasure when I do not go to race courses or associate with the licentious. It is my pleasure to keep far off from the pleasures of those men of pleasure, in whose company I was forced to spend that evening. The pleasures of this world are so full of dust, dirt, and grit, that he who has once washed his mouth clean of them declines another meal of such dregs. You will lose no pleasure if you come to Christ.

I hear one other person say, "I cannot come." Why not? "Well, sir, I do not mean that I shall not come one of these days, but it would not be convenient just now. I could not yield my heart to the Lord tonight." No. I know. You have an engagement tomorrow which must be attended to, but it would not be quite the thing for a Christian. Just so. It would not be convenient tonight, nor on Monday, nor will it be on Tuesday; depend upon it. Your anxious thoughts will be gone by then. It will not be convenient to be saved! You want to see a little "life," do you not? "Life" in London means death. "Oh, but just now I am only an apprentice!"

Then at once be bound as an apprentice to Christ. "But I am a journeyman. When I get a little business of my own, then will be the time." Will it? Oh, that you would become a journeyman to Christ! "But I have associations just now that render it difficult." That is to say, God must wait for your convenience. Is that the way the poor treat the doctors who receive patients for free? Do they say, "Doctor, it is not convenient for me to call upon you before ten or eleven o'clock in the morning. It is not convenient for me to come to your house. I shall be glad to see you if you come to my house about half-past eleven in the evening." Would you send a message to a physician in the West End, that you will be pleased for him to attend to you for nothing if he will come at your time?

"Oh," say you, "I would not think of insulting a doctor like that, if he is kind enough to attend to me for nothing." And yet you will insult your God! You mean that God is not worthy of your strength and health; but when you are old, and worn-out, then you mean to sneak into heaven, and cheat the devil. It is dirty mean of you! I can say no better. Though the Lord is exceedingly gracious and merciful, yet, when men make up their minds to it that they will only give him the leftovers of life, it is small wonder that they die in their sins. What must God think of such treatment? Do not say, "I cannot come." Come at once. The Lord help you to come!

I have heard people say, "I cannot come, sir, for I cannot understand it. I am a poor man, I never had any education." What is it that you cannot understand? Can you not understand that you have broken God's law, and that the just God must punish you for it? You can understand that. Can you not understand that if you trust the Lord Jesus Christ, then it is certain that he took your sin, and bore it in his own body on the tree, and put your sin away, for his name is *the Lamb of God, which taketh away the sin of the world* (John 1:29)? Can you not understand that if you trust in him, you have him to stand in your room, and place, and stead; for the Scripture says, *He hath made him to be sin for us, who knew no sin; that we might be made the righteousness of God in him* (2 Corinthians 5:21). You *can* understand it, if you wish to do so.

There is nothing in the gospel which the poorest and the least educated cannot understand if their minds be made willing to know and receive the truth. If the Spirit of God will come upon them, they cannot only understand the gospel, but also grasp it, and enjoy it, and begin to teach it to others, too; for the Lord makes the babes to have knowledge and discretion in his ways, while the wise and learned in scientific matters often miss the way to the eternal kingdom.

I am done. The sound of the bell tells me that my time has fled. Another bell will one day warn *you* that you are done, and that your life is over, even as my sermon is over. But I wanted just to say this. If there is any man here who says, "I cannot come," I beg him to express himself properly and speak out the sad fact as it ought to be spoken. Here is the style: "Unhappy wretch, I cannot come to Christ! Millions in heaven have come, but I cannot come. My mother died in a good hope; but, 'Mother, I cannot come.' My father has gone home to be with Jesus; but I cannot come."

I thank God that this statement is not true; but if you say it, and believe it, you ought never to rest anymore; for if you cannot come to Christ, you are the unhappiest person in the world. Is there any woman that cries, "I cannot come," or any man that pleads, "I cannot come"? Wherever you are sitting or standing, let the bell that told out the death of the last hour warn you of your spiritual death; for if you cannot come to Christ, and eat of his supper, you cannot be saved. You cannot escape from the wrath to come: you are doomed forever.

May I ask you to do another thing? If you still intend to say, "I cannot come," will you speak the truth now? Will you alter a word, and get nearer the truth? Say, "I will not come." "I cannot come" is Greek, or double Dutch; but the plain English is "I will not come." I wish you would say *that* rather than the other, because the recoil of saying, "I will not come; I will not believe in Jesus; I will not repent of sin; I will not turn from my wicked ways" – the recoil, I say, from that might be blessed by God to you to make you see your desperate state. I wish you would then cry, "I cannot sit down, and make my own damnation sure by saying that I will not come to Christ."

Will you now, instead of refusing to come, resolve to come at once? Say, "I will come to Jesus. Tell me how." You can only come to Christ by trusting him. Trust yourself with him, and he will save you. Never did anyone trust Jesus in vain. Trust has a powerful influence over the Lord Jesus. He comes to the rescue of a soul that leans wholly upon him. He will do all things for you: he will change your nature as well as forgive your sin; and your nature being changed, you shall lead a new life from this time forth, and grow in grace until you become like him in whom you trust; and then he will take you to be forever with him. Washed in the blood of the Lamb, you shall walk with him in white amidst the glorified.

Thus I have talked in a very simple way. I pray the Lord to bless words which are intended to be faithful, plain, and impressive. May we meet in heaven! There are very many strangers here tonight; may you not be strangers to the Lord Jesus! Many of our friends are away, and some of you have come out although it is a nasty, rainy evening: I take this as a token for good. God bless you! I pray that you may get the double blessing, and may remember this gloomy, dark, Decembery evening in May by the blessing that God shall put upon you through Jesus Christ his Son. Amen.

Chapter 10

Come In

Compel them to come in. (Luke 14:23)

I feel in such a haste to go out and obey this commandment this morning, by compelling those to come in who are now delaying in the highways and hedges, that I cannot wait for an introduction, but must at once set about my business.

Hear then, O you that are strangers to the truth as it is in Jesus – hear then the message that I have to bring you. You have fallen, fallen in your father Adam; you have fallen also in yourselves, by your daily sin and your constant iniquity; you have provoked the anger of the Most High; and as assuredly as you have sinned, so certainly must God punish you if you persevere in your iniquity, for the Lord is a God of justice, and will by no means spare the guilty. But have you not heard, has it not long been spoken in your ears, that God, in his infinite mercy, has devised a way whereby, without any infringement upon his honor, he can have mercy upon you, the guilty and the undeserving? To you I speak; and my voice is unto you, O sons of men; Jesus Christ, very God of very God, has descended from heaven, and was made in the likeness of sinful flesh.

Begotten of the Holy Spirit, he was born of the Virgin Mary; he lived in this world a life of exemplary holiness, and of the deepest suffering, until at last he gave himself up to die for our sins, *the just for the unjust, that he might bring us to God* (1 Peter 3:18). And now the plan of salvation is simply declared unto you – Whosoever believes in the Lord Jesus Christ shall be saved. For you who have violated all the precepts of God, and have disdained his mercy and dared his vengeance, there is yet mercy proclaimed, *for whosoever shall call upon the name of the Lord shall be saved* (Romans 10:13).

This is a faithful saying, and worthy of all acceptation, that Christ Jesus came into the world to save sinners; of whom I am chief (1 Timothy 1:15). *Him that cometh to [him he] will in no wise cast out* (John 6:37), for *he is able also to save them to the uttermost that come unto God by him, seeing he ever liveth to make intercession for [us]* (Hebrews 7:25).

Now all that God asks of you – and this he gives you – is that you will simply look at his bleeding, dying Son, and trust your souls in the hands of him whose name alone can save from death and hell. Is it not a marvelous thing that the proclamation of this gospel does not receive the unanimous consent of men? One would think that as soon as ever this was preached: *That whosoever believeth in him should not perish, but have eternal life* (John 3:15), every one of you, casting away every his sins and his iniquities, would lay hold on Jesus Christ, and look alone to his cross.

But alas! such is the desperate evil of our nature, such is the wicked depravity of our character, that this message is despised, the invitation to the gospel feast is rejected, and there are many of you who are this day enemies of God by wicked works, enemies to the God who preaches Christ to you today, enemies to him who sent his Son to give his life a ransom for many. Strange I say it is that it should be so, yet nevertheless it is the fact, and thus the necessity for the command of the text – *Compel them to come in.*

Children of God, you who have believed, I shall have little or nothing to say to you this morning; I am going straight to my business – I am going after those that will not come – those that are in the byways and hedges, and God going with me, it is my duty now to fulfill this command: *Compel them to come in.*

First, I must *find you out*; secondly, I will go to work to *compel you to come in.*

First, I must find you out. If you read the verses that precede the text, you will find an amplification of this command: *Go out quickly into the streets and lanes of the city, and bring in hither the poor, and the maimed, and the halt, and the blind* (Luke 14:21); and then, afterwards, *Go out into the highways,* bring in the vagrants, the highwaymen, *and [into the] hedges,* and bring in those that have no resting place for their heads, and are lying under the hedges to rest, bring them in also, and *compel them to come in* (Luke 14:23). Yes, I see you this morning, you that are *poor.* I am to compel *you* to come in. You are poor in circumstances, but this is no barrier to the kingdom of heaven, for God has not exempted from his grace the man who shivers in rags, and who is destitute of bread. In fact, if there be any distinction made, the distinction is on your side, and for your benefit – *To you is the word of this salvation sent* (Acts 13:26); for *the poor have the gospel preached to them* (Matthew 11:5).

But especially I must speak to you who are poor *spiritually.* You have no faith, you have no virtue, you have no good work, you have no grace, and what is worse poverty still, you have no hope. Ah, my Master has sent *you* a gracious invitation; come and welcome to the marriage feast of his love. *Whosoever will, let him take the water of life freely* (Revelation 22:17). Come, I must lay hold upon you, though you be defiled with the foulest filth, and though you have nothing but rags upon your back, though your own righteousness has become as filthy rags, yet must I lay hold upon you, and invite you first, and even compel you to come in.

And now I see you again. You are not only poor, but you are also *maimed.* There was a time when you thought you could work out your own salvation without God's help, when you could perform good works, attend to ceremonies, and get to heaven by yourselves; but now you are maimed, the sword of the law has cut off your hands, and now you can work no longer; you say, with bitter sorrow,

> The best performance of my hands,
> Dares not appear before thy throne.

You have lost all power now to obey the law; you feel that when you would do good, evil is present with you. You are maimed; you have given up, as a forlorn hope, all attempt to save yourself, because you are maimed and your arms are gone. But you are worse off than that, for if you could not work your way to heaven, yet you could walk your way there along the road by faith; but you are maimed in the feet as well as in the hands; you feel that you cannot believe, that you cannot repent, that you cannot obey the stipulations of the gospel. You feel that you are utterly undone, powerless in every respect to do anything that can be pleasing to God. In fact, you are crying out,

> Oh, could I but believe,
>   Then all would easy be,
> I would, but cannot, Lord relieve,
>   My help must come from thee.

To you am I sent also. Before *you* I am to lift up the bloodstained banner of the cross, to *you* I am to preach this gospel: *Whosoever shall call upon the name of the Lord shall be saved;* and unto you am I to cry, *Whosoever will, let him take the water of life freely* (Revelation 22:17).

There is yet another class. You are *lame.* You are faltering between two opinions. You are sometimes seriously inclined, and at another time worldly gaiety calls you away. What little progress you do make in religion is but a limp. You have a little strength, but that is so little that you make but painful progress. Ah, limping brother, to you also is the word of this salvation sent. Though you falter between two opinions, the Master sends me to you with this message: *How long halt ye between two opinions? if the Lord be God, follow him: but if Baal, then follow him* (1 Kings 18:21). *Consider your ways* (Haggai 1:7). *Set thine house in order; for thou shalt die, and not live* (2 Kings 20:1). *Because I will do this unto thee, prepare to meet thy God, O Israel* (Amos 4:12). Halt no longer, but decide for God and his truth.

And yet I see another class – *the blind.* Yes, you who cannot see yourselves, who think yourselves good when you are full of evil, who put bitter for sweet and sweet for bitter, darkness for light and light for darkness – to you I am sent. You blind souls who cannot see your lost estate, who do not believe that sin is so exceedingly sinful as it is, and who will not be persuaded to think that God is a just and righteous God – to you I am sent. To you too who cannot see the Savior, who see no beauty in him that you should desire him; who see no excellence in virtue, no glories in religion, no happiness in serving God, no delight in being his children – to you also I am sent.

Alas, to whom am I not sent if I take my text? For it goes further than this – it not only gives a particular description, so that each individual case may be met, but afterwards it also makes a general sweep, and says, *Go out into the highways and hedges* (Luke 14:23). Here we bring in all ranks and conditions of men – my lord upon his horse in the highway, and the woman trudging about her business, the thief waylaying the traveler – all these are in the highway, and they are all to be compelled to come in, and there away in the hedges there lie some poor souls whose refuges of lies are swept away, and who are seeking now to find some little shelter for their weary heads – to you also we are sent this morning. This is the universal command – *Compel them to come in.*

Now, I pause after having described the character, I pause to look at the herculean labor that lies before me. Well did Melanchthon say, "Old Adam was too strong for young Melanchthon." As well might a little child seek to compel a Samson, so is it as I seek to lead a sinner to the cross of Christ. And yet my Master sends me on the errand. Lo, I see the great mountain before me of human depravity and empty indifference, but by faith I cry, *Who art thou, O great mountain? before Zerubbabel thou shalt become a plain* (Zechariah 4:7). Does my Master say, *Compel them to come in*? Then, though the sinner be like Samson and I a child, I shall lead him with a thread. If God says, *Do* it, if I attempt it in faith, *it shall be done,* and if with a groaning, struggling, and weeping heart, I so seek this day to compel sinners to come to Christ, then the sweet compulsions of the Holy Spirit shall go with every word, and some indeed shall be compelled to come in.

And now to the work – directly to the work. Unconverted, unreconciled, obstinate men and women, I am to compel you to come in. Permit me first of all to aggressively approach you in the highways of sin and tell you over again my errand. The King of heaven this morning sends a gracious invitation to you. He says, *As I live, saith the Lord God, I have no pleasure in the death of the wicked; but that the wicked turn from his way and live* (Ezekiel 33:11). *Come now, and let us reason together, saith the Lord: though your sins be as scarlet, they shall be as white as snow; though they be red like crimson, they shall be as wool* (Isaiah 1:18).

Dear brother, it makes my heart rejoice to think that I should have such good news to tell you, and yet I confess my soul is heavy because I see you do not think it is good news, but turn away from it, and do not give it due regard. Permit me to tell you what the King has done for you. He knew your guilt, he foresaw that you would ruin yourself. He knew that his justice would demand your blood, and in order that this difficulty might be escaped, that his justice might have its full due, and that you might yet be saved, *Jesus Christ has died.* Will you just for a moment glance at this picture?

You see that man there on his knees in the garden of Gethsemane, sweating drops of blood. You see this next: you see that miserable sufferer tied to a pillar and lashed with terrible scourges, until the shoulder bones are seen like white islands in the midst of a sea of blood. Again you see this third picture: it is the same man hanging on the cross with hands extended, and with feet nailed fast, dying, groaning, bleeding; it seems to me the picture spoke and said, *It is finished* (John 19:30). Now all this has Jesus Christ of Nazareth done, in order that God might consistently with his justice pardon sin; and the message to you this morning is this – *Believe on the Lord Jesus Christ, and thou shalt be saved.* That is, trust him, renounce your works, and your ways, and set your heart alone on this man, who gave himself for sinners.

Well brother, I have told you the message, what do you say unto it? Do you turn away? You tell me it is nothing to you; you cannot listen to it; that you will hear me by and by; but you will go your ways this day and attend to your farm and merchandise. Stop brother. I was not told merely to tell you and then go about my business. No; I am told to compel you to come in; and permit me to observe to you before I further go, that there is one thing I can say – and to which God is my witness this morning, that I am in earnest with you in my desire that you should comply with this command of God.

You may despise your own salvation, but I do not despise it; you may go away and forget what you shall hear, but you will please remember that the things I now say cost me many a groan before I came here to utter them. My inmost soul is speaking out to you, my poor brother, when I implore you by him that lives and was dead, and is alive forevermore, to consider my Master's message which he bids me now to address to you.

But do you spurn it? Do you still refuse it? Then I must change my tone a minute. I will not merely tell you the message, and invite you as I do with all earnestness, and sincere affection – I will also go further. Sinner, in God's name I *command* you to repent and believe. Do you ask me from where my authority comes? I am an ambassador of heaven. My credentials, while some of them are secret, and in my own heart, others of them open before you this day in the seals of my ministry, sitting and standing in this hall, where God has given me many souls for my hire. As God the everlasting one has given me a commission to preach his gospel, I command you to believe in the Lord Jesus Christ; not on my own authority, but on the authority of him who said, *Go ye into all the world, and preach the gospel to every creature;* and then annexed this solemn sanction: *He that believeth and is baptized shall be saved; but he that believeth not shall be damned.*

Reject my message, and remember: *He that despised Moses' law died without mercy under two or three witnesses: of how much sorer punishment, suppose ye, shall he be thought worthy, who hath trodden under foot the Son of God* (Hebrews 10:28-29). An ambassador is not to stand below the man whom he deals with, for we stand higher. If the minister chooses to take his proper rank, girded with the omnipotence of God, and anointed with his holy fervor, he is to command men, and speak with all authority compelling them to come in: *reprove, rebuke, exhort with all long suffering* (2 Timothy 4:2).

But do you turn away and say you will not be commanded? Then again will I change my note. If that does not help, all other means shall be tried. My brother, I come to you simple of speech, and I *exhort* you to flee to Christ. O my brother, do you know what a loving Christ he is? Let me tell you from my own soul what I know of him. I too once despised him. He knocked at the door of my heart and I refused to open it. He came to me, times without number, morning by morning, and night by night; he checked me in my conscience and spoke to me by his Spirit, and when, at last, the thunders of the law prevailed in my conscience, I thought that Christ was cruel and unkind. O, I can never forgive myself that I should have thought so ill of him. But what a loving reception did I have when I went to him.

I thought he would strike me, but his hand was not clenched in anger but opened wide in mercy. I thought for sure that his eyes would dart lightning-flashes of wrath upon me; but, instead of that, they were full of tears. He fell upon my neck and kissed me; he took off my rags and clothed me with his righteousness, and caused my soul to sing aloud for joy; while in the house of my heart and in the house of his church there was music and dancing, because his son whom he had lost was found, and he who was dead was made alive.

I exhort you, then, to look to Jesus Christ and to be lightened. Sinner, you will never regret – I will be a slave for my Master that you will never regret it – you will have no sigh to go back to your state of condemnation; you shall go out of Egypt and shall go into the promised land and shall find it flowing with milk and honey. The trials of Christian life you shall find heavy, but you will find grace that will make them light. And as for the joys and delights of being a child of God, if I lie this day, you shall charge me with it in days to come. If you will taste and see that the Lord is good, I am not afraid but that you shall find that he is not only good, but also better than human lips ever can describe.

I know not what arguments to use with you. I appeal to your own self-interests. Oh, my poor friend, would it not be better for you to be reconciled to the God of heaven than to be his enemy? What are you getting by opposing God? Are you the happier for being his enemy? Answer, pleasure-seeker: have you found delights in that cup? Answer me, self-righteous man: have you found rest for the sole of your foot in all your works? Oh, you who go about to establish your own righteousness, I charge you to let conscience speak. Have you found it to be a happy path? Ah, my friend, *wherefore do ye spend money for that which is not bread? and your labour for that which satisfieth not? hearken diligently unto me, and eat ye that which is good, and let your soul delight itself in fatness* (Isaiah 55:2).

I exhort you by everything that is sacred and solemn, everything that is important and eternal, flee for your lives, look not behind you, stay not in all the plain, stay not until you have proved, and found an interest in, the blood of Jesus Christ, that blood which *cleanseth us from all sin* (1 John 1:7). Are you still cold and indifferent? Will not the blind man permit me to lead him to the feast? Will not my maimed brother put his hand upon my shoulder and permit me to assist him to the banquet? Will not the poor man allow me to walk side by side with him?

Must I use some stronger words? Must I use some other compulsion to compel you to come in? Sinners, this one thing I am resolved upon this morning: if you be not saved, you shall be without excuse. You, from the gray-headed down to the tender age of childhood, if you this day do not lay hold upon Christ, your blood shall be on your own head.

If there be power in man to bring his fellow man (as there is when man is helped by the Holy Spirit), that power shall be exercised this morning, God helping me. Come, I am not to be put off by your rebuffs; if my exhortation fails, I must come to something else. My brother, I implore you, I beg you to stop and consider. Do you know what it is you are rejecting this morning? You are rejecting Christ, your only Savior. *Other foundation can no man lay* (1 Corinthians 3:11); *there is none other name under heaven given among men, whereby we must be saved* (Acts 4:12). My brother, I cannot bear that you should do this, for I remember what you are forgetting: the day is coming when you will want a Savior. It is not long before weary months shall have ended, and your strength begins to decline; your pulse shall fail you, your strength shall depart, and you and the grim monster – death – must face each other.

What will you do in the swellings of Jordan without a Savior? Deathbeds are stony things without the Lord Jesus Christ. It is an awful thing to die anyhow; he that has the best hope, and the most triumphant faith, finds that death is not a thing to laugh at. It is a terrible thing to pass from the seen to the unseen, from the mortal to the immortal, from time to eternity; and you will find it hard to go through the iron gates of death without the sweet wings of angels to conduct you to the gates of the skies.

It will be a hard thing to die without Christ. I cannot help thinking of you. I see you acting the suicide this morning, and I picture myself standing at your bedside and hearing your cries, and knowing that you are dying without hope. I cannot bear that. I think I am standing by your coffin now, and looking into your clay-cold face, and saying, "This man despised Christ and neglected the great salvation." I think what bitter tears I shall weep then, if I think that I have been unfaithful to you, and how those eyes closed fast in death shall seem to chide me and say, "Minister, I attended the music hall, but you were not in earnest with me; you amused me, you preached to me, but you did not plead with me. You did not know what Paul meant when he said, *As though God did beseech you by us: we pray you in Christ's stead, be ye reconciled to God* (2 Corinthians 5:20).

I beg you to let this message enter your heart for another reason. I picture myself standing at the bar of God. As the Lord lives, the day of judgment is coming. You believe that? You are not an infidel; your conscience would not permit you to doubt the Scripture. Perhaps you may have pretended to do so, but you cannot. You feel there must be a day when God shall judge the world in righteousness. I see you standing in the midst of that throng, and the eye of God is fixed on you. It seems to you that he is not looking anywhere else, but only upon you, and he summons you before him; and he reads your sins, and he cries, *Depart from me, ye cursed, into everlasting fire [in hell]!*

My friend, I cannot bear to think of you in that position; it seems as if every hair on my head must stand on end to think of any hearer of mine being damned. Will you picture yourselves in that position? The word has gone forth: *Depart from me, ye cursed.* Do you see the pit as it opens to swallow you up? Do you listen to the shrieks and the yells of those who have preceded you to that eternal lake of torment? Instead of picturing the scene, I turn to you with the words of the inspired prophet, and I say, *Who among us shall dwell with the devouring fire? who among us shall dwell with everlasting burnings?* (Isaiah 33:14).

Oh! my brother, I cannot let you thus put away religion; no, I think of what is to come after death. I should be destitute of all humanity if I should see a person about to poison himself, and did not smash the cup; or if I saw another about to plunge from London Bridge, if I did not assist in preventing him from doing so; and I should be worse than a fiend if I did not now, with all love, and kindness, and earnestness, implore you to *lay hold on eternal life* (1 Timothy 6:12), to *labour not for the meat which perisheth, but for that meat which endureth unto everlasting life* (John 6:27).

Some hyper-Calvinist would tell me I am wrong in doing so. I cannot help it. I must do it. As I must stand before my judge at last, I feel that I shall not make full proof of my ministry unless I entreat with many tears that you would be saved, that you would look unto Jesus

Christ and receive his glorious salvation. But does not this help? Are all our appeals lost upon you; do you turn a deaf ear? Then again, I change my note.

Sinner, I have pleaded with you as a man pleads with his friend, and were it for my *own* life I could not speak more earnestly this morning than I do speak concerning *yours*. I did feel earnest about my own soul, but not a bit more than I do about the souls of my congregation this morning; and therefore, if you put away these pleadings, I have something else – I must *threaten* you.

You shall not always have such warnings as these. A day is coming, when hushed shall be the voice of every gospel minister, at least for you; for your ear shall be cold in death. It shall not be anymore threatening; it shall be the fulfillment of the threatening. There shall be no promise, no proclamations of pardon and of mercy, no peace-speaking blood; but you shall be in the land where the Sabbath is all swallowed up in everlasting nights of misery, and where the preachings of the gospel are forbidden because they would be unprofitable.

I charge you, then, to listen to this voice that now addresses your conscience; for if not, God shall speak to you in his wrath, and say unto you in his hot displeasure, *Because I have called, and ye refused; I have stretched out my hand, and no man regarded; [therefore] I also will laugh at your calamity; I will mock when your fear cometh* (Proverbs 1:24, 26). Sinner, I threaten you again. Remember, it is but a short time you may have to hear these warnings. You imagine that your life will be long, but do you know how short it is? Have you ever tried to think how frail you are? Did you ever see a body when it has been cut in pieces by the anatomist? Did you ever see such a marvelous thing as the human frame?

> Strange, a harp of a thousand strings,
> Should keep in tune so long.

Let but one of those cords be twisted, let but a mouthful of food go in the wrong direction, and you may die. The slightest chance, as we have it, may send you swiftly to death, when God wills it. Strong men have been killed by the smallest and slightest accident, and so may you. In the chapel, in the house of God, men have dropped down dead. How often do we hear of men falling in our streets – rolling out of time into eternity, by some sudden stroke. And are you sure that heart of yours is quite sound? Is the blood circulating with all accuracy? Are you quite sure of that? And if it be so, how long shall it be? O, perhaps there are some of you here who shall never see Christmas Day; it may be that the mandate has gone forth already: *Set thine house in order; for thou shalt die, and not live* (2 Kings 20:1).

Out of this vast congregation, I might with accuracy tell how many will be dead in a year; but certain it is that the whole of us shall never meet together again in any one assembly. Some out of this vast crowd, perhaps some two or three, shall depart before the new year shall be ushered in. I remind you, then, my brother, that either the gate of salvation may be shut, or else you may be out of the place where the gate of mercy stands. Come, then, let the threatening have power with you.

I do not threaten because I would alarm without cause, but in hopes that a brother's threatening may drive you to the place where God has prepared the feast of the gospel. And now, *must I turn hopelessly away?* Have I exhausted all that I can say? No, I will come to you again. Tell me what it is, my brother, that keeps you from Christ. I hear one say, "Oh sir, it is because I feel myself too guilty." That cannot be, my friend, that cannot be. "But sir, I am the chief of sinners." Friend, you are not.

The chief of sinners died and went to heaven many years ago; his name was Saul of Tarsus, afterwards called Paul the apostle. He was the chief of sinners, and I know he spoke the truth. "No," but you say still, "I am too vile." You cannot be viler than the *chief* of sinners. You must, at least, be second worst. Even supposing you are the worst now alive, you are second worst, for he was chief. But suppose you are the worst; is not that the very reason why you should come to Christ? The worse a man is, the more reason he should go to the hospital or the physician. The poorer you are, the more reason you should accept the charity of another.

Now, Christ does not want any merits of yours. He gives freely. The worse you are, the more welcome you are. But let me ask you a question: Do you think you will ever get better by stepping away from Christ? If so, you know very little as yet of the way of salvation at all. No sir, the longer you stay the worse you will grow; your hope will grow weaker, your despair will become stronger; the nail with which Satan has fastened you down will be more firmly clenched, and you will be less hopeful than ever. Come, I implore you, recollect that there is nothing to be gained by delay, but by delay everything may be lost. "But," cries another, "I feel I cannot believe." No, my friend, and you never will believe if you look first at your believing. Remember, I am not come to invite you to faith, but am come to invite you to Christ.

But you say, "What is the difference?" Why, just this: if you first of all say, "I want to believe a thing," and you never do it. But your first inquiry must be: "What is this thing that I am to believe?" Then will faith come as the consequence of that search. Our first business has not to do with faith, but with Christ. Come, I beg you, on Calvary's mount, and see the cross. Behold the Son of God, he who made the heavens and the earth, dying for your sins. Look to him; is there not power in him to save? Look at his face so full of pity. Is there not love in his heart to prove him *willing* to save?

Sinner, the sight of Christ will help you to believe. Do not believe first, and then go to Christ, or else your faith will be a worthless thing; go to Christ without any faith, and cast yourself upon him, sink or swim. But I hear another cry, "Oh sir, you do not know how often I have been invited, how long I have rejected the Lord." I do not know, and I do not want to know; all I know is that my Master has sent me to compel you to come in, so come along with him now.

You may have rejected a thousand invitations; don't make this the thousandth-and-one. You have been up to the house of God, and you have only been gospel hardened. But do I not see a tear in your eye; come, my brother, and don't be hardened by this message.

O, Spirit of the living God, come and melt this heart, for it has never been melted, and compel him to come in! I cannot let you go on such idle excuses as that; if you have lived so many years making light of Christ, there are so many reasons why now you should not make light of him. But did I hear you whisper that this was not a convenient time? Then what must I say to you? When will that convenient time come? Shall it come when you are in hell? Will that time be convenient? Shall it come when you are on your dying bed, and the death throttle is in your throat – shall it come then? Or when the burning sweat is scalding your brow; and then again, when the cold, clammy sweat is there, shall those be convenient times? When pains are racking you, and you are on the borders of the tomb? No, sir, this morning is the convenient time. May God make it so.

Remember, I have no authority to ask you to come to Christ *tomorrow*. The Master has given you no invitation to come to him next Tuesday. The invitation is, *To day if ye will hear his voice, harden not your hearts, as in the provocation* (Hebrews 3:15), for the Spirit says "today." *Come **now**, and let us reason together* (Isaiah 1:18, emphasis added); why should you put it off? It may be the last warning you shall ever have. Put it off, and you may never weep again in the chapel. You may never have so earnest a conversation addressed to you. You may not be pleaded with as I would plead with you now. You may go away, and God may say, "He *is joined to idols: let him alone*" (Hosea 4:17). He shall throw the reins upon your neck; and then, mark – your course is sure, but it is sure damnation and swift destruction.

And now again, is it all in vain? Will you not now come to Christ? Then what more can I do? I have but one more resort, and that shall be tried. I can be permitted to weep for you; I can be allowed to pray for you. You shall scorn the address if you like; you shall laugh at the preacher; you shall call him a fanatic if you will; he will not chide you, he will bring no accusation against you to the great judge. Your offense, so far as he is concerned, is forgiven before it is committed; but you will remember that the message that you are rejecting this morning is a message from one who loves you, and it is given to you also by the lips of one who loves you.

You will recollect that you may play your soul away with the devil, that you may listlessly think it a matter of no importance; but there lives at least one who is in earnest about your soul, and one who before he came here wrestled with his God for strength to preach to you, and who, when he has gone from this place, will not forget his audience of this morning.

I say again, when words fail us, we can give tears – for words and tears are the arms with which gospel ministers compel men to come in. You do not know, and I suppose could not believe, how anxious a man whom God has called to the ministry feels about his congregation, and especially about some of them. I heard but the other day of a young man who attended here a long time, and his father's hope was that he would be brought to Christ. He became acquainted, however, with an infidel; and now he neglects his business, and lives in a daily course of sin. I saw his father's poor ashen face; I did not ask him to tell me the story himself, for I felt it was raking up a trouble and opening a sore.

I fear, sometimes, that good man's gray hairs may be brought with sorrow to the grave. Young men, you do not pray for yourselves, but your mothers wrestle for you. You will not think of your own souls, but your father's anxiety is exercised for you. I have been at prayer meetings, when I have heard children of God pray there, and they could not have prayed with more earnestness and more intensity of anguish if they had been each of them seeking their own soul's salvation. And is it not strange that we should be ready to move heaven and earth for your salvation, and that still you should have no thought for *yourselves,* no regard for eternal things?

Now I turn for one moment to some here. There are some of you here who are members of Christian churches, who make a profession of religion, but unless I be mistaken in you – and I shall be happy if I am – your profession is a lie. You do not live up to it, you dishonor it; you can live in the perpetual practice of absenting yourselves from God's house, if not in sins worse than that. Now I ask such of you who do not adorn the doctrine of God your Savior, Do you imagine that you can call me your pastor, and yet that my soul cannot tremble over you and in secret weep for you? Again, I say it may be but little concern to you how you defile the garments of your Christianity, but it is a great concern to God's hidden ones, who sigh and cry, and groan for the iniquities of the mere professing Christians of Zion.

Now does anything else remain to the minister besides weeping and prayer? Yes, there is one thing else. God has given to his servants not the power of regeneration, but he has given them something akin to it. It is impossible for any man to regenerate his neighbor; and yet how are men born to God? Does not the apostle say of such a one that he was begotten by him in his bonds? Now the minister has a power given him of God, to be considered both the father and the mother of those born to God, for the apostle said he labored in birth for souls until Christ was formed in them. What can we do then? We can now appeal to the Spirit.

I know I have preached the gospel, that I have preached it earnestly; I challenge my Master to honor his own promise. He has said it shall not return unto me void, and it shall not. It is in his hands, not mine. I cannot compel you, but you, O Spirit of God who has the key of the heart, you can compel. Did you ever notice in that chapter of Revelation, where it says, *Behold, I stand at the door, and knock* (Revelation 3:20), that a few verses before, the same person is described as *he that hath the key of David* (Revelation 3:7)? So that if knocking will not help, he has the key and can and will come in. Now if the knocking of an earnest minister prevails not with you this morning, there remains still that secret opening of the heart by the Spirit, so that you shall be compelled.

I thought it my duty to labor with you as though *I* must do it; now I throw it into my Master's hands. It cannot be his will that we should labor in birth, and yet not bring forth spiritual children. It is with *him;* he is master of the heart, and the day shall declare it, that some of you constrained by sovereign grace have become the willing captives of the all-conquering Jesus, and have bowed your hearts to him through these words.

Chapter 11

Counting the Cost

For which of you, intending to build a tower, sitteth not down first, and counteth the cost, whether he have sufficient to finish it? lest haply, after he hath laid the foundation, and is not able to finish it, all that behold it begin to mock him, saying, This man began to build, and was not able to finish. (Luke 14:28-30)

This passage is peculiar to Luke, and he tells us that at the time when our Lord uttered it great multitudes followed him. It is observable that when our Lord was forsaken by the crowd, he was not depressed, and when his ministry became popular, he was not elated. He was calm and wise in the midst of the excitement of the thronging multitudes. This passage is sufficient evidence of that fact. On this occasion our Lord spoke with a view to the winnowing of the great heap of nominal discipleship which lay before him, that the chaff might be driven away and only the precious wheat might remain. The discourse before us reminds us of Gideon's process of diminishing that vast but motley host of which the Lord said, *The people that are with thee are too many for me* (Judges 7:2).

After having bidden the fainthearted to go, he next brought down the remaining thousands to the river, and bade them to drink; and then only kept for himself those who lapped in a certain peculiar manner, which indicated their zeal, their speed, their energy, and their experience. Our Lord tested his followers so that he might have only those remaining who would be fit for the conquest of the world. To carry his precious treasure, he would select vessels whom grace had made fit for his use; the rest he could dispense with.

Our Lord Jesus was far too wise to pride himself upon the number of his converts; he cared rather for quality than quantity. He rejoiced over one sinner that repented, but ten thousand sinners who merely professed to have repented would have given him no joy whatever. His heart longed after the real, he loathed the counterfeit; he panted after the substance, and the shadow could not content him. His fan was in his hand with which to thoroughly purge his floor, and his axe was laid to the root of the trees to cut down the fruitless.

He was anxious to leave a living church like good seed in the land, as free as possible from all intermixture. Therefore in this particular instance, one might even think that he was repelling men rather than attracting them to his leadership; but, indeed, he was doing nothing of the kind. He understood very well that men to be truly won must be won by truth, that the truest love is ever honest, and that the best disciple is not he who joins the class of the great Master in a hurry, and then afterwards discovers that the learning is not such as he expected, but one who comes sighing after just such knowledge as the teacher is prepared to give.

Moreover, our Lord knew what sometimes we may forget – that there is no heartbreak in the world to the godly worker like that which comes of disappointed hopes, when those who have said, *Lord, I will follow thee whithersoever thou goest* (Luke 9:57), turn back to hell, and when the hot breath which shouted, "Hosanna!" turns into the cruel, cold-blooded cry, *Crucify him, crucify him* (Luke 23:21). Nothing is more injurious to a church than a large dilution with halfhearted members, and nothing more dangerous to the persons themselves than to allow them to put on an untrue profession.

Therefore did the Master take most care at the time when that care was most needed, that none should follow him under misunderstanding, but should be made fully aware of what was meant by being his disciples, so that they would not say afterwards, "We have been misled;

we have been beguiled into a service which disappoints us." Unlike the enlisting sergeant who sets forth all the glories of military service in glowing colors in order to gain a recruit, the great Captain of our salvation would have his followers take all things into consideration before they cast in their lot with him.

This morning our text may be equally suitable, and its warning may be as necessary and as beneficial as when first the Master pronounced it; for great multitudes are just now following Christ; a revival has come and stirred the mass of you. Among the would-be disciples (blessed be God!) are many whom the Lord himself has called, for every one of whom we give most hearty thanks; but with them necessarily, and of course (for when was it ever different?) there are others who are not called of God at all, but who are moved by the natural impulse of imitating others, and stirred by feelings which are nonetheless fleeting because just now they are intense; and therefore in Christ's name it is ours to address you even as he did, and warn you in his own words: *If any man come to me, and hate not his father, and mother, and wife, and children, and brethren, and sisters, yea, and his own life also, he cannot be my disciple. And whosoever doth not bear his cross, and come after me, cannot be my disciple. For which of you, intending to build a tower, sitteth not down first, and counteth the cost, whether he have sufficient to finish it? Lest haply, after he hath laid the foundation, and is not able to finish it, all that behold it begin to mock him, saying, This man began to build, and was not able to finish* (Luke 14:26-30).

To assist our memories, we will divide our meditation into three parts. The first will be headed in this manner: *true religion is a costly thing*; the second shall bear this motto: *wisdom suggests that before we enter upon it, we should estimate the cost*; and the third shall bear this inscription: *cost what it may, it is worth what it costs*.

First, then, it is clear from our text that true religion is costly. Far be it from us to create any confusion of thought here. The gifts of God's grace cost us nothing, neither could his salvation be purchased with money, nor with merit, nor by vows and confessions. *If a man would give all the substance of his house for love, it would utterly be contemned* (Song of Solomon 8:7). The gospel motto is: "Without money and without price we are *justified freely by his grace through the redemption that is in Christ Jesus*" (Romans 3:24). Yet, for all that, if a man will be a Christian, it will cost him something. Consider a moment.

Here is a blind man sitting by the wayside begging; he asks to have his eyes opened. Will it cost him anything? No, the Savior would not accept all the gold in the world for the cure, he will freely open his eyes; but when they are opened it will cost that blind man something. Obtaining his sight, he will be called upon to discharge the duties of one who has eyes. He will not be allowed after that to sit there and beg, or, if he tries to do so, he will lose the sympathy which is bestowed upon blindness; now that his eyes are opened, he must use them, and earn his own bread. It will cost him something, for he will now be conscious of the darkness of the night which he knew nothing of before! And there are sad sights which now he must look upon which never grieved him before, for often what the eye does not see the heart does not regret.

A man cannot gain a faculty except at some expense; he that increases knowledge or the means of gaining it, increases both sorrow and duty. Take another case. A poor man is suddenly made a prince: it will cost him the giving up of his former manners and will involve him in new duties and cares. A man is set on the road to heaven as a pilgrim: does he pay anything to enter by the Wicket Gate[1]? I think not; free grace admits him to the sacred way.

But when that man is put on the road to heaven it will cost him something. It will cost him earnestness to knock at the Wicket Gate, and sweat by which to climb the Hill Difficulty; it will cost him tears to find his roll again when he has lost it in the arbor of ease; it will cost him great care in going down the Valley of Humiliation; it will cost him resistance unto blood when he stands foot to foot with Apollyon in conflict; it will cost him many fears when he has to travel in the Valley of the Shadow of Death; it may cost him his life when he comes to Vanity Fair, if like Faithful he is called to bear testimony at the stake. True religion is the gift of God, and there is nothing we can do to purchase it; at the same time, if we receive it, certain consequences will flow from it, and we ought to consider whether we shall be able to put up with them.

---

1   The Wicket Gate in *The Pilgrim's Progress* represents Jesus Christ, the only door through which we can enter heaven (John 10:9).

You may be sure that the cost must be great, since our Lord compares it to the building of a tower. The word here used for *tower* has often been employed to signify a turreted house, a villa, or a country mansion. "Which of you," says he to the people, "intending to build for himself a mansion in which to reside at your ease, would not first of all count the cost?" The building is to be a costly one. Doddridge is wrong in the supposition that a temporary tower is intended here. That it would cost a considerable sum is clear from the Savior's saying that the wise man sits down and counts the cost.

He does not merely stand up and pass his hand over his brow and say, "This tower will cost me so many hundred pounds"; but it is to be an elaborate construction, an almost palatial edifice, and therefore he sits down, like a merchant at his desk, and thoughtfully considers the undertaking; he consults the architect and the mason, and calculates what will be the expense of the outer walls, what of the roof, what of the interior fittings, and the like, and he does not make a rough guess, but counts the cost as men count their gold. It is evidently a matter of consequence with him, and so is true religion – it is no trifle, but an all-important business. He who thinks that a careless, hit-or-miss, headlong venture will suffice for his eternal interests is the reverse of wise.

True godliness is the building up of a character which will endure the day of judgment. It begins in laying deep the foundations in faith and love and a renewed heart; it is carried on by the putting patiently and carefully, and often painfully, stone upon stone the materials of the fair edifice, diligently adding *to your faith virtue; and to virtue knowledge; and to knowledge temperance; and to temperance patience; and to patience godliness; and to godliness brotherly kindness; and to brotherly kindness charity* (2 Peter 1:5-7). Our life-work consists in *building up [our]selves on [our] most holy faith* (Jude 1:20). Do you not see that it is a glorious palace to which the Christian character is likened?

But, lest we should still think the expense small, our Lord compares it to a war, and he speaks of the number of troops engaged in that war, showing that it is no petty skirmish of two insignificant tribes. He likens it to a war in which upon one side there is an array of ten thousand, and on the other a host of twenty thousand. Now, warfare is always expensive work; besides the cost for equipment and ammunition, there is the cost of human life and blood; there is the removal of strong arms from work at home, and the direr risks of defeat, captivity, and devastation.

The Lord compares religion, then, in its externals, to a battle between the gracious man and the evils rampant in the outside world. The disciple of Jesus has to defend himself against a gigantic foe, and he has within himself a power which, so far as he is concerned, is not sufficient for the contest; the odds are fearful – ten thousand against twenty thousand. Well does the Savior say in the latter case that it is well to sit down to consult. The king with the smaller army consults, asks his scholarly senators, takes counsel from experience, calls in good advisers, and debates whether the thing can be done or not. So should we consider the matter of our souls, for religion is a costly thing, and not to be entered on, as the Frenchman said, "with a light heart." That light heart cost his nation dearly, and so it will ourselves if we indulge it.

We might have inferred this, I think, from some other considerations – namely, first from the fact that true religion is a lasting thing. It lasts for life. False religion comes and goes; true conversion is never repeated, and it is the commencement of a life that will know no end, either in time or in eternity. Now anything that is to last must be expensive. You shall get your glass colored, if you will, cheaply, but the sun will soon remove all its beauty. If you would obtain a glass that shall retain its color for centuries, every single step in the process of its manufacture will be costly, involving much labor and great care.

So it is with true religion. You may get it cheaply if you will; it will look quite as good as the real thing, and for a little while it will bring you almost all the comfort and respect that the genuine article would have brought you, but it will not last; soon will its color fly, and the beauty and the excellence, which were there but in pretense, will soon be gone. You want, dear friend (I am sure you do), you want a godliness that will last you until you die; well then, it must cost you something, be sure of that.

Remember also that true religion will have to bear a strain, for it is certain to be opposed. This tower will not be built without opposition. It is like the wall of Jerusalem; Sanballat and Tobiah will be sure to hinder the building of it. True religion must be able to endure hardness; if it cannot do that, it is good for nothing. The old Toledo blade cost the warrior much at firsthand, but when he had once procured it, he knew that it would cut through joint and marrow in the day of battle, and he was not afraid to dash into the thick of the fray, trusting to its unrivaled temper and keen edge. Could he not find a cheaper sword? I suppose he could have found it easily enough, and with small expense of gold; but then in the moment when his sword hit upon his enemy's helmet, instead of splitting through the skull, it snapped in the warrior's hand and cost him his life.

Such is the cheap religion with that so many take up. There is no self-denial in it, no forsaking of the world, no giving up of carnal amusements – they are just the same as the world; their religion costs them nothing, and at last when they want it, it will fail them; it will snap like the ill-made sword in the day of battle, and leave them defenseless.

Oh, if you want that which will endure the conflict, you must spend a price upon it. Jesus Christ knew that the persons to whom he spoke would not be able to bear the tests which awaited his disciples; they did not know that he would be crucified, for just then he was popular, and they hoped that he was to be the King of Israel. But the Savior knew that there would come dark days in which the King of the Jews would be hanged upon a gallows, and his disciples, even his true ones, would forsake him for the moment and would flee; and therefore he in effect said to them, "You must be prepared for cross-bearing; you must be prepared to follow me amid derision and shame and reproach, and if you are not ready for this, your discipleship is a mistake." In their case it did not stand the test; these people were nowhere when the time of trial came.

And remember, dear friends, and I dwell with great emphasis upon this point: we want a religion that will withstand the inspection of the great judge at the last day. Now, there are things in the world that will endure for a while, but if they are closely looked at, and especially if they are placed under a microscope, they will be seen to have many flaws. Now, no microscopic examination can for a moment be compared with the glance of the Lord; he will read us through and through. Oh, what a withering will there be for fair professions in the day when his fiery eye shall gaze upon them.

Never does the grass dry up under a sirocco one-half so swiftly as the fair plains of pretended Christianity will wither beneath the divine glance in the last tremendous day. He will look upon what men call Christendom, and it will almost – if not altogether – vanish; for *when the Son of man cometh, shall he find faith on the earth?* (Luke 18:8). Will it not, then, be evidently true that *many are called, but few are chosen* (Matthew 22:14)? *Strive to enter in at the strait gate* is still the voice of Christ to all of us, *for many . . . will seek to enter in, and shall not be able* (Luke 13:24). If our religion is to be weighed in the balances, and may perhaps be found lacking, it is well for us to see to it, and to know that it must be sincere, genuine, and costly, if it is to pass that ordeal.

What, then, is the expense? What is the cost of building this tower or fighting this war? The answer is given by our Savior, not by me. I should not have dared to invent such tests as he has ordained; it is for me to be the echo of his voice and no more. What does he say? Why, first, that if you would be his, and have his salvation, you must love him beyond every other person in this world. Is not that the meaning of this expression: *If any man come to me, and hate not his father, and mother* (Luke 14:26)?

Dear names! Dear names! *Father, and mother*! Does there live a man with a soul so dead that he can pronounce either of these words without emotion, and especially the last – *mother*? Men and brethren, this is a dear and tender name to us, and it touches a chord which thrills our being; yet far more powerful is the name of *Savior,* the name of *Jesus.*

Less loved must father and mother be than Jesus Christ. The Lord also demands precedence over the best beloved "wife." Here he touches another set of heartstrings. Dear is that word "wife," partner of our being, comfort of our sorrow, delight of our eyes – "wife." Yet, wife, you must not take the chief place; you must sit at Jesus' feet, or else you are an idol, and Jesus will not accept your rivalry. And "children," the dear babes that nestle in the bosom, and clamber to the knee, and pronounce the parent's name in accents of music, they must not be our chief love, and they must not come between us and the Savior; nor for their sakes, to give them pleasure or to promote their worldly advantage, must we grieve our Lord.

Many a child is master of his father, many a daughter has been mistress to the mother; but if it be for evil, this must be ended at once. If they tempt us to evil, they must be treated as if we hated them; yes, the evil in them must be hated for Christ's sake. If you be Christ's disciples, your Lord must be first, and then mother, father, wife, children, brethren, and sisters will follow in due rank and order.

I am afraid that many professing Christians are not prepared for this. They would be Christians if their family would approve, but they must consult their brother, father, or wife. They would make a stand against worldly pleasures if others would, but they cannot bear to appear peculiar, or to oppose the views of relatives. They say, "My father wishes it, and I dare not tell him that it is wrong." "My mother says that we must not be too straitlaced, and therefore, though my conscience tells me it is wrong, yet will I do it, or else they will say, 'My girls are growing up and must have amusement, and my boys must be allowed their pleasures, and therefore I must wink at sin.'" Ah, my brethren, this must not be, if you are indeed Christ's disciples.

You must put them all aside. The dearest must go sooner than Jesus be forsaken; for does he not say in the Psalms, *Hearken, O daughter, and consider, and incline thine ear; forget also thine own people, and thy father's house; so shall the king greatly desire thy beauty: for he is thy Lord; and worship thou him* (Psalm 45:10-11)?

Mark you, you will best prove your love to your relatives by being decided for the right, since you will be the more likely to win their souls. Love them too much to indulge the wrong in them; love them so truly that you hate that in them which would injure you and ruin them. You must be prepared to suffer from those who are bound to you by the dearest ties; sin must not be tolerated whatever may happen. We cannot yield in the point of sin, our determination is invincible; come hate or come love, we must follow Christ.

The next item of cost is this – self must be hated. I am afraid there are some who would sooner hate father or wife than hate their own life. Yet such is the demand. It means this: that where my own pleasure, or my own gain, or my own repute, or even my own life shall come in the way of Christ's glory, I am so little to make any account of myself, that I must even hate myself if self shall stand in the way of Christ. I am to look upon father, mother, brother, sister, and myself also, as foes, so far as they are opposed to the Lord Jesus and his holy will. I am to love them and desire their good as I also desire good for myself, but I am not to desire any good for them or for myself at the cost of sinning, and robbing the Lord Jesus of his glory.

As for myself, if I see anything in myself opposed to Jesus, I must do away with it. I must mortify the flesh with its affections and lusts, denying myself anything and everything that would grieve the Savior, or would prevent my realizing perfect conformity to him.

Next, the Savior goes on to say that if we would follow him, we must bear our cross. *Whosoever doth not bear his cross, and come after me, cannot be my disciple* (Luke 14:27). Sometimes that cross comes in the shape of confessing our faith before opposers. "Ah," says the timid heart, "if I do so I shall have all my friends against me." Take up your cross! It is a part of the cost of true discipleship. "I shall scarcely be able to bear myself in the house if I profess my religion." Take up your cross, my brother, or you cannot be Christ's disciple. "Well, but it will involve a change even in my daily life." Make the change, my brother, or you cannot be the Lord's disciple.

"I know there is one very dear to me whom I have looked upon as likely to be my future companion, and he will leave me if I forsake the ways of the world." Then, heavy as the loss may be, let him go, if it be so that you cannot follow Christ and unite with him; for Jesus you must follow, or be lost forever.

What hard words these are! What detectors of the hypocrisy of many professing Christians! Did they ever separate from the world? No, not they; they fall in with its ways as the dead fish floats with the current. Have they any cross to bear? Does anybody reproach them for being too rigid and too strictly moral? Oh no! for theirs is the religion that the world praises, and consequently the religion that God abhors. *If any man love the world, the love of the Father is not in him* (1 John 2:15), and he who has the smile of the ungodly must look for the frown of God.

But, more than this, the Savior, as another item of cost, requires that his disciple should take up his cross, and *come after him;* that is to say, he must act as Christ acted. If we are not prepared to make Christ our example, yes, if it be not our highest ambition to live as he lived, to give ourselves up to act as he did, we cannot be his disciples.

Last of all, we must make an unreserved surrender of all to Jesus. Listen to these words: *Whosoever he be of you that forsaketh not all that he hath, he cannot be my disciple* (Luke 14:33). It may yet come to this, that persecution may arise, and you may have to actually give up all. You must be prepared for the event. You may not have to give up anything, but the surrender must be just as real in your heart as if it had to be carried out in act and deed. No man has truly given himself to Christ unless he has also said, "My Lord, I give to you this day my body, my soul, my powers, my talents, my goods, my house, my children, and all that I have. From this point on I will hold them at your will, as a steward under you. Yours they are. As for me, I have nothing; I have surrendered all to you."

You cannot be Christ's disciples at any less expense than this: if you possess a farthing that is your own and not your Master's, Christ is not your Master. It must be all his, every single jot and tittle, and your life also, or you cannot be his.

These are very searching words, but I would remind you once again that they are none of mine. If in expounding them I have erred, then I am grieved that it should be so, but I am persuaded that I have not erred on the side of too great severity. I confess I may have spoken too leniently. The words of the text lay the axe to it and are sweeping to the last degree. Oh, count you, then, the cost! And if any of you have taken up a religion that costs you nothing, put it down and flee from it, for it will be your curse and your ruin.

Is there any getting to heaven without this cost? No. But may we not be Christians without these sacrifices? You may be counterfeits, you may be hypocrites, you may be brethren of Judas, but you cannot be real Christians. This cost is unavoidable; it cannot be decreased one solitary mite. God grant you may be enabled to submit to it.

The second topic is this: Wisdom suggests that we should count the cost. You feel you would like to be a Christian. Dear friend, give me your hand. I am glad you have such a liking. But as I grasp your hand and would willingly draw you towards Christ, I look you in the face and say, "Do you know what you desire? Are you sure you desire it?" There are men lying on beds of sickness who cry for help, but when they recover and have to go out and battle with the world, the time may come when they will say, "I want leave to be on the bed of sickness again." I should not like a time to come when any one of you shall say, "I joined the church, but it was a mistake. I did not weigh the matter rightly. I am now in for it, and I am sorry I am, for I ought not to be where I am."

If you are honest, you ought to give up your profession, if such is the case. If you have no grace, I hope you will have enough of common honesty not to stick to a practical falsehood. I should grieve indeed if that should happen, and therefore this morning, I pray you, count the cost. For observe, if you do not count the cost, you will not be able to carry out your resolves. It is a great building, it is a great war. No mistake can be greater than the notion that in order to be saved there is only needed a measure of emotion during a few days, and the belief at one decisive hour. If I preached such doctrines, I would be deceiving your souls.

Faith and repentance are not the work of a week or two, they are a lifework; as long as the Christian is on earth he must repent; and as for faith, it is not saying, "I believe in Jesus, and therefore I am saved," but it is a daily grace, the trust of a lifetime; the Christian continues still to believe and repent until he commences to triumph in eternal glory.

Moreover, faith is continually producing sanctifying results upon the life of the believer, or otherwise he is not possessed of the right faith. He who believes in Jesus Christ is saved; but if there were such a thing as a temporary faith, there would be such a thing as a temporary salvation. He who truly repents of sin is a renewed man, but if repentance of sin were only a transient thing, and were soon over, the life which it indicated would be over too. You must not be content with false and fleeting religion. You are beginning to build a tower of which the top stone will never be laid until you are taken up to heaven, and you are commencing a war which will never end until you exchange the sword for the palm branch.

Remember, also, that to fail in this great enterprise will involve terrible defeat, for what says our Lord? He says that not to be able to finish will expose you to ridicule. I beg you to notice the form of that ridicule. *All that behold it begin to mock him, saying [one to another]* [for that is the force of the expression], *This man began to build, and was not able to finish* (Luke 14:29-30). Our Lord does not represent them as saying to the foolish builder, "You began to build and were not able to finish," but as speaking about him as a third person – *This man.*

Now, halfhearted Christians and halfhearted religious men may not be scoffed at in the public streets to their faces, but they are common butts of ridicule behind their backs. You false professing Christians are universally despised. Worldlings laughingly say, "Ah, these are pretty specimens of church members!" The world looks upon a worldly church with utter disdain, and for my part, little do I regret that such derision is poured upon an object that so well deserves it. To be a mere pretender of Christian discipleship is to become an object of scorn in time and in eternity, and such will be the false professing Christian's fate.

Sir, if you mean to be a Christian, resolve that it shall be the right thing, thorough and decided; for then, though men will not go around and praise you to your face, they will honor you, and even those who hate you will know your value. But if you are only half a Christian, and not thorough, they may not come to your face and show their contempt, but as they pass by, they will sneer, and will have more respect for a downright worldling than for you, because he is what he says he is, and makes no claim of being anything else; but as for you, you began to build and could not finish. What a wretched object is a sham Christian! We have sometimes seen great buildings which have been commenced and deserted by over speculative persons, and the neighbors have called them "Smith's Folly," or "Brown's Folly," or "Robinson's Folly," or the like; these are but fleeting causes of derision. But the pretender, the man who in appearance commenced to be a Christian and then broke down at it, will be pointed at even by the lost in hell.

The drunkard will cry, "And you? Have you also come to this place? You who were so eloquent about sobriety, and so ready to rebuke the drunkard?" "Aha!" cries another, "you are the man who lived down our street, and made so much show of your religion; you told me I was very wicked, but how are you better off than I am?" Behold, I see the openly profane elevate themselves from their racks of remorse to exclaim, "Are you become like one of us? You church-member, are you in hell? Is the taste of the sacramental wine upon your lips still? Why, then, do you demand a drop of water to cool your tongue? That sacramental bread that you swallowed so readily, does it not even now stick in your hypocritical throat? You liar before God and man, fitting and right it is that you are cast out even as we are."

Oh, if you must be lost, be lost as anything but hypocrites; if you must perish, perish rather outside the church than in it. Do not mimic the Lord of glory! I know of no worse act than to mimic the excellencies of the Savior with lively imitations of his graces. What worse offense can you render to the majesty of his sacred virtue than to imitate his holiness and mimic his perfection?

The last word shall be this, that cost whatever it may, true religion is worth the cost. We are like a man with the black pest upon him who knows that he is dying, and yet yonder is a drug that will heal him. "Physician," says he, "you ask so great a price that each drop costs me a diamond; you are demanding more than its weight in choicest pearls; but it does not matter, I must have it. If I do not, I am a dead man, and then what will it profit me that I have kept my gold?" It is the case of every one of us present here; we must have Christ or perish forever, and it will be better for us to cut off our right arm and to pluck out our right eye than that we should be cast into hellfire.

Observe, brethren, that the present blessings of true religion are worth all the cost. What if I have to tear some fond connection? Jesus, you are better to me than husband, wife, or child. If it must be so that she who lies in my bosom shall count me as her enemy, then you shall be in my heart, my Savior, better than a Rachel, or a Rebekah. Yes, if it must be so that the father shall say, "You shall never darken my doors again if you follow Christ," he must say it, for *when my father and my mother forsake me, then the Lord will take me up* (Psalm 27:10). The immediate joy will recompense for the immediate loss; yes, doubtless you may count all things but loss for the excellency of the knowledge of Christ Jesus your Lord, and yet remain a gainer.

And again, what recompense comes for all cost in the consolation afforded by true godliness in the article of death? To lie dying, why, it will give no pain to be able to say then, "I was cast out of my family for Jesus." It will be no sorrow to remember, "I was ridiculed for Christ." It will cause us no pangs to say, "I was counted too precise and too much of a Puritan." No, my brethren, those are not the things which put thorns into death pillows. Oh, no! there we shall see how sweet it was to have borne any part of Jesus' cross; a sliver of his cross will be worth a king's ransom on a dying day. Moreover, at the judgment, when the trumpet rings out, and the dead are rising, we shall not say, "I suffered too much for Christ."

When to the right his chosen go, and we among them, we shall not look back with regret to the fact that we lost caste in society and position among the refined for Jesus' sake. We shall not lament that we attended a despised meetinghouse and worshipped among the poor of this world out of love for Jesus, and fidelity to his gospel. Oh, no! I warrant you in that day he shall shine brightest who was most blurred for his Lord's sake. Amidst the bright ones, doubly bright shall be the martyr band of whom the world was not worthy, who were counted as the outcast of all things; and while each one of the disciples shall receive a hundredfold for all he may have given up for his Lord's cause, these shall have the fairest portion.

Moreover, let me remind you, beloved, that Christ asks you to give up nothing that will injure you. If you must hate father and mother, it is only in this sense – that you will not yield to their wrong requests, nor will you leave Christ for them. If you must give up any pleasure, it is because it is not a fitting pleasure for you; it is poisonous sugar of lead, and not true sweetness. Christ will give you greater enjoyments by far.

Moreover, I remember that our Redeemer does not ask any one of us to do what he has not done himself. That thought pierces me to the heart; I wish it might affect you also. Master, do you say, Give up father? Did you not leave your Father? Do you bid me even to leave my father's house if it must be for your sake? Did you not leave the glorious mansions of heaven? What if I am called to bear reproach? They called the Master of the house Beelzebub. What if I am cast out? They also cast you out. When we think of the scourgings, and the shame, and the spitting that the Lord endured, what are our griefs? And if for his sake we should even be condemned to death, we know how he hung on the cross, stripped of his all, that he might save us from the wrath to come.

O believer, can you follow your Lord to whatever place he goes? Soldiers of the cross, can you follow him? Is the path smooth enough for those dear feet and too rough for you? There he is in the center of the battle where the blows fall fastest; will you follow him? Dare you follow him, or do you long for the tents of ease, and the soft couches of the cowards yonder who are shrinking back, and deserting to the Enemy? Oh, by everything that is good, if you are indeed his followers, I charge you to cry, "Where he is, there let his servant be; as he copes, so let his servant cope; in this world let his humiliation be ours, so that in the world to come we may be partakers of his glory."

This is strong preaching, you tell me, but the Savior meant all that I have said. His was a testing discourse, but there are truths to be remembered which may console us while hearing them. It is true that *you* cannot build the tower; Joshua said to the people in his time, *Ye cannot serve the Lord* (Joshua 24:19), to test them and to see if they'd choose the Lord over false gods. If you have counted the cost, you know by this time that you cannot wage the war. Ten thousand cannot stand against twenty thousand. But yet, it must be done, for inevitable necessity drives on behind; whatever may be in front, we dare not turn back.

Remember Lot's wife (Luke 17:32). What, then, must we do? Hear the Lord's words: *With men it is impossible, but not with God: for with God all things are possible* (Mark 10:27). Are you willing? Then the Spirit of God will help you. You shall give up the world and the flesh without a sigh; you shall fight against your lusts, and you shall overcome them through the blood of the Lamb. The tower shall be built and the Lord shall inhabit it. Cast yourselves on Jesus by a simple faith: rest in his power, and from day to day believe in his strength, and he will bear you safely through.

Do you notice the verse that follows this passage in Luke 14? I wonder whether anything like it will follow my message. It is astonishing that though Jesus thundered out as from the top of Sinai, and his words seemed harsh, yet it is written, *Then drew near unto him all the publicans and sinners for to hear him* (Luke 15:1), as if they said to themselves, "This man tells us the truth; therefore we will hear him." And then he began to tell them the precious truths of his free grace, acting just as the husbandman does who puts in the plow and turns up the soil; and when he sees the earth breaking in the furrow, then he scatters the golden seed, but not until then. Ho, every one of you who would have Christ, come, and have him!

You who would have salvation, accept it as the gift of his sovereign grace, but do not receive it under misunderstanding; understand what is meant by it. Salvation is not deliverance from hell alone; it is deliverance from sin. It is not merely the rescue of men from eternal pain; it is also their redemption from this world's vain and wicked ways. It cannot be divided; it is a garment without seams, woven from the top to bottom. If you would have justification, you must have sanctification; if you would have pardon, you must have holiness; if you would be one with Christ, you must be separate from sinners. If you would walk the streets of gold above, you must walk the road of holiness below. God grant you his Holy Spirit to enable you so to do, and his shall be the praise forever. Amen.

Chapter 12

Consider before You Fight

Or what king, going to make war against another king, sitteth not down first, and consulteth whether he be able with ten thousand to meet him that cometh against him with twenty thousand? Or else, while the other is yet a great way off, he sendeth an ambassage, and desireth conditions of peace. (Luke 14:31-32)

Every sensible man endeavors to adapt his purposes to his strength. He does not begin to build a house that he will not be able to finish, nor commence a war that he cannot hope to fight through. The religion of Christ is the most reasonable one in the world, and Jesus Christ never desires to have any disciples who shall blindly follow him without counting the cost. We always esteem it to be a happy thing when we can get men to sit down and consider.

Most of you are so full of other thoughts, so occupied with the world, ever running here and there about your ordinary business, that we cannot get you to think, or calmly sit down, and soberly look at things as in the light of eternity, and weigh them deliberately as you ought. And, yet it is only reasonable that the Master should ask of you to do for him with regard to your own spiritual matters what you will admit that every sensible man does in his business continually.

You are poor traders if you never have any inventory; you are likely to be before long in the bankruptcy court if there is no periodical examination of accounts. And so Christ would have you sit down sometimes, and take stock as to where you are, and what you are, and then to figure up by some sort of arithmetic by which you may come to a truthful calculation what you are able to do, and what you are not able to do; what therefore it is reasonable for you to undertake, and what is unreasonable; and where your position ought to be, and where it ought not to be.

I especially invite this evening, those who are unconverted in this assembly, to some few thoughts upon the war in which they are engaged with God, hoping that perhaps if they consider a little upon it, they will send an embassy, and desire peace. When I have spoken upon that, there will be some, perhaps, who will be running away with the idea that they will at once be at peace with God, and make war with Satan; but I will want to pin them down for a moment, and make them estimate their chances of victory in such a war as that, and see whether they are able to meet the wicked Prince of Darkness in their own strength. We will try and see if we cannot make it tonight the subject of a little simple talk about our souls, and a little earnest personal consideration about our future.

First, then, there are some here who are not the friends of God, and in this case he that is not with him is against him.

If you cannot look up to God and say, "My Father," and feel that your heart beats true to him, then remember it is a fact that you are his enemy. If you could have what you wish, there would be no God. If it were in your power, you would never trouble yourself again with thoughts of him. You would like to live, you say, as you choose, and I know how you would choose to live. It would be, anyhow, different from what God commands. Now, as you are engaged in antagonism with him, just think a while – Can you expect to succeed? Are you likely to win the day? You have entered into a conflict with his law; you do not intend to keep it; with his day, you do not regard it; you are thus at war with God.

Now, is it likely that you will be successful? Is there a chance for you? If there is, why then, perhaps, it may be as well to go on. If you can conquer him, if the battlements of glory may yet see the flag of sin waved triumphantly there, why, man, then try it. There will be at least an ambition worthy of Satan who desired sooner to reign in hell than to be ruled by heaven. But is there any hope for you? Let me put a few things before you which may, perhaps, make you think the conflict too unequal and thus lead you to abandon the thought at once.

Think of God's *stupendous power*! What is there that he cannot do? We see but little of God's power comparatively in our land. Now and then there comes a crash of thunder in a storm, and we look up with amazement when he sets the heavens on a blaze with his lightning. But go and do business on the deep waters; let your vessel fly before the howling hurricane; observe how every staunch timber seems to crack as though it were but matchboard, and the steady mast goes by the board, and snaps, and is broken to shivers. Observe what God does when he stirs up the great deep, and seems to bring heaven down, and lifts the earth up until the elements mingle in a common mass of tempest.

Then go to the Alps and listen to the thunder of the avalanche. Stand amazed as you look down some grim precipice, or peer with awestruck wonder into the blue mysteries of a crevasse; see the leaping waterfalls, and observe those frozen seas – the glaciers – as they come sweeping down the mountainside. Stay a while until a storm shall gather there, and Alp shall talk to Alp, and those white prophetic heads shall seem to bow while the wings of tempest cover them! There you may learn something of the power of God amidst the crash of nature. If you could have stood by the side of Dr. Woolfe who, when rising early one morning, went out of Aleppo, and upon turning his head, saw that Aleppo was no more, it having been in a single moment swallowed up by an earthquake; then again you might see what God can do. But why do I need to feebly recapitulate what you all know so well?

Think of what that Book records of his deeds of prowess, when he unloosed the depths, and bade the fountains of the great deep to be broken up, so that the whole world that then was, might be covered with water. Think of what he did at the Red Sea, when the depths stood upright as a heap for a time, while his people went through, and when afterwards with eager joy the floods clasped their hands, and buried the enemy in the deep, never to rise again! Let such names as Og, king of Bashan; Sihon, king of the Amorites; and Sennacherib, the mighty, rise before your recollection, and observe what God has done! Who has ever smashed upon the studs of his shield without being wounded? What iron has he not broken? What spear has he not shattered?

Millions came against him, but by the blast of the breath of his nostrils they fell, or they flew, like the chaff before the wind. *Let the sea roar, and the fulness thereof* (Psalm 98:7), but the rocks stand still and hurl off the waves in flakes of foam, and so does God, when his foes are most enraged and passionate. *He that sitteth in the heavens shall laugh: the Lord shall have them in derision* (Psalm 2:4); and he breaks them in pieces without a stroke of his hand, or even the glance of his eye.

Think, sinner, think, of him with whom you contend. Have you an arm like God's? Can you thunder with a voice like his? Can you stomp with your foot, and shake the mountains? Can you touch the hills, and make them smoke? Can you say to the sea, "Be stirred to your depths," or can you call to the winds, and bid the steeds of tempest to be unloosed? If you cannot, then think of the battle! Attempt to do no more but hasten yourself back to your bed, and there commune with your heart, and make your peace with him against whom you cannot hope successfully to contend.

Think, again, O rebellious man, that you have to deal not only with almighty power, but also with an *ever-surrounding power.* Please think how much you are in God's power as it regards your worldly position. You are prospering in business, but the tide of prosperity may be turned in a way unknown to you. God has a thousand ways of stripping those whom he formerly seemed to clothe most lavishly. You dote upon that wife of yours: she may be struck before your eyes and waste away with tuberculosis or decline, or, more rapidly still, she may be taken from you in a heartbeat, and then where is your joy?

Those children, those happy babblers who make glad your heart – could you hold them for a moment if God should call back their spirits? If he said, *Return, ye children of men* (Psalm 90:3), your prayers, the physician, your love – what could all these profit you? You have but to buy the coffin, and the shroud, and the grave, and bury your dead out of your sight. God can sweep away all, if he will, and leave you penniless, childless, a widower, and without comfort in the world.

I would not contend with him who has so many ways to wound me. I am vulnerable at so many points, and he knows how to pierce me to the heart in them all. I will, therefore, make him my friend rather than my foe. I had better not strive with him who has the key of the back gate, and of the front gate, and of the iron gate, and who can storm every position along my bastion whenever he shall please.

Think, again, how much you are personally in his hand! You are strong, you say; you will do a day's work with any man; there are few who can lift a load more readily than you can perhaps; and yet one second would be enough to paralyze every limb. Your faculties are clear; you can write with clearness, and no one can see through an intricate account more rapidly than you can, or find out a secret more speedily; and yet one tick of that clock is time enough to reduce either you or me to a drooling idiot, or to a raving madman. A mysterious hand falls on that brain and cools it, so that there is no longer the light of intellect within it, or else an awful breath fans its flame, until it burns like Nebuchadnezzar's furnace, and the soul walks within it as a martyr, doomed to live in the midst of fire.

Think of this – not many yards from here there stands in Bedlam an awful proof of what the providence of God can do in one moment with those who seemed the most sane, the most witty, and the most able of men. And you do not have to go far in either direction before at the gate of some hospital you will find how soon the body may become very, very low, even to the dust, if God but wills it. I would not.

O sinner, I would not have God be other than my friend, while I am thus helplessly in his control. If the moth is in my hand, and I can crush it at my will and pleasure, surely if that moth had a mind and sense, it would not provoke me to anger, nor seek to bring down my plagues upon it, but, if it could, it would seek to nestle near my heart, that I, so able to crush it, might use my power for its protection, and might make what sense I have to be its wisdom for its shelter and defense.

It is well also to remember the *mighty army* of the Lord of Hosts, and that you live amidst the creatures of God who all are ready to do his bidding. As the children of Israel journeyed in the wilderness, they were preserved by God from many foes and innumerable dangers that lurked around them, waiting to destroy them. Once God gave the fiery serpents permission to assault the host, what death and terror immediately filled the camp! They must have seen, then, that it was no small thing to be not in harmony with God, when he had so many allies waiting to do his bidding. How clearly this was shown in the plagues of Egypt, when frogs, locusts, and lice, hail and fire, plague and death, flooded the ill-fated land when beckoned on by the uplifted finger of God.

He can still call to his help the forces of creation. The stars in their courses fought against Sisera, and God can still make all things work for evil as well as for good, if he be pleased to command them. When Herod contended with God, he was struck with worms and died, and God has still a countless army of servants who do his commandments, listening to the voice of his Word. You had better wait a while and think how you can meet them. Are your friends as numerous? Can you muster an army like unto God's? Is the muster roll of your hosts like unto his? Consider the heavens, for he mobilizes yonder starry multitudes and calls them all by name; because he is great in strength, not one fails. Be wise and enter into covenant with him through blood, and rush not on to certain defeat by seeking to outrival God.

Remember, moreover, what is the extent of *God's wisdom,* and that his foolishness is greater than your highest knowledge. A good general is worth more than a regiment of men. When Stonewall Jackson was killed, his enemies and friends alike felt that his death was more than the loss of ten thousand men. Our Iron Duke, when alive, was a strength to our army beyond all calculation.

Now mark the skill and infinite wisdom of the God who leads the army of the skies. All light and knowledge are his. He is the Ancient of Days, and his experience runs back to all eternity. You are but of yesterday and know nothing. His plans are beyond your conception, but he knows the way you take. He is far above your thoughts and ever out of your sight; but he can see you through and through, and knows you better than you know yourself. Do not show your folly by weighing your wisdom against his in the scales, or by expecting to outshine him so as to triumph over him. Poor moth rushing into the flame, you will be consumed amidst the pity of good men and the derision of evil ones.

Yet there is another matter I want you to recollect, you who are the enemies of God – that you have a *conscience.* You have not gotten rid of it yet. You have a thief in that candle of the Lord, it is true, but still it is ablaze. It is not put out; and God has ways of making it to become a terrible plague to you if you do not accept it as a friend. Conscience is meant to be man's armor-bearer, beneath whose shield he may fight the battles of the right; but if you make it your enemy, then conscience often places a sword in such a way as to cut and wound you severely. You have a conscience, and that is a very awkward thing for a man to have who is an enemy of God. If I were God's enemy, I would prefer having no monitor to call my attention to the holy character and righteous law of the Most High; I would be glad to get rid of every particle of moral sense.

But you have consciences, and most of you are not yet dead to all feelings of guilt and shame. You cannot, therefore, sin so cheaply as others; and if you do for the present time manage to put Mr. Conscience down, yet since he is still in you, the time will come when you will find his voice growing louder, and there will be a terror in that voice that will make it a terror for you to sleep, and hard for you to go about your daily business with your accustomed regularity. Those men who serve God most faithfully still find that their conscience, when it can accuse them of anything wrong, though it is their best friend, is no very pleasant companion.

It is said that David's heart struck him. I would sooner have anybody strike me than my own heart, for it strikes with so hard a blow, and hits the place where one may most tenderly feel it. And it will be so with you unless you get your conscience seared with a hot iron. I am afraid there will come a time when you will not rest in your beds, nor be able anywhere to find peace or satisfaction. I think therefore, if I had a friend of God inside my heart, I would not like to fight with God, so long as he continued within me. Oh, that you would be at peace with him, and *thereby good shall come unto thee* (Job 22:21).

One other reflection, for I must not keep you thinking on this point long, is this: Remember, *you must die,* and therefore, it is a pity to be at enmity with God. You may put it off and say, "I shall not die yet"; but you do not know. How can you tell? It is possible that you may die tomorrow. But suppose that you live for the next twenty or thirty years; why, what is that? I am only some thirty years of age, and yet I confess that I never thought time so short as I feel it to be now. When we were children, we thought twelve months a great length of time; when we were twenty, a year seemed to be a very respectable period; but now it flies, and some of my friends here, whose hair is turning gray, will tell you that whether it is fifty, sixty, or seventy years, it all seems but a mere dream, a snap of the finger, and it is gone so soon.

Well, just push through a little interval of time, and then you must die. My dear friend, will it not be a very dreadful thing to die when you are at war with God? If you could fight this out forever under such circumstances as those in which you now are, I could not then commend the struggle; but since it must come to such an awful pause, since there must be that death rattle in your throat, since there must be that clammy sweat upon your brow, O you will want some better business than to be carrying arms against the God of heaven in your dying moments. They that have God for their friend still find death no very pleasant task; but what will *you* find it, who will have to strike yourselves in every blow that you are aiming against the Most High, whom you have made, and continue to make your enemy?

Here is this, too, to think of: there is a *future state,* so that when you die, you have to live again. We know very little about that next state, and I do not intend to say much about it . You are launched without your earthly body, an unclothed spirit, into a world that you have not yet seen. Will you find companions there, or will you be alone? Where will it be? What sort of place will it be like?

I would not choose to enter upon the realm of spirits without having God to be my friend; for it would be a dreadful thing to get into that mysterious unknown country, having nothing to take with me across its border except this – an entrenched animosity toward the King that reigns supreme in it. If I must cross the border, and go into a land I have never trodden, I would like, at least, to carry a passport with me, or to be able to say, "I am a friend of the King that reigns here"; but to go there as God's enemy – why, how terrible it must be!

Besides, let me say, you cannot hope to succeed, because *all experience is against you.* There never was one yet, that either in this state or the next has fought with God and conquered, and you will not be the first; for they who contend with God all come to this one conclusion: "He comes forth in his strength, and his enemies are given like stubble to the fire, and like wax to the flame. He lifts up his voice, and they melt away. He looks at them, and that one flash of fire withers them forever, and out of the bottomless pit of despair they weep and wail the pite-ous but useless regret, that their harvest is past, and their summer is ended, and that they are not saved; for they have spent their strength against their God, and so have brought themselves where ruin is eter-nal, and hope can never come." Oh, that you would send an embassy, and be at peace!

It seems to me that I hear some say, "Well, we wish to give up the contest; but what is to be done, so as to be at peace with God?" I ask, Have you got an ambassador to go to God for you? That is the first thing. He cannot look at *you,* for Jesus Christ is the ambassador between God and man; can you commit your case into his hand? Will you do so? If so, your case will succeed well. God cannot deny him any request. He has a right to all he ever asks the Father to give, and the Father is always well pleased in him, and delights to grant him whatever he desires. That Savior is willing to plead your cause. He waits to be gracious.

I am sent to tell you the good news of his love and mercy; to warn you of the certain doom that awaits all who turn from Christ; and to bid you and every sin-sick rebel to come at once, just as you are, to the footstool of mercy; and I can pledge the honor of God (as being Christ's ambassador for this purpose,) that if you come, he will in no wise cast you out. And the terms of peace are very brief. They are these: *give up the traitors;* there can be no peace between you and God while you harbor sin. Give them up and be willing to renounce every sin of every sort and kind, for one harbored traitor will prevent God effect-ing peace with you.

Sinner, what say you? Is it hard to give up your sin? Does that con-dition strike you as unreasonable? Out with the knife, man, and cut the throat of every iniquity. Why, there is no sin for which it is worth your while to be damned. A little rioting, and accommodating, and unruliness – is that worth hellfire forever? What, to have your giddy amusements for an hour or two, is this a due recompense for an eternity of fire unmitigated by a drop of water?

I pray you, be reasonable. Barter not away your soul for trifles; pawn not eternity for the mere fictions of an instant. God give you grace, sinner, not to kick at that condition, but at once to cast out your enemies and gods, and then *lay hold on Christ,* on Jesus Christ alone, and let him stand as ambassador for you. You cannot fight it out. Let peace be made. Oh, may it be made tonight, through the blood of Jesus Christ, God's dear Son.

Then next, *confess* that you deserve the King's wrath. Bow that head; put the rope around your neck as though you felt you deserved to have the executioner lead you forth. *Pray to God* for pardon, and cry, *God be merciful to me a sinner,* and then cling to the skirts of that appointed Savior, the Lord Jesus Christ, who on yonder bloody tree made atonement for the sin of God's enemies, that they might thereby become God's friends.

God demands of you a confession of your guilt. He will be honored by your humbling yourself before him. Your sin has aimed at his glory, and now he will glorify himself by your repentance. It would be only just on his part if he rejected you and cast you out into the pit that has no bottom, but he has said that whoever confesses his sin shall obtain forgiveness.

Go, therefore, in the spirit of the publican, and strike your breast, and say, *God be merciful to me a sinner.* Confess that you deserve hell, but ask for heaven, and you shall not plead in vain. Only honor God's justice, and appeal to his mercy through the Lord Jesus Christ. This, surely, is not much for God to expect at your hands. If you will not submit, what can you say when God shall crush you? You refuse to bend the knee, and to bow the head; what will you do when God shall trample on you in his fury, and tread you in his hot displeasure? You must, therefore, now in the accepted time, while it is still the day of mercy, seek his face, and with weeping and supplication *take with you words, and turn to the Lord* (Hosea 14:2), *and he will have mercy upon [you]; and to our God, for he will abundantly pardon* (Isaiah 55:7).

And now we turn the subject, so as to look at the second contest, in which I trust many are anxious to be engaged.

Some young spirit that has been touched with a sense of its own condition, and somewhat aroused, may be saying, "I will be God's enemy no longer, I will be his friend." Bowing the knee, that heart cries, "Oh God, reconcile me unto yourself by the death of your dear Son. I throw down all my weapons; I confess my guilt; I plead for mercy. For Jesus' sake grant it to me." "But," says that soul, "if I am the friend of God, I must be the foe of Satan, and from this day I pledge myself to fight forever with Satan until I get the victory, and am free from sin."

My dear friend, I want you to stop. I do not wish you to make peace with the Evil One, but I want you to consider where you are at. There are a few things I would whisper in your ear, and one is that *sin is sweet*. The uppermost drops of sin's cup glitter and sparkle. There is pleasure in sin of a certain sort and for a certain season. It is a poisoned sweet; it is but a temporary delusion, but still the world does promise handsomely; its gingerbread is gold, and though it wears nothing but tinsel, and a little gold leaf now and then, yet it does look very much like gold.

Can you, can you resist sin when it seems so charming? The next time the cup is brought to you – you know the flavor of it – oh, it is rich – can you turn away? Are you certain that you will be able to thrust it from your lips? Ah, man, you will find it different when the hour of trial comes, than what it is now that you are sitting in the tabernacle and resolving, away from the temptation, that you will do right.

Remember, again, you may be *enticed by friends* who will be very pressing. You can give up sin just now, but you do not know who may be the tempter at some future time. Perhaps *she* would allure you, who has tempted you so well before! Perhaps *he – he* should speak! He! The very word has wakened up your recollection. If he should speak as he alone can speak, and look as only he can look, can you then resist, and stand out? That witching voice, that fascinating eye! Oh, how many souls have been damned for what men call love! Oh, that they had but a little *true* love of themselves and others and would not thus pander to the prince of hell. But alas, alas, while the cup itself looks sweet, there is to be added to it the hand that holds it out.

It is not so easy to contend with Satan when he employs the service of someone whom you esteem highly and love with all your heart. Remember the case of Solomon whose wisdom was marvelous, but who was enticed by his wives, and fell a prey into the hands of the Evil One. It needs a spirit like the Master's to be able to say, *Get thee behind me, Satan* (Luke 4:8) to the tempter, when he has the appearance of one of your best loved friends. The devil is a crafty being, and if he cannot force the door, he will try and get the key that fits the notch of the lock, and, by the means of our most tender love and affections, will make a way for himself into our hearts; you will find it no easy task therefore to contend with him.

Then again, remember, man, there is *habit*. You say you will all of a sudden give up your sins and fight Satan. Do not tell me that; can the Ethiopian change his skin, or the leopard his spots? If so, then he that is accustomed to doing evil may learn to do well. If you had never sinned as you have sinned, there would not be this difficulty with you; but he that has gone day after day, and year after year into sin, is not so easily turned from it. It is as well to hope to make Niagara leap up instead of down, as to make human nature flow back to virtue instead of going downward to sin.

You do not know yourself. Habit is an iron bond, and he that is once enveloped in it may pull and strain, but he will tear away his flesh sooner than break the links of that dread chain. We have seen men who, convinced of the error of their ways, have sought to turn from them without asking for God's help. For a time they have made some little progress in appearance, but it has only been like the retreating of the waves at the rising of the tide; their evil habits have returned upon them with a rush, and have covered them deeper than before.

Read the parable of our Lord concerning the unclean spirit that went out of the man, and roamed through dry places, seeking rest but finding none, and it said, *I will return unto my house whence I came out* (Luke 11:24). It came back, and found it swept and furnished, and then took to it seven other evil spirits, more wicked than itself, so the last end of that man was worse than the first. Thus it is with those who enter upon the work of saving themselves without looking up by faith to God for his needed help. Satan will triumph over you. You are like the fly in the snares of the spider's web: the more it struggles, the more it will be enclosed. You must cry for help as you are quite unable by yourself to escape from the snares of the wicked one. He has you bound fast, hand and foot, and you will never break his cords, nor be able to cast his bonds from you. You have no seven locks of strength like Samson, but you will certainly be overcome.

Again, you think you will give up sin, but *ridicule* is very unpleasant. When the finger comes to be pointed at you, and they say, "Ah, so you have set yourself up for a saint, I see"; when they put it as they only can put it, in such a sharp, cutting, and grating manner; when it is wrapped up so wittily in an epigram that is told all around the shop against you; and when, moreover, there is some foible of yours, some giddy weakness, and they know how to hook on your attempt at saint-ship to your weakness, and they bandy that all around, and there are fifty laughing faces at you, can you stand that? Yes, it is a very pretty thing for you to come here on Sundays, and say what you will do, but it is different to do it on Mondays.

To be laughed at is not really to a sensible man anything very won-derful, for, it seems to me, you have only to get used to it, and then you will just as much expect to hear people laugh at you as to hear birds singing when you walk out into a morning. But at first that is a very sharp trial, that trial of *cruel mockings* (Hebrews 11:36); and many who have been going to fight Satan have drawn back, for they found they could not stand it.

When the Jews were rebuilding the walls of Jerusalem after their return from captivity, one of the most severe tests of their zeal and devotion was the laughter of their enemies who came and looked on and said, *What do these feeble Jews? . . . Even that which they build, if a fox go up, he shall even break down their stone wall* (Nehemiah 4:2-3). The words of their foes were more cutting than swords, and keenly did they feel in their spirits the derision of the scoffers.

It is as painful now for the sensitive spirit as it was of old, but you must not be daunted. Heaven is worth buying, even though it should cost a life heaped full of stinging words and malicious sayings from a deriding and taunting world. Did not Christ himself show us how to endure this trial? See his foes gathered around him when he hung dying on the cross. They laugh at him even there. *He saved others; himself he cannot save*, they said as they wagged their heads, and mocked equally his dignity and his woe. *If thou be the Son of God, come down from the cross, and we will believe [thee]* (Matthew 27:40, 42). These sayings must have been bitterer to his spirit than the wormwood mingled with gall was to his lips. You must follow Christ here also if you would contend, as he did, with Satan. Then count the cost. Can you drink his cup, and be baptized with his baptism?

And yet further, let me say to you, you that are for going to heaven so zealously – *gain*; gain is a very pretty thing, a very pleasant affair. Who does not like to make money? You know, if you can be religious, and grow rich at the same time, that will just suit some of you. Oh yes, the two going together, that will be admirable; you will kill the two birds with one stone. Mr. By-ends said, "Now, if a man by being religious can get a good wife who has a considerable sum of money; and if by being religious he gets a good shop, and many customers, why," says he, "then religion is a good thing"; for to get a good wife is a good thing, and to get customers, that is another good thing, and so, he says, "The whole is a good thing put together." But he that knows Mr. By-ends, knows that he is an old rogue, notwithstanding that he puts it prettily.

I have known him. He is a member of this church, I am sorry to say; I never went into a church where he was not a member. I have tried to turn him out, and did once, but there was another one of the family left inside, and however many you may expel, there are sure to be more of that breed remaining.

But there sometimes comes a pinch with Mr. By-ends. Now if you should find that shutting up your shop on Sundays would ruin your business, well, what then? Would you stand it? Now there are some of you that try it every now and then when you get spasmodically godly, but it does not pay you, you find, and so you begin once more to open shop on the Lord's Day. Some of you Sunday traders discover that it gets a little hot and strong for you when you come to the tabernacle occasionally, and you shut up for a season; but soon you say, "Well, people must live."

Yes, and people must die, and people must be damned too, if they try to live by breaking God's laws. Remember that it will not pay to be religious, as some people imagine. We have heard of a man saying, "I cannot afford to keep a conscience; it is too expensive an article for me." Ah, but keep in mind the saying of the Lord: *What shall it profit a man, if he shall gain the whole world, and lose his own soul? Or what shall a man give in exchange for his soul?* (Mark 8:36-37). There is such a thing as being "penny-wise and pound-foolish," and there is such a thing also as being "worldly wise and eternally foolish." Think of this then, for the trial will come to you in the shape of yellow gold, and it will be hard to keep yourself from the glittering bait that the god of this world will lay before you.

I am putting these things to you so that you may calculate whether you can carry on the war against the devil with all these fearful odds against you. If I were a recruiting sergeant I would not do this. He puts the shilling into the country lad's hand, and the lad may say fifty things. "Oh, never mind," says the gallant soldier, "you know it is all glory, nothing but glory. There, I will just tie these ribbons around your hat. There are some long strips of glory to begin with, and then all your days it will be just glory, glory forever; and you will die a general, and be buried at Westminster Abbey, and they will play the 'Dead March in Saul,' and all that kind of thing."

Now, I cannot thus deceive or try to cheat men to enlist under the banner of the cross. I do not desire to raise objections to it; all I want of you is to count the cost, lest you should be like him who began to build without being able to finish. That is the misery of so many. I advise you, if you are about to declare war with Satan, to see whether you are able to carry it out and win the victory.

"Well," says one, "it is hard to be saved." Nobody ever thought it was not, I hope. What does Peter say? *If the righteous scarcely be saved, where shall the ungodly and the sinner appear?* (1 Peter 4:18). "It is hard to be saved," you say. Whoever said it was not? But it is not hard to be saved if a man is willing to be received according to the plan that God has appointed. If Christ undertakes it, then it is done, and my counsel to those of you who are about making war with Satan is to remember that it is too much for you, and therefore do not attempt it in your own strength. Beware of this.

I know Satan will tempt you first of all to believe that you need no Savior, and then if you are not convinced of this but are disturbed because of sin, he suggests that you can save yourself. He speaks of *Abana and Pharpar, rivers of Damascus,* which flow close by your own door. He says, "*May I not wash in them, and be clean?* (2 Kings 5:12). Stay where you are and help yourself"; but if you listen to the words of the seducer of souls, you are lost and undone forever. Can the man born blind see to operate upon his own scale-covered eyes so as to give himself sight? Can the crippled man run away from his lameness, and outrun the feebleness of his feet? Can the dead man exert himself to make the tide of life flow once more in his veins, and flush his cheeks anew with the glow of health? Can he call back his departed spirit from the shades of the unseen world, and make it reoccupy its decaying habitation, and bid the marks of the mighty consumer to be gone, and leave no trace of Death's conquest behind, to remind the returning inhabitant that the palace had been occupied by the ruthless spoiler?

We answer, No. A mighty finger must touch and open the eyes. An omnipotent arm must lift up the paralyzed and impotent man into strength and power; and most evidently, if life is to be secured, the voice of God alone can speak the word that shall make the dead to live. On this point we wish to be clearly understood. You will never of yourself successfully resist sin so as to escape its enslavement; how much less can you remove its guilt? The cancer is in your blood, and you can never get it out. The wicked deed is done, and it is written, *The soul that sinneth, it shall die* (Ezekiel 18:20). Oh, then at once ask help of him who alone can save you from the wrath to come.

Remember, poor feeble one, nothing is too hard for God, and therefore ask Almighty strength to come to your help. It is true you cannot contend with your obsessive sins; your passions, your corruptions of whatever sort they may be, are much too strong for you; old Adam is too mighty for you with your best intentions. But there is a strong one whose hand, once pierced, is always ready and at the service of every sinner who would have Satan cast out.

There is one *mighty to save* (Isaiah 63:1) who can come to the rescue and do for you what you cannot do for yourself. Oh, that you had Christ, so that at once you might cry to him, "Jesus, save me; I see the fight is too unequal for me. I cannot drive out my sins, I cannot fight my way to heaven; come and help me, Lord Jesus. I put myself into your hands; wash me in your blood; fill me with your Spirit; save me with your great salvation; and let me be with you where you are at the end."

"No man can save himself," says one. Yet the situation is very like that of the master who sent his servant with a letter. The servant was rather lazy, and came back with it. "Why did you not deliver it?" the master asked.

"I could not," the servant answered.

"Could not deliver it?"

"No, master."

"Why not?"

"A deep river, sir, very deep river, I could not get across."

"A deep river?" said he.

"Yes."

"Is not there a ferryman there?"

"Do not know, sir; if there was, he was on the other side."

"Did you call across, 'Boat, ahoy!'"

"No sir."

"Why then, you rascal," said he, "what does it matter; it is no excuse. It is true, you could not get across the river, but then there was one there who could take you, and you never cried to him."

And so it is in your case. You say, "I cannot save myself." Quite true; but there is one who can, and you have never cried to him, for, mark you, if you cry to him, if your heart says, "Oh Savior, come and save me," and your spirit rests in him, deep as that river of your sin certainly is, he knows how to bear you safely through it, and land you on the other shore. May he do that with each of you. *With God all things are possible* (Matthew 19:26), though with man it is impossible. May the blessing of the Most High rest upon us this night for Jesus' sake. Amen.

Chapter 13

The Lost Silver Piece

*Either what woman having ten pieces of silver, if she lose
one piece, doth not light a candle, and sweep the house,
and seek diligently till she find it? And when she hath found
it, she calleth her friends and her neighbours together,
saying, Rejoice with me; for I have found the piece which
I had lost. Likewise, I say unto you, there is joy in the presence of the angels of God over one sinner that repenteth.*
(Luke 15:8-10)

This chapter is full of grace and truth. Its three consecutive parables
have been thought to be merely a repetition of the same doctrine
under different metaphors, and if that is so, the truth that it teaches
is so important that it could not be rehearsed too often in our hearing. Moreover, it is one that we are apt to forget, and it is well to have
it again and again impressed upon our minds. The truth here taught
is just this – that mercy stretches forth her hand to misery; that grace
receives men as sinners, that it deals with faults, unworthiness, and
worthlessness; that those who think themselves righteous are not the
objects of divine compassion, but the unrighteous, the guilty, and the
undeserving are the proper subjects for the infinite mercy of God; in a
word, that salvation is not of merit but of grace.

This truth I say is most important, for it encourages repentant ones to return to their Father; but it is very apt to be forgotten, for even those who are saved by grace too often fall into the spirit of the elder brother, and speak as if, after all, their salvation depended on the works of the law.

But, my dear friends, the three parables recorded in this chapter are not repetitions; they all declare the same main truth, but each one reveals a different phase of it. The three parables are three sides of a vast pyramid of gospel doctrine, but there is a distinct inscription upon each one. Not only in the similarity, but also in the teaching covered by the similarity, there is variety, progress, enlargement, and discrimination.

We have need only to read attentively to discover that in this trinity of parables, we have at once unity of essential truth and distinctness of description. Each one of the parables is needful to the other, and when combined, they present us with a far more complete exposition of their doctrine than could have been conveyed by any one of them.

Note for a moment the first of the three that brings before us a shepherd seeking a lost sheep. To whom does this refer? Who is the shepherd of Israel? Who brings again that which has gone astray? Do we not clearly discern the ever-glorious and blessed chief Shepherd of the sheep, who lays down his life that he may save them? Beyond question, we see in the first parable the work of our Lord Jesus Christ. The second parable is most suitably placed where it is. It, I doubt not, represents the work of the Holy Spirit, working through the church, for the lost but precious souls of men. The church is that woman who sweeps her house to find the lost piece of money, and in her the Spirit works his purposes of love.

Now the work of the Holy Spirit follows the work of Christ. As here we first see the shepherd seeking the lost sheep, and then read of the woman seeking the lost piece of money, so the Great Shepherd redeems, and then the Holy Spirit restores the soul. You will perceive that each parable is thoroughly understood in its minute details when so interpreted. The shepherd seeks a sheep that has willfully gone astray, and so far, the element of sin is present; the lost piece of money does not bring up that idea, nor was it needful that it should, since the parable does not deal with the pardon of sin as the first parable does. The sheep, on the other hand, though stupid, is not altogether senseless and dead; but the piece of money is altogether unconscious and powerless, and therefore all the more suitable an emblem of man as the Holy Spirit begins to deal with him, dead in trespasses and sins.

The third parable evidently represents the Divine Father in his abundant love receiving the lost child who comes back to him. The third parable would likely be misunderstood without the first and the second. We have sometimes heard it said – here is the prodigal received as soon as he comes back – with no mention being made of a Savior who seeks and saves him. Is it possible to teach all truths in one single parable? Does not the first one speak of the shepherd seeking the lost sheep? Why would it be necessary to repeat what had been said before? It has also been said that the prodigal returned of his own free will, for there is no hint of the operation of a superior power upon his heart; it seems as if he himself spontaneously says, *I will arise and go to my father.*

The answer is that the Holy Spirit's work had been clearly described in the second parable, and needed not to be introduced again. If you put the three pictures in a line, they represent the whole compass of salvation. The shepherd, with much pain and self-sacrifice, seeks the reckless, wandering sheep; the woman diligently searches for the insensible but lost piece of money; the father receives the returning prodigal. *What therefore God hath joined together, let not man put asunder* (Matthew 19:6). The three life sketches are one, and one truth is taught in the whole three; yet each one is distinct from the other, and by itself instructive.

May we be taught of God while we try to discover the mind of the Spirit in this parable, which, as we believe, represents the work of the Holy Spirit in and through the church. The church is always represented as a woman, either the spotless bride of Christ, or the shameless prostitute of Babylon. As for good a woman sweeps the house, so for evil a woman takes the leaven and hides it in the meal until all is leavened. Towards Christ a wife and towards men a mother, the church is most suitably set forth as a woman. A woman with a house under her control is the full idea of the text, with her husband away and herself in charge of the treasure. Just such is the condition of the church ever since the departure of the Lord Jesus to the Father.

To bring each part of the text under inspection, we shall notice man in three conditions – *lost, sought, found.*

First, the parable treats the man, the object of divine mercy, as lost.

Notice, first, the treasure was *lost in the dust.* The woman had lost her piece of silver, and in order to find it she had to sweep for it, which proves that it had fallen into a dusty place, fallen to the earth, where it might be hidden and concealed amid rubbish and dirt. Every man born of Adam is as a piece of silver lost, fallen, dishonored, and some buried amid foulness and dust. If we should drop many pieces of money, they would fall into different positions; one of them might fall into actual mire, and be lost there; another might fall upon a carpet, a cloth, or a clean, well-polished floor, and be lost there. If you have lost your money, it is equally lost into whatever place it may have fallen. So all men are alike lost, but they have not all fallen into the same condition of apparent defilement.

One man from the surroundings of his childhood and the influences of education has never indulged in the coarser and more brutalizing vices; he has never been a blasphemer, perhaps never openly even a Sabbath breaker, yet he may be lost for all that. Another, on the other hand, has fallen into great excess of riot; he is familiar with unruliness and strife, and all manner of evil; he is lost, he is lost with an emphasis, but the more respectable sinner is lost also.

There may be some here this morning (and we wish always to apply the truth as we go on) who are lost in the very worst of corruption. I wish to God that they would take hope and learn from the parable before us, that the church of God and the Spirit of God are seeking after them, and they may be among the found ones yet.

Since, on the other hand, there are many here who have not dropped into such unclean places, I would affectionately remind them that they are nevertheless lost, and they need as much to be sought after by the Spirit of God as if they were among the vilest of the vile. To save the moral needs divine grace as certainly as to save the immoral. If you be lost, my dear friend, it will be small benefit to you that you perished respectably, and were accursed in decent company. If you lack but one thing, yet if the deficiency be fatal, it will be but a poor consolation that you had only one lack. If one leak sent the vessel to the bottom, it was no comfort to the crew that their ship only leaked in one place.

One disease may kill a man; he may be sound everywhere else, but it will be a sorry comfort to him to know that he might have lived long had but that one organ been sound. If, dear hearer, you should have no sin whatever except an evil heart of unbelief, if all your external life should be lovely and amiable, yet if that one fatal sin be in you, you can draw small consolation from all else that is good about you. You are lost by nature, and you must be found by grace, whoever you may be.

In this parable, that which was lost was *altogether ignorant of its being lost*. The silver coin was not a living thing, and therefore had no consciousness of its being lost or sought after. The piece of money lost was quite as content to be on the floor or in the dust, as it was to be in the purse of its owner among its kind. It knew nothing about its being lost and could not know. And it is just so with the sinner who is spiritually dead in sin: he is unconscious of his state, nor can we make him understand the danger and terror of his condition. When he feels that he is lost, there is already some work of grace in him. When the sinner knows that he is lost, he is no longer content with his condition, but begins to cry out for mercy, which is evidence that the finding work has already begun.

The unconverted sinner will confess that he is lost because he knows the statement to be scriptural, and therefore out of compliment to God's Word he admits it to be true. But he has no idea of what is meant by it, or else he would either deny it with proud indignation, or he would rouse himself to pray that he might be restored to the place from which he has fallen, and be numbered with Christ's precious property. O my friends, this it is that makes the Spirit of God so needful in all our preaching and in every other soul-saving exercise, because we have to deal with insensible souls.

The man who puts the fire escape against the window of a burning house may readily enough rescue those who are aware of their danger, and who rush to the front and help him, or at least are submissive to him in his work of delivering them. But if a man were insane, if he played with the flames, if he were idiotic and thought that some grand illumination was going on, and knew nothing of the danger but was only "glamoured by the glare," then it would be hard work for the rescuer. Even thus it is with sinners. They know not, though they profess to know, that sin is hell, that to be an alien from God is to be condemned already, and that to live in sin is to be dead while you live.

The insensibility of the piece of money fairly pictures the utter indifference of souls uninvigorated by divine grace.

The silver piece was *lost but not forgotten.* The woman knew that she had ten pieces of silver originally. She counted them over carefully, for they were all her little store, and she found only nine, but she well remembered that one more was hers and ought to be in her hand. This is our hope for the Lord's lost ones; they are lost but not forgotten, and the heart of the Savior remembers them and prays for them. O soul, I trust you are one whom Jesus calls his own. If so, he remembers the pangs that he endured in redeeming you, and he recollects the Father's love that was reflected on you from old eternity, when the Father gave you into the hands of his beloved Son. You are not forgotten by the Holy Spirit who seeks you for the Savior.

This is the minister's hope, that there is a people whom the Lord remembers and whom he never will forget, though they forget him. Strangers to him, far off, ignorant, callous, careless, and dead, yet the everlasting heart in heaven throbs towards them with love; and the mind of the Spirit, working on earth, is directed to them. These, who were numbered and reckoned up of old are still in the inventory of the divine memory; and though lost, they are earnestly remembered still. In some sense this is true of every sinner here. You are lost, but that you are remembered is evident, for I am sent today to preach the gospel of Jesus to you. God has thoughts of love concerning you, and bids you to turn to him and live. Have respect, I pray you, to the word of his salvation.

Next, the piece of silver was *lost but still claimed.* Observe that the woman called the money *the piece which I had lost* (Luke 15:9, emphasis added). When she lost possession of it, she did not lose her right to it; it did not become somebody else's when it slipped out of her hand and fell upon the floor. Those for whom Christ has died, whom he has uniquely redeemed, are not Satan's even when they are dead in sin. They may come under the devil's usurped dominion, but the monster shall be chased from his throne.

Christ has received them of old from the Father, and he has bought them with his precious blood, and he will have them; he will chase away the intruder and claim his own. Thus says the Lord, *Your covenant with death shall be disannulled, and your agreement with hell shall not stand* (Isaiah 28:18). *Ye have sold yourselves for nought; and ye shall be redeemed without money* (Isaiah 52:3). Jesus shall have his own, and none shall pluck them from his hold; he will defend his claim against all comers.

Further, observe that the lost piece of money was not only remembered and claimed, but *it was also valued.* In these three parables the value of the lost article steadily rises. This is not very clear at first sight, because it may be said that a sheep is of more value than a piece of money; but notice that the shepherd only lost one sheep out of a hundred, but the woman lost one piece out of ten, and the father lost one son out of two. Now, it is not the value of the thing in itself which is set forth here, for the soul of a man, as absolutely valued in comparison with the infinite God, is of small esteem; but because of his love it is of great value to him. The one piece of money to the woman was a tenth part of all she had, and it was very valuable in her esteem. To the Lord of love a lost soul is very precious: it is not because of its intrinsic value, but it has a relative value that God sets at a high rate.

The Holy Spirit values souls, and therefore the church prizes them too. The church sometimes says to herself, "We have but few conversions, few members; many are called, but few chosen." She counts her few converts, her few members, and one soul is to her all the more precious because of the few there are who in these times are in the treasury of Christ, stamped with the image of the great King, and made of the precious genuine silver of God's own grace.

O dear friend, you think yourself of small value, you who are conscious that you have sinned, but the church does not think you of small value, and the Holy Spirit does not despise you. He sets a high price upon you, and so do his people. We value your souls, we only wish we knew how to save them; we would spare no expense or pains if we might but be the means of finding you, and bringing you once more into the great Owner's hand.

The piece of money was lost, but *it was not lost hopelessly.* The woman had hopes of recovering it, and therefore she did not despair, but set to work at once. It is a dreadful thing to think of those souls that are lost hopelessly.

Their state reminds me of a paragraph I have cut from this week's newspaper: "The fishing smack Veto, of Grimsby, S. Cousins, master, arrived in port from the Dogger Bank on Saturday night. The master reports that on the previous Wednesday, when about two hundred miles from Spurn, he sighted to the leeward what at first appeared to be a small schooner in distress, but on bearing down to her found her to be a full-sized lifeboat, upwards of twenty-feet long, and full of water up to her corks.

"There was no name on the boat, which had evidently belonged to some large ship or steamer. It was painted white both inside and out, with a brown streak around the rim. When alongside, on closer examination, three dead sailors were perceived lying aft, huddled together, and a fourth athwart in the bow, with his head hanging over the rowlocks. They seemed from their dress and general appearance to be foreigners, but the bodies had been frightfully washed about, and were in a state of decomposition, and had evidently been dead some weeks.

"The water-logged waif drifted on with its ghastly cargo, and the horrible sight so shocked the crew of the Veto that afterwards they were almost too unnerved to attend to their trawling, and the smack, in consequence, returned to port with a comparatively small catch, and sooner than expected." Do you wonder at the men sickening in the presence of this mystery of the sea?

I shudder as I think I see that Charon-like boat floating on and on; mercy need not follow it, she can confer no aid; love need not seek it, no deed of hers can save. My soul sees, as in a vision, souls hopelessly lost, drifting on the waves of eternity, beyond all hope or help. Alas! Alas! Millions of our race are now in that condition. Upon them has passed the second death, and powerless are we all to save them. Towards them even the gospel has no aspect of hope. Our joy is that we have to deal today with lost souls who are not yet hopelessly lost. They are dead in sin, but there is an invigorating power that can make them live. O mariner of the sea of life, fisher of men upon this stormy sea, those castaways whom you meet with are accessible to your efforts of compassion, they can be rescued from the pitiless deeps; your mission is not a hopeless one.

I rejoice over the ungodly man here today that he is not in torment, not in hell, he is not among those whose *worm dieth not, and [whose] fire is not quenched* (Mark 9:44). I congratulate the Christian church too, that her piece of money has not fallen where she cannot find it. I rejoice that the fallen around us are not past hope; yes, though they dwell in the worst dens of London, though they be thieves and harlots, they are not beyond the reach of mercy. Up, O church of God, while possibilities of mercy remain! Gird up your loins, you soul winners, and resolve by the grace of God that every hour of hope shall be well employed by you.

One other point is worthy of notice. The piece of silver was lost, but it was *lost in the house,* and the woman knew it to be so. If she had lost it in the streets, the probabilities are she would not have looked for it again, for other hands might have closed over it. If she had lost it in a river, or dropped it in the sea, she might very fairly have concluded that it was gone forever; but evidently, she was sure that she had lost it in the house.

Is it not a consolation to know that those here, who are lost, are still in the house? They are still under the means of grace, within the sphere of the church's operations, within the habitation of which she is the mistress, and where the Holy Spirit works. What thankfulness there ought to be in your minds that you are not lost as heathens, nor lost amid Roman Catholic or Mohammedan superstition; but that you are lost where the gospel is faithfully and plainly preached to you; where you are lovingly told that whosoever believes in Christ Jesus is not condemned; that you are lost, but lost where the church's business is to look after you, where it is the Spirit's work to seek and to find you.

This is the condition of the lost soul, depicted as a lost piece of silver.

Secondly, we shall notice the soul under another condition: we shall view it as sought.

By whom was the piece of silver sought? It *was sought by its owner personally.* Notice, she who lost the money lit a candle and swept the house, and sought diligently until *she* found it. So, brethren, I have said that the woman represents the Holy Spirit, or rather the church in which the Holy Spirit dwells. Now, there will never be a soul found until the Holy Spirit seeks after it. He is the great soul finder. The heart will continue in the dark until he comes with his illuminating power. He is the owner, he possesses it, and he alone can effectively seek after it. The God to whom the soul belongs must seek the soul. But he does it by his church, for souls belong to the church too; they are sons and daughters of the chosen mother, they are her citizens and treasures.

For this reason, the church must personally seek after souls. She cannot delegate her work to anybody else. The woman did not pay a servant to sweep the house, but she swept it herself. Her eyes were much better than a servant's eyes, for the servant's eyes would only look after somebody else's money, and perhaps would not see it; but the mistress would look after her own money, and she would be certain to light upon it if it were anywhere within sight. When the church of God solemnly feels, "It is our work to look after sinners; we must not delegate it even to the minister, or to the city missionary, or to the Bible woman, but the church as a church must look after the souls of sinners," then I believe souls will be found and saved.

When the church recognizes that these lost souls belong to her, she will be likely to find them. It will be a happy day when every church of God is actively at work for the salvation of sinners. It has been the curse of Christendom that she has ventured to delegate her sacred duties to men called priests, or that she has set apart certain persons to be called *the religious,* who are to do works of mercy and charity and of evangelization. We are, every one of us who are Christ's, bound to do our own share; no, we should deem it a privilege of which we will not be deprived, to personally serve God, to personally sweep the house and search after the lost spiritual treasures. The church herself, in the power of the indwelling Spirit of God, must seek lost souls.

Note that this seeking became *a matter of chief concern* with the woman. I do not know what other business she had to do, but I do know that she put it all aside to find the piece of money. There was the wheat to be ground for the morning meal, perhaps that was done; at any rate, if not, she left it unprepared. There was a garment to be mended, or water to be drawn, or the fire to be kindled, or the friends and neighbors to be conversed with – never mind, the mistress forgets everything else, she has lost her piece of money, and she must find it at once. So with the church of God: her chief concern should be to seek the perishing sons of men.

To bring souls to know Jesus, and to be saved in him with a great salvation should be the church's great longing and concern. She has other things to do. She has her own edification to consider, she has other matters to be attended to in their place; but this first, this evermore and always first. The woman evidently said, "The money is lost, I must find that first." The loss of her piece of silver was so serious a matter that if she sat down to do her mending, her hands would miss their nimbleness, or if any other household work demanded her attention, it would be an irksome task to her, for she was thinking of that piece of money. If her friend came and talked with her, she would say to herself, "I wish she were gone, for I want to be looking for my lost money."

I wish the church of God had such an engrossing love for poor sinners that she would feel everything to be an irrelevance that hindered her from soul-saving. We have every now and then, as a church, a little to do with politics, and a little to do with finance, for we are still in the world; but I love to see in all churches everything kept in the background, compared with soul-saving work. This must be first and foremost.

Educate the people – yes, certainly; we take an interest in everything that will do good to our fellow citizens, for we are men as well as Christians. But first and foremost our business is to win souls, to bring men to Jesus, to hunt for those who bear heaven's image, though lost and fallen. This is what we must be devoted to, this is the main and chief concern of believers, the very reason for the existence of a church; if she regards it not, she forgets her highest end.

Now note, that the woman having thus set her heart to find her money, *she used the most fit and proper means* to accomplish her end. First, she lit a candle. So does the Holy Spirit in the church. In Eastern dwellings it would be necessary, if you lost a piece of money and wanted to find it, to light a candle at any time; for in our Savior's day glass was not used, and the windows of houses were only slits in the side of the wall, and the rooms were very dark. Almost all the Oriental houses are very dark to this day, and if anything be dropped as small as a piece of silver, it must be looked for with a candle even at high noon. Now, the sphere in which the church moves here on earth is a dim twilight of mental ignorance, and moral darkness; and in order to find a lost soul, light must be brought to bear upon it.

The Holy Spirit uses the light of the gospel; he convinces men of sin, of righteousness, and of judgment to come. The woman lit a candle, and even thus the Holy Spirit lights up some chosen man whom he makes to be a light in the world. He calls to himself whomsoever he wills and makes him a lamp to shine upon the people. Such a man will have to be consumed in his calling: like a candle he will be burned up in light-giving. Earnest zeal, and laborious self-sacrifice will eat him up. So, may this church, and every church of God, be continually using up her anointed men and women, who shall be as lights in the midst of a crooked and perverse generation, to seek out lost souls.

But she was not content with her candle; she also fetched her broom, and she swept the house. If she could not find the silver as things were in the house, she brought the broom to bear upon the accumulated dust. Oh, how a Christian church, when it is moved by the Holy Spirit, cleanses herself and purges all her work! "Perhaps," says she, "some of our members are inconsistent, and so men are hardened in sin; these offenders must be put away. The tone of religion is low – that may be hindering the conversion of souls; it must be raised. Perhaps our statements of truth, and our ways of proclaiming it are not the most likely to command attention – we must amend them; we must use the best possible methods; we must in fact sweep the whole house."

I delight to see an earnest house-sweeping by confession of sin at a prayer meeting, or by a searching discussion – a house-sweeping when everyone is earnest to reform himself, and to get nearer to God himself by a revival of his own personal devoutness. This is one of the means by which the church is enabled to find the hidden ones. Besides this, all the neighborhood around the church (for the house is the sphere in which the church moves) must be ransacked, stirred, turned over, and in a word, "swept." A church that is really in earnest after souls will endeavor to penetrate the gloom of poverty and stir the heaps of immorality. She will hunt high and hunt low if by any means she may rescue from destruction the precious thing upon which her heart is set.

Carefully note that this seeking after the lost piece of silver with proper instruments, the broom and the candle, was *accompanied by no small state of activity*. She swept the house – there was dust for her eyes; if any neighbors were in the house there was dust for them. You cannot sweep a house without causing some confusion and temporary discomfort. We sometimes hear persons complain of certain Christians for making too much ado about religion. The complaint shows that something is being done, and in all probability some success is being achieved. Those people who have no interest in the lost silver are annoyed at the dust; it is getting down their throats, and they cough at it. Never mind, good woman, sweep again, and make them grumble more.

Another will say, "I do not approve of religious excitement; I am for quiet and orderly modes of procedure." I dare say that this good woman's neighbor, when she came in to make a call, exclaimed in disgust, "Why, mistress, there is not a chair to sit down upon in comfort, and you are so taken up about this lost money that you scarce give me an answer. Why, you are wasting a candle at a great rate, and you seem quite in a fever." "Well," the good woman would answer, "but I must find my piece of silver, and in order to seek it out I can bear a little dust myself, and so must you if you wish to stop here while I am searching."

An earnest church will be sure to experience a degree of excitement when it is soul hunting, and very cautious, very fastidious, very critical people will find fault. Never mind them, my brethren, sweep on and let them talk on. Never mind making a dust if you find the money. If souls be saved, irregularities and singularities are as the small dust of the balance. If men be brought to Jesus, care nothing about what nit-pickers say. Sweep on, sweep on, even though men exclaim, *These that have turned the world upside down are come hither also* (Acts 17:6). Though confusion and activity, and even persecution be the present results, yet if the finding of an immortal soul be the ultimate effect, you will be well repaid for it.

It is to be remarked, also, that in the seeking of this piece of silver the coin was *sought in a most engaging manner.* For a time, nothing was thought of but the lost silver. Here is a candle: the good woman does not read by the light of it, nor mend her garments; no, but the candlelight is all spent on that piece of money. All its light is consecrated to the search. Here is a broom: there is other work for the broom to do, but for the present it sweeps for the silver and for nothing else. Here are two bright eyes in the good woman's head: alas, but they look for nothing but the lost money; she does not care what else may be in the house or out of it – her money she cares for, and that she must find; and here she is with candle, broom, strength, eyesight, faculties of mind, and limbs of body, all employed in searching for the lost treasure.

It is just so when the Holy Spirit works in a church. The preacher, like a candle, yields his light, but it is all with the view of finding out the sinner and letting him see his lost condition. Whether it be the broom of the law or the light of the gospel, all is meant for the sinner. All the Holy Spirit's wisdom is engaged to find the sinner, and all the living church's talent and substance and power are put forth if by any means the sinner may be saved. It is a fair picture, may I see it daily. How earnestly souls are sought for when the Spirit of God is truly in his church!

One other thought only. This woman *sought for her piece of silver continuously – till she [found] it.* May you and I, as parts of the church of God, look for wandering souls until we find them. We say they discourage us. No doubt that piece of silver did discourage the woman who sought it. We complain that men do not appear inclined to religion. Did the piece of money lend the housewife any help? Was it any assistance to her? She did the seeking, she did it all.

And the Holy Spirit through you, my brother, seeks the salvation of the sinner, not expecting the sinner to help him, for the sinner is averse to being found. What, were you repulsed the other day by one whose spiritual good you longed for? Go again! Were your invitations laughed at? Invite again! Did you become the subject of ridicule through your earnest pleadings? Plead again! Those are not always the least likely to be saved who at first repel our efforts.

A harsh reception is sometimes only an indication that the heart recognizes the power of the truth, though it does not desire at present to yield to it. Persevere, brother, until you find the soul you seek. You who spend so much effort in your Sunday school class, use still your candle, enlighten the child's mind still, sweep the house until you find what you seek; never give up the child until it is brought to Christ. You, in your senior class, dealing with that young man or young woman, cease not from your private prayers and from your personal admonitions, until that heart belongs to Jesus.

You who can preach in the streets, or visit the lodging houses, or go from door to door with tracts, I charge you all, for you can all do something, never give up the pursuit of sinners until they are safely lodged in Jesus' hands. We must have them saved! With all the intense perseverance of the woman who turned everything upside down, and counted all things but loss that she might but find her treasure, so may we also, the Spirit of God working in us, upset everything of rule and conventionality, and form and difficulty, if we may but by any means save some, and bring out of the dust those who bear the King's image, and are dear to the King's heart.

Now I must close with the third point, which is the piece of silver found.

Found! In the first place, this was *the woman's ultimatum, and nothing short of it.* She never stopped until the coin was found. So it is the Holy Spirit's purpose, not that the sinner should be brought into a hopeful state, but that he should be actually saved; and this is the church's great concern, not that people be made hearers, not that they be made orthodox professing Christians, but that they be really changed and renewed, regenerated and born again.

The woman herself found the piece of money. It did not turn up by accident, nor did some neighbor step in and find it. The Spirit of God himself finds sinners, and the church of God herself, as a rule, is the instrument of their recovery.

Dear brethren, a few years ago there was a kind of slur cast upon the visible church by many enthusiastic but mistaken persons who dreamed that the time had come for doing away with organized effort, and for irregular agencies outside of the visible church were to do all the work. Certain remarkable men sprang up whose ferocious rebukes almost amounted to attacks upon the recognized churches. Their efforts were apart from the regular ministry, and in some cases flamboyantly in opposition to it. It was as much their aim to pull down the existing church as to bring in converts.

I ask any man who has fairly watched these efforts, What they have come to? I never condemned them, nor will I; but I do venture to say today in the light of their history, that they have not superseded regular church work and never will. The masses were to be aroused, but where are the boasted results? What has become of many of these much-boasted works?

Those who have worked in connection with a church of God have achieved permanent usefulness; those who acted as separatist agencies, though they blazed for a while before the public eye and filled the corners of the newspapers with spiritual hype, are now either altogether or almost extinct. Where are the victories that were to be won by these free-shooters? Echo answers, Where? We have to fall back on the old disciplined troops.

God means to bless the church still, and it is through the church that he will continue to send a benediction upon the sons of men. I am glad to hear of anybody preaching the gospel; if Christ is preached, in that I do rejoice, yes, and will rejoice. I remember the Master's words: *Forbid them not* (Luke 18:16). *He that is not against us is for us* (Luke 9:50). Still the mass of conversions will come through the church and by her regular organized efforts. The woman who lights the candle and sweeps the house, to whom the silver belongs, will herself find it.

Now notice when she had found it what she did: *She rejoiced.* The greater her trouble in searching, the higher her joy in finding. What joy there is in the church of God when sinners are converted! We have our high holidays, we have our cheerful days downstairs in the lecture hall, when we hear of souls turned from the paths of the destroyer; and in the vestries behind, your pastors and elders often experience such joy as only heaven can equal, when we have heard the stories of souls emancipated from the slavery of sin, and led into the perfect liberty that Jesus gives. The church rejoices.

Next, she *calls her friends and neighbors* to share her joy. I am afraid we do not treat our friends and neighbors with quite enough respect, or remember to invite them to our joys. Who are they? I think the angels are meant here; not only the angels in heaven, but also those who are watching here below. Note well, that when the shepherd took the sheep home, it is written, *Joy shall be in heaven over one sinner that repenteth* (Luke 15:7), but it does not mention heaven here, nor speak of the future; but it is written, *There is joy in the presence of the angels of God* (Luke 15:10).

Now, the church is on earth, and the Holy Spirit is on earth, at work; when there is a soul saved, the angels down below, who keep watch and protection around the faithful, and so are our friends and neighbors, rejoice with us. Know you not that angels are present in our assemblies? For this reason the apostle tells us that the woman has her head covered in the assembly. He says, *Because of the angels* (1 Corinthians 11:10), for they love order and decorum. The angels are wherever the saints are, beholding our orders and rejoicing in our joy. When we see conversions, we may bid them to rejoice too, and they will praise God with us. I do not suppose the rejoicing ends there; for as angels are always ascending and descending upon the Son of Man, they soon convey the tidings to the hosts above, and heaven rejoices over one repenting sinner.

The joy is a present joy; it is a joy in the house, in the church in her own sphere; it is the joy of her neighbors who are round about her here below. All other joy seems swallowed up in this: as every other occupation was suspended to find the lost silver, so every other joy is hushed when the precious thing is found. The church of God has a thousand joys – the joy of her saints ascending to the skies, the joy of her saints ripening for glory, the joy of such as contend with sin and overcome it, and grow in grace and receive the promise; but the chief joy in the church, which swallows all others, as Aaron's rod swallowed up the other rods, is the joy over the lost soul which, after much sweeping and searching, is found at last.

The practical lesson to the unconverted is just this. Dear friend, *see what value is set upon you.* You think that nobody cares for you – why, heaven and earth care for you! You say, "I am as nothing, a castaway, and I am utterly worthless." No, you are not worthless to the blessed Spirit, nor worthless to the church of God – she longs for you.

See, again, *how false that suspicion of yours is that you will not be welcome* if you come to Christ. Welcome! Why, the church is searching for you; the Spirit of God is searching for you. Do not talk of welcome, for you will be a great deal more than welcome. Oh, how glad will Christ be, and the Spirit be, and the church be to receive you!

Ah! but you complain that you have done nothing to make you fit for mercy. Talk not so; what had the lost piece of money done? What could it do? It was lost and helpless. They who sought it did all; he who seeks you will do all for you. O poor soul, since Christ now bids you to come, then come! If his Spirit draws you, yield! Since the promise now speaks, *Come now, and let us reason together, saith the Lord: though your sins be as scarlet, they shall be as white as snow; though they be red like crimson, they shall be as wool* (Isaiah 1:18), accept the promise. Believe in Jesus. God bless you and save you, for Jesus' sake. Amen.

Chapter 14

Bread Enough to Spare

And when he came to himself, he said, How many hired
servants of my father's have bread enough and to spare,
and I perish with hunger! (Luke 15:17)

*H*e came to himself. The phrase may be applied to one waking out
of a deep swoon. He had been unconscious of his true condition,
and he had lost all power to deliver himself from it; but now he was
coming around again, returning to consciousness and action.

The voice that shall awaken the dead aroused him; the visions of
his sinful trance all disappeared; his foul but fascinating dreams were
gone; *he came to himself.* Or the phrase may be applied to one recovering from insanity. The Prodigal Son had played the madman, for sin is
madness of the worst kind. He had been demented, he had put bitter
for sweet and sweet for bitter, darkness for light and light for darkness;
he had injured himself, and had done for his soul what those possessed
of devils in our Savior's time did for their bodies, when they wounded
themselves with stones, and cut themselves with knives.

The insane man does not know himself to be insane, but as soon as
he comes to himself, he painfully perceives the condition from which
he is escaping. Returning then to true reason and sound judgment, the
prodigal came to himself. Another illustration of the phrase may be
found in the old-world fables of enchantment: when a man was liberated

from the magician's spell, *he came to himself.* Classic story has its legend of Circe, the enchantress who transformed men into swine. Surely this young man in our parable had been degraded in the same manner. He had lowered his manhood to the level of the brutes.

It should be the property of man to have love for his kindred, to have respect for righteousness, to have some care for his own interest; but this young man had lost all these proper attributes of humanity, and so had become as the beast that perishes. But as the poet sings of Ulysses, that he compelled the enchantress to restore his companions to their original form, so here we see the prodigal returning to manhood, looking away from his sensual pleasures, and commencing a course of conduct more consistent with his birth and parentage.

There are men here today perhaps who are still in this swoon; O God of heaven, arouse them! Some are here who are morally insane; may the Lord recover them, may the divine Physician put his cooling hand upon their fevered brow and say to them, *I will; be thou clean* (Matthew 8:3). Perhaps there are others here who have allowed their animal nature to reign supreme; may he who destroys the works of the devil deliver them from the power of Satan, and give them power to become the sons of God. He shall have all the glory!

It appears that when the prodigal came to himself, he was shut up to two thoughts. Two facts were clear to him: that there was plenty in his father's house, and that he himself was famishing. May the two kindred spiritual facts have absolute power over all your hearts, if you are yet unsaved; for they were most certainly all-important and pressing truths. These are no delusions of one in a dream; no ravings of a maniac; no imaginations of one under fascination. It is most true that there is plenty of all good things in the Father's house, and that the sinner needs them. Nowhere else can grace be found or pardon gained, but with God there is abundance of mercy; let none venture to dispute this glorious truth.

Equally true is it that the sinner without God is perishing. He is perishing now, he will perish everlastingly. All that is worth having in his existence will be utterly destroyed, and he himself shall only remain as a desolation; the owl and the heron of misery and anguish shall haunt the ruins of his nature forever and forever. If we could shut up unconverted men to those two thoughts, what hopeful congregations we would have.

Alas! they forget that there is mercy only with God, and imagine that it is to be found somewhere else. They try to slip away from the humbling fact of their own lost condition, and imagine that perhaps there may be some back door of escape; that, after all, they are not so bad as the Scripture declares, or that perhaps it shall be right with them at the end, however wrong it may be with them now.

Alas! my brethren, what shall we do with those who willfully shut their eyes to truths of which the evidence is overwhelming, and the importance overpowering? I earnestly entreat those of you who know how to approach the throne of God in faith, to breathe the prayer that he would now bring into captivity the unconverted heart, and put these two strong fetters upon every unconverted soul. There is abundant grace with God, there is utter destitution with themselves. Bound with such fetters, and led into the presence of Jesus, the captive would soon receive the liberty of the children of God.

I intend only to dwell this morning, or mainly, upon the first thought, the master thought, as it seems to me, that was in the prodigal's mind – that which really constrained him to say, *I will arise and go to my father.* It was not, I think, the home-bringing thought that he was perishing with hunger, but the impulse towards his father found its mainspring in the consideration, *How many hired servants of my father's have bread enough and to spare!* The plenty, the abundance, the superabundance of the father's house was that which attracted him to return home; and many, many a soul has been led to seek God when it has fully believed that there was abundant mercy with him.

My desire this morning shall be to put plainly before every sinner here the exceeding abundance of the grace of God in Christ Jesus, hoping that the Lord will find out those who are his sons, and that they may catch these words, and as they hear of the abundance of the bread in the Father's house, they may say, *I will arise and go to my father.*

First, then, let us consider for a short time the more than abundance of all good things in the Father's house. What do you need this morning, awakened sinner? Of all that you need, there is with God an all-sufficient, a superabounding supply; *bread enough and to spare.* Let us prove this to you. First, *consider the Father himself* and whosoever shall rightly consider the Father, will at once perceive that there can be no limit to mercy, no bounds to the possibilities of grace. What is the nature and character of the Supreme Being? "Is he harsh or loving?" says one. The Scripture answers the question, not by telling us that God is loving, but by assuring us that God *is* love.

God himself is love; it is his very essence. It is not that love is in God, but that God himself is love. Can there be a more concise and more positive way of saying that the love of God is infinite? You cannot measure God himself; your conceptions cannot grasp the grandeur of his attributes, neither can you tell the dimensions of his love, nor conceive of the fullness of it. Only know this, that high as the heavens are above the earth, so are his ways higher than your ways, and his thoughts than your thoughts. His mercy endures forever. He pardons iniquity, and passes by the transgression of the remnant of his heritage. He retains not his anger forever, because he delights in mercy. *Thou, Lord, art good, and ready to forgive; and plenteous in mercy unto all them that call upon thee* (Psalm 86:5). *Thy mercy is great above the heavens* (Psalm 108:4). *The Lord is very pitiful, and of tender mercy* (James 5:11).

If divine love alone would not seem sufficient for your salvation, remember that with the Father to whom the sinner returns, there is as much wisdom as there is grace. Is your case a very difficult one? He that made you can heal you. Are your diseases strange and complex? He that fashioned the ear, can he not remove its deafness? He that made the eye, can he not enlighten it if it be blind? No mischief can have happened to you but what he who is your God can recover you from it. Matchless wisdom cannot fail to meet the intricacies of your case.

Neither can there be any failure of power with the Father. Do you not know that he who made the earth, and stretched out the heavens like a tent to dwell in, has no bounds to his strength, nor limits to his might? If you need omnipotence to lift you up from the swamp into which you have fallen, omnipotence is ready to deliver you, if you cry to the strong for strength. Though you should need all the force with which the Creator made the worlds, and all the strength with which he bears up the pillars of the universe, all that strength and force should be laid out for your good, if you would believingly seek mercy at the hand of God in Christ Jesus. None of his power shall be against you, none of his wisdom shall plan your overthrow; but love shall reign in all, and every attribute of God shall become subservient to your salvation.

Oh, when I think of sin, I cannot understand how a sinner can be saved; but when I think of God, and look into his heart, I understand how readily he can forgive. "Look into his heart," says one. "How can we do that?" Has he not laid bare his heart to you? Do you inquire where he has done this? I answer, yonder, upon Calvary's cross. What was in the very center of the divine heart? What, but the person of the Well-beloved, his only begotten Son. And he has taken his only begotten and nailed him to the cross, because, if I may venture so to speak, he loved sinners better than his Son. He spared not his Son, but he spares the sinner; he poured out his wrath upon his Son and made him the substitute for sinners, that he might lavish love upon the guilty who deserved his anger.

O soul, if you are lost, it is not from any lack of grace, or wisdom, or power in the Father. If you perish, it is not because God is hard to move or unable to save. If you be a castaway, it is not because the Eternal refused to hear your cries for pardon or rejected your faith in him. On your own head be your blood if your soul be lost. If you starve, you starve because you will starve, for in the Father's house there is *bread enough and to spare.*

But now, consider a second matter which may set this more clearly before us. Think of *the Son of God,* who is indeed the true Bread of Life for sinners. Sinner, I return to my personal address. You need a Savior; and you may well be encouraged when you see that a Savior is provided – provided by God, since it is certain he would not make a mistake in the provision. But consider who the Savior is. He is himself God. Jesus who came from heaven for our redemption was not an angel, or else we might tremble to trust the weight of our sin upon him. He was not a mere man, or he could but have suffered as a substitute for one, if indeed for one; but he was very God of very God, in the beginning with the Father.

And does such a one come to redeem? Is there room to doubt as to his ability if that be the fact? I do confess this day, that if my sins were ten thousand times heavier than they are, yes, and if I had all the sins of this crowd in addition piled upon me, I could trust Jesus with them all at this moment, now that I know him to be the Christ of God. He is the mighty God, and by his pierced hand the burden of our sins is easily removed; he blots out our sins, he casts them into the depths of the sea.

But think of what Jesus the Son of God has done. He who was God, and thus blessed forever, left the throne and royalties of heaven, and stooped to yonder manger. There he lies; his mother wraps him in swaddling clothes, he hangs upon her breast; the Infinite is clothed as an infant, the Invisible is made manifest in flesh, the Almighty is linked with weakness for our sakes. Oh, matchless stoop of condescension! If the Redeemer God does this in order to save us, shall it be thought a thing impossible for him to save the vilest of the vile? Can anything be too hard for him who comes from heaven to earth to redeem?

Pause not because of astonishment, but press onward. Do you see him who was God over all, blessed forever, living more than thirty years in the midst of the sons of men, bearing the infirmities of manhood, taking upon himself our sicknesses, and sharing our sorrows; his feet weary with treading the acres of Palestine; his body faint oftentimes with hunger and thirst, and labor; his knees knit to the earth with midnight prayer; his eyes red with weeping (for Jesus wept often), tempted in all points like as we are? Matchless spectacle! An incarnate God dwells among sinners and endures their contradiction!

What glory flashed forth ever and immediately from the midst of his lowliness! A glory that should render faith in him inevitable. You who did walk the sea, you who did raise the dead, it is not rational to doubt your power to forgive sins! Did you not yourself put it so, when you bade the man to take up his bed and walk? *Whether is easier, to say, Thy sins be forgiven thee; or to say, Rise up and walk?* (Luke 5:23). Assuredly he is able to save to the uttermost them that come unto God by him; he was able even here on earth in weakness to forgive sins, much more now that he is seated in his glory. He is exalted on high to be a Prince and a Savior, to give repentance and remission of sins.

But, ah! the master-proof that in Christ Jesus there is *bread enough and to spare* is the cross. Will you follow me a moment, will you follow him, rather, to Gethsemane? Can you see the bloody sweat as it falls upon the ground in his agony? Can you think of his scourging before Herod and Pilate? Can you trace him along the Via Dolorosa of Jerusalem? Will your tender hearts endure to see him nailed to the tree, and lifted up to bleed and die? This is but the shell; as for the inward kernel of his sufferings, no language can describe it, neither can concept peer into it. The everlasting God laid sin on Christ, and where the sin was laid there fell the wrath. *It pleased the Lord to bruise him; he hath put him to grief* (Isaiah 53:10).

Now he that died upon the cross was God's only begotten Son. Can you conceive a limit to the merit of such a Savior's death? I know there are some who think it necessary to their system of theology to limit the merit of the blood of Jesus: if my system of theology needed such a limitation, I would cast it to the winds. I cannot, dare not allow the thought to find a lodging in my mind; it seems so near akin to blasphemy. In Christ's finished work I see an ocean of merit; my plummet finds no bottom, my eye discovers no shore. There must be sufficient effectualness in the blood of Christ, if God had so willed it, to have saved not only all this world, but also ten thousand worlds, had they transgressed the Maker's law.

Once infinity is admitted into the matter, limit is out of the question. Having a divine person for an offering, it is not consistent to conceive of limited value; bounds and measure are terms inapplicable to the divine sacrifice. The intent of the divine purpose fixes the application of the infinite offering but does not change it into a finite work. In the atonement of Christ Jesus there is *bread enough and to spare;* even as Paul wrote to Timothy, *[He] is the Saviour of all men, specially of those that believe* (1 Timothy 4:10).

But now let me lead you to another point of solemnly joyful consideration, and that is *the Holy Spirit.* To believe and love God is to possess the key to theology. We spoke of the Father, we spoke of the Son; let us now speak of the Holy Spirit. We do the Spirit all too little honor, for the Holy Spirit stoops to come to earth and dwell in our hearts; and notwithstanding all our provocations, the Lord in this way still abides within his people. Now, sinner, you need a new life and you need holiness, for both of these are necessary to make you fit for heaven. Is there a provision for this? The Holy Spirit is provided and given in the covenant of grace; and surely in him there is *enough and to spare.* What can the Holy Spirit not do? Being divine, nothing can be beyond his power.

Look at what the Holy Spirit has already done. The Holy Spirit moved upon the face of chaos and brought it into order; all the beauty of creation arose beneath his breath that molded it. We ourselves must confess with Elihu, *The spirit of God hath made me, and the breath of the Almighty hath given me life* (Job 33:4). Think of the great deeds of the Holy Spirit at Pentecost, when unlearned men spoke with tongues of which they knew not a syllable formerly, and the flames of fire upon them were also within them, so that their hearts burned with zeal and courage to which they up to this time had been strangers.

Think of the Holy Spirit's work on such a one as Saul of Tarsus. That persecutor foams blood, he is an utter wolf; he would devour the saints of God at Damascus, and yet, within a few moments, you hear him say, *Who art thou, Lord?* (Acts 9:5); and yet again, *Lord, what wilt thou have me to do?* (Acts 9:6). His heart is changed; the Spirit of God has newly created it; the stone is melted in a moment into wax.

Many of us stand before you as the living monuments of what the Holy Spirit can do, and we can assure you from our own experience, that there is no inward evil that he cannot overcome, no lustful desire of the flesh that he cannot subdue, no callousness of the affections that cannot melt. Is anything too hard for the Lord? Is the Spirit of the Lord hampered by anything? Surely no sinner can be beyond the possibilities of mercy when the Holy Spirit stoops to be the agent of human conversion.

O sinner, if you perish, it is not because the Holy Spirit lacks power, or the blood of Jesus lacks effectualness, or the Father fails in love. It is because you believe not in Christ, but abide in willful rebellion, refusing the abundant Bread of Life that is placed before you.

A few rapid sentences I will give upon other things, which will go to show still further the greatness of the provision of divine mercy. Observe well that *throughout all the ages God has been sending one prophet after another,* and these prophets have been succeeded by apostles, and these by martyrs and confessors, and pastors and evangelists, and teachers; all these have been commissioned by the Lord in regular succession, and what has been the message they have had to deliver? They have all pointed to Christ, the great deliverer. Moses and the prophets all spoke of him, and so have all truly God-sent ambassadors.

Do you think, sinner, that God has made all this fuss about a trifle? Has he sent all these servants to call you to a table insufficiently furnished? Has he multiplied his invitations through so long a time to bid you and others to come to a provision that is not, after all, sufficient for you? Oh, it cannot be! God is not mocked, neither does he mock poor needy souls. The stores of his mercy are sufficient for the utmost emergencies.

> Rivers of love and mercy here
>> In a rich ocean join;
> Salvation in abundance flows,
>> Like floods of milk and wine.
>
> Great God, the treasures of thy love
>> Are everlasting mines,
> Deep as our helpless miseries are,
>> And boundless as our sins.

Recollect, again, that *God has been pleased to stake his honor upon the gospel.* Men desire a name, and God also is jealous for his glory. Now, what has God been pleased to select for his name? Is it not the conversion and salvation of men? When *instead of the thorn shall come up the fir tree, and instead of the brier shall come up the myrtle tree: and it shall be to the Lord for a name, for an everlasting sign that shall not be cut off* (Isaiah 55:13). And do you think God will get a name by saving little sinners by a little Savior?

Ah! his great name comes from washing out stains as black as hell, and pardoning sinners who were the foulest of the foul. Is there one monstrous rebel here who is qualified to glorify God greatly, because his salvation will be the wonder of angels and the amazement of devils? I hope there is.

O you most degraded, wicked, loathsome sinner, nearest to being a damned sinner, if this voice can reach you, I challenge you to come and prove whether God's mercy is not a match for your sin. You Goliath sinner, come you to this place; you shall find that God can slay your hostility, and make you yet his friend, and the more his loving and adoring servant, because great forgiveness shall secure great love. Such is the greatness of divine mercy, that *where sin abounded, grace [doth] much more abound* (Romans 5:20).

Do you think, again, O sinner, that Jesus Christ came out of heaven to do a little deed, and to provide a meager store of mercy? Do you think he went up to Calvary, and down to the grave, and all, that he might do a commonplace thing, and provide a stinted, narrow, limited salvation, such as your unbelief would imagine his redemption to be? No. We speak of the labors of Hercules, but these were child's play compared with the labors of Christ who slew the lion of hell, turned a purifying stream through the Augean Stables of man's sin and cleansed them, and performed ten thousand miracles besides. And will you so depreciate Christ as to imagine that what he has accomplished is, after all, little, so little that it is not enough to save you?

If it were in my power to single out the man who has been the most dishonest, most licentious, most drunken, most profane – in three words, most earthly, sensual, devilish – I would repeat the challenge which I gave just now, and bid him to draw near to Jesus, and see whether the fountain filled with Christ's atoning blood cannot wash him white. I challenge him at this instant to come and cast himself at the dear Redeemer's feet, and see if he will say, "I cannot save you; you have sinned beyond my power." It shall never, never, never be, for he is able to the uttermost to save. He is a Savior, and a great one. Christ will be honored by the grandeur of the grace that he bestows upon the greatest of offenders. There is in him pardon *enough and to spare.*

I must leave this point, but I cannot do so without adding that I think *bread enough and to spare* might be taken for the motto of the gospel. I believe in particular redemption, and that Christ laid down his life for his sheep; but, as I have already said, I do not believe in the limited value of that redemption; how else could I dare to read the words of John: *He is the propitiation for our sins: and not for ours only, but also for the sins of the whole world* (1 John 2:2)? There is a sure portion for his own elect, but there is also over and above *to spare.* I believe in the electing love that will save all its objects – *bread enough* – but I believe in boundless benevolence: *bread enough **and to spare*** (emphasis added).

We, when we have a purpose to accomplish, put forth the requisite quantity of strength and no more, for we must be economical, we must not waste our limited supply; even charity gives the poor man no more than he absolutely needs; but when God feeds the multitude, he spreads the board with imperial bounty. Our water cart runs up and down the favored road, but when heaven's clouds would favor the good man's fields, they deluge whole nations, and even pour themselves upon the sea. There is no real waste with God; but at the same time there is no limitation. *Bread enough and to spare;* write that inscription over the house of mercy, and let every hungry passerby be encouraged thereby to enter in and eat.

We must now pass on to a second consideration, and dwell very briefly on it. According to the text, there was not only bread enough in the house, but also the lowest in the Father's house enjoyed enough and to spare.

We can never make a parable run on all fours; therefore, we cannot find the exact counterpart of the *hired servants* (Luke 15:17, 19). I understand the prodigal to have meant this, that the very lowest humble servant employed by his father had bread to eat and had *bread enough and to spare.* Now, how should we translate this? Why, sinner, the very lowest creature that God has made, that has not sinned against him, is well supplied and has abounding happiness. There are adaptations for pleasure in the organizations of the lowest animals. See how the gnats dance in the summer's sunbeam; hear the swallows as they scream with delight when on the wing. He who cares for birds and insects will surely care for men. God who hears the ravens when they cry, will he not hear the returning repentant ones? He gives these insects happiness; did he mean me to be wretched? Surely, he who opens his hand and supplies the lack of every living thing will not refuse to open his hand and supply my needs if I seek his face.

Yet I must not make these lowest creatures to be the hired servants. Whom shall I then select among men? I will put it thus. The very worst of sinners that have come to Christ have found grace *enough and to spare,* and the very least of saints who dwell in the house of the Lord find love *enough and to spare.* Take, then, *the most guilty of sinners,* and see how bountifully the Lord treats them when they turn unto him. Did not some of you, who are yourselves unconverted, once know persons who were at least as bad, perhaps more outwardly immoral than yourselves?

Well, they have been converted, though you have not been; and when they were converted, what was their testimony? Did the blood of

Christ serve to cleanse them? Oh yes, and more than cleanse them, for it added to beauty that was not their own. They were naked once; was Jesus able to clothe them? Was there a sufficient covering in his righteousness? Ah, yes! and adornment was superadded; they received not bare apparel, but a royal garment. You have seen others thus liberally treated; does not this induce you also to come? Some of us need not confine our remarks to others, for we can speak personally of ourselves.

We came to Jesus as full of sin as ever you can be, and felt ourselves beyond measure lost and ruined; but oh, his tender love! I could sooner stand here and weep than speak to you of it. My soul melts in gratitude when I think of the infinite mercy of God to me in that hour when I came seeking mercy at his hands. Oh! why will you not also come? May his Holy Spirit sweetly draw you! I proved that there was bread enough, mercy enough, forgiveness enough, and to spare. Come along, come along, poor guilty one; come along, there is room enough for you.

Now, if the chief of sinners bears this witness, so do *the most obscure of saints.* If we could call forth from his seat a weak believer in God, who is almost unknown in the church, one who sometimes questions whether he is indeed a child of God, and would be willing to be a hired servant so long as he might belong to God, and if I were to ask him, "Now, after all, how has the Lord dealt with you?" what would be his reply? You have many afflictions, doubts, and fears, but have you any complaints against your Lord? When you have waited upon him for daily grace, has he denied you? When you have been full of troubles, has he refused you comfort? When you have been plunged into distress, has he declined to deliver you?

The Lord himself asks, *Have I been a wilderness unto Israel?* (Jeremiah 2:31). Testify against the Lord, you his people, if you have anything against him. Hear, O heavens, and give ear, O earth, whosoever there be in God's service who has found him a hard taskmaster, let him speak.

Among the angels before Jehovah's throne, and among men redeemed on earth, if there be any one that can say he has been dealt with unjustly or treated with ungenerous rudeness, let him lift up his voice. But there is not one. Even the devil himself, when he spoke of God and of his servant Job, said, *Doth Job fear God for nought?* (Job 1:9). Of course he did not. God will not let his servants serve him for nothing; he will pay them superabundant wages, and they shall all bear witness that at his table there is *bread enough and to spare*. Now, if these still enjoy the bread of the Father's house, these who were once great sinners, these who are now only very commonplace saints, surely, sinner, it should encourage you to say, *I will arise and go to my father* (Luke 15:18), for his hired servants *have bread enough and to spare*.

Notice in the third place, that the text dwells upon the multitude of those who have *bread enough and to spare*. The prodigal lays an emphasis upon that word: **How many** hired servants of my father's (emphasis added). He was thinking of their great number and counting them over. He thought of those that tended the cattle, of those that went out with the camels, of those that watched the sheep, and those that minded the wheat, and those that waited in the house; he ran them over in his mind. His father was great in the land, and had many servants; yet he knew that they all had of the best food *enough and to spare*.

"Why should I perish with hunger? I am only one at any rate; though my hunger seems insatiable, it is but one belly that has to be filled, and lo, my father fills hundreds, thousands every day; why should I perish with hunger?" Now, O you awakened sinner, you who feel this morning your sin and misery, think of the numbers upon whom God has bestowed his grace already. Think of the countless hosts in heaven: if you were introduced there today, you would find it as easy to count the stars, or the sands of the sea, as to count the multitudes that are before the throne even now.

They have come from the east and from the west, and they are sitting down with Abraham, with Isaac, and with Jacob, and there is room enough for you. And beside those in heaven, think of those on earth. Blessed be God, his elect on earth are to be counted by millions, I believe, and the days are coming, brighter days than these, when there shall be multitudes upon multitudes brought to know the Savior, and to rejoice in him. The Father's love is not for a few only, but for an exceedingly great company. A number that no man can number will be found in heaven. Now, a man can number a very great amount. Set to work your Newtons, your calculators, and they can count great numbers; but God and God alone can count the multitude of his redeemed.

Now, sinner, you are but one at any rate, great sinner as you are, and the mercy of God that embraces millions must have room enough in it for you. The sea which holds the whales and creeping things innumerable, do you say, "It will overflow its banks if I bathe in it"? The sun which floods the universe with light, can you say, "I should exhaust his beams if I would ask him to enlighten my darkness"? Say not so. If you come to yourself you will not tolerate such a thought, but you will remember with hope the richness of the Father's grace, even though your own poverty stares you in the face.

Let us add a few words to close with, familiar grappling words to some of you to whom God has sent his message this morning, and whom he intends to save. O you who have been long hearers of the gospel, and who know it well in theory, but have felt none of the power of it in your hearts, let me now remind you where and what you are! You are perishing.

As the Lord lives, there is but a step between you and death; but a step, no, but a breath between you and hell. Sinner, if at this moment your heart should cease its beating, and there are a thousand causes that might produce that result before the clock ticks again, you would be in the flames of divine wrath. Can you bear to be in such peril? If you were hanging over a rock by a slender thread that must soon break, and if you would then fall headlong down a terrible precipice, you would not sleep, but be full of alarm. May you have sense enough, intelligence enough, and grace enough to be alarmed until you escape from the wrath to come.

Recollect, however, that while you are perishing, you are perishing in sight of plenty; you are famishing where a table is abundantly spread. What is more, there are those whom you know now sitting at that table and feasting. What a sad perversity for a man to persist in being starved in the midst of a banquet, where others are being satisfied with good things!

But I think I hear you say, "I fear I have no right to come to Jesus." I will ask you this: Have you any right to say that until you have been denied? Did you ever try to go to Christ? Has he ever rejected you? If then you have never received a rejection, why do you wickedly imagine that he would reject you? Wickedly, I say, for it is an offense against the Christ who opened his heart upon the cross, to imagine that he could repel a repentant one. Have you any right to say, "But I am not one of those for whom mercy is provided"? Who told you so? Have you climbed to heaven and read the secret records of God's election? Has the Lord revealed a strange decree to you and said, "Go and despair, I will have no pity on you"?

If you say that God has so spoken, I do not believe you. In this sacred Book is recorded what God has said; here is the sure word of testimony, and in it I find it said of no humble seeker that God has shut him out from his grace. Why have you a right to invent such a fiction in order to secure your own damnation? Instead of that, there is much in the Word of God and elsewhere to encourage you in coming to Christ. He has not turned away one sinner yet; that is good to begin with. It is not likely that he would, for since he died to save sinners, why should he reject them when they seek to be saved? You say, "I am afraid to come to Christ." Is that wise?

I have heard of a poor navigator who had been converted, who had but little education, but who knew the grace of our Lord Jesus Christ, and when dying, very cheerfully and joyfully longed to depart. His wife said to him, "But, mon, ain't ye afeared to stand before the judge?" "Woman," said he, "why should I be afeared of a man as died for me?"

Oh, why should you be afraid of Christ who died for sinners? The idea of being afraid of him should be banished by the fact that he shed his blood for the guilty. You have much reason to believe from the very fact that he died, that he will receive you. Besides, you have his word for it, for he says, *Him that cometh to me I will in no wise cast out* – for no reason, and in no way, and on no occasion, and under no pretense, and for no motive. "I will not cast him out," says the original. *Him that cometh to me I will in no wise cast out.* You say it is too good to be true that there can be pardon for you; this is a foolish measuring of God's wheat with your bushel, and because it seems too good a thing for you to receive, you imagine it is too good for God to bestow. Let the greatness of the good news be one reason for believing that the news is true, for it is so like God.

> Who is a pardoning God like thee?
> Or who hath grace so rich and free?

Because the gospel assures us that he forgives great sins through a great Savior, it looks as if it were true, since he is so great a God.

What should be the result of all this with every sinner here at this time? I think this good news should arouse those who have almost gone to sleep through despair. The sailors have been pumping the vessel, the leaks are gaining, she is going down, the captain is persuaded she must be a wreck. Depressed by such evil tidings, the men refuse to work; and since the boats are all smashed in and they cannot make a raft, they sit down in despair. Presently the captain has better news for them. "She will float," he says. "The wind is abating too, the pumps direct themselves upon the water, the leak can be reached yet." See how they work; with what cheery courage they toil on, because there is hope! Soul, there is hope! *There is hope!* There is hope for the harlot, for the thief, for the drunkard.

"There is no hope," says Satan. Liar that you are, get back to your den; for you there is no hope, but for fallen man, though he be in the mire of sin up to his very neck, though he be at the gates of death, yet while he lives there is hope. There is hope for hopeless souls in the Savior.

In addition to arousing us this ought to elevate the sinner's thoughts. Some years ago, there was a crossing-sweeper in Dublin, with his broom, at the corner, and in all probability his highest thoughts were to keep the crossing clean and look for the pence. One day, a lawyer put his hand upon his shoulder and said to him, "My good fellow, do you know that you are heir to a fortune of ten thousand pounds a year?"

"Do you mean it?" said he.

"I do," he said. "I have just received the information; I am sure you are the man." He walked away, *and he forgot his broom.*

Are you astonished? Why, who would not have forgotten a broom when they were suddenly made possessor of ten thousand a year? So, I pray that some poor sinners, who have been thinking of the pleasures of the world, when they hear that there is hope, and that there is heaven to be had, will forget the deceitful pleasures of sin, and follow after higher and better things.

Should it not also purify the mind? The prodigal, when he said, *I will arise and go to my father,* became in a measure reformed from that very moment. How, say you? Why, he left the swine-trough; but even more, he left the wine cup, and he left the harlots. He did not go with the harlot on his arm, and the wine cup in his hand, and say, "I will take these with me, and go to my father." It could not be. These were all left, and though he had no goodness to bring, yet he did not try to keep his sins and come to Christ. I shall close with this remark, because it will act as a sort of *caveat*, and be a suitable word to season the wide invitations of the free gospel.

Some of you, I fear, will make mischief even out of the gospel, and will dare to take the cross and use it for a gallows for your souls. If God is so merciful, you will go therefore and sin the more; and because grace is freely given, therefore you will continue in sin that grace may abound. If you do this, I would solemnly remind you that I have no grace to preach to such as you. *[Your] damnation is just* (Romans 3:8); it is the word of inspiration, and the only one I know that is applicable to such as you are. But every needy, guilty soul that desires a Savior is told today to believe in Jesus; that is, trust in the substitution and sacrifice of Christ, trust him to take your sin and blot it out, trust him to take your soul and save it.

Trust Christ entirely, and you are forgiven this very moment; you are saved this very instant, and you may rejoice now in the fact that being justified by faith you have peace with God through Jesus Christ our Lord. O come, come, come; come and welcome; come now to the Redeemer's blood. Holy Spirit, compel them to come in, that the house of mercy may be filled. Amen, and Amen.

Chapter 15

Confession of Sin

My message here will have seven texts, and yet I pledge myself that there shall be but three different words in the whole of them; for it so happens that the seven texts are all alike occurring in seven different portions of God's Holy Word. I shall request, however, to use the whole of them to exemplify different cases; and I must request those of you who have brought your Bibles with you to refer to the texts as I shall mention them.

The subject of this discourse will be this – confession of sin. We know that this is absolutely necessary to salvation. Unless there be a true and hearty confession of our sins to God, we have no promise that we shall find mercy through the blood of the Redeemer. *Whoso confesseth [his sins] and forsaketh them shall have mercy* (Proverbs 28:13). But there is no promise in the Bible to the man who will not confess his sins. Yet, as upon every point of Scripture there is a probability of being deceived, so more especially in the matter of confession of sin. There be many who make a confession, and a confession before God, who, notwithstanding, receive no blessing because their confession does not have in it certain marks that are required by God to prove it genuine and sincere, and that demonstrate it to be the work of the Holy Spirit.

My text this morning consists of three words: *I have sinned*. And you will see how these words, on the lips of different men, indicate very different feelings. While one says, "I have sinned," and receives forgiveness, another we shall meet with says, "I have sinned," and goes his way to blacken himself with worse crimes than before, and dive into greater depths of sin than before now he had discovered.

The Hardened Sinner
Pharaoh – *I have sinned.* (Exodus 9:27)

The first case I shall bring before you is that of the hardened sinner, who, when under terror, says, *I have sinned.* And you will find the text in the book of Exodus, the ninth chapter, and the twenty-seventh verse: *And Pharaoh sent, and called for Moses and Aaron, and said unto them, I have sinned this time: the Lord is righteous, and I and my people are wicked.*

But why this confession from the lips of the haughty tyrant? He was not often accustomed to humbling himself before the Lord. Why does the proud one bow himself now? You will judge the value of his confession when you hear the circumstances under which it was made. *And Moses stretched forth his rod toward heaven: and the Lord sent thunder and hail, and the fire ran along upon the ground; and the Lord rained hail upon the land of Egypt. So there was hail, and fire mingled with the hail, very grievous, such as there was none like it in all the land of Egypt since it became a nation* (Exodus 9:23-24).

"Now," says Pharaoh – while the thunder is rolling through the sky, while the lightning flashes are setting the very ground on fire, and while the hail is descending in big lumps of ice – "Now," says he, *I have sinned.* He is but a type and specimen of multitudes of the same class. How many a hardened rebel on shipboard, when the timbers are strained and creaking, when the mast is broken, and the ship is drifting before the gale, when the hungry waves are opening their mouths to swallow the ship up alive and quick as those that go into the pit – how many a hardened sailor has then bowed his knee, with tears in his eyes, and cried, "I have sinned!" But of what benefit and of what value was his confession?

The repentance that was born in the storm died in the calm; that repentance of his that was begotten amidst the thunder and lightning ceased as soon as all was hushed in quiet, and the man who was a pious mariner when aboard ship became the most wicked and abominable of sailors when he placed his foot on *terra firma.* How often, too, have we seen this in a storm of thunder and lightning? Many a man's cheek is dulled when he hears the thunder rolling; the tears spring to his eyes, and he cries, "O God, I have sinned!" while the rafters of his house are shaking, and the very ground beneath him is reeling at the voice of God which is full of majesty. But alas, for such a repentance! When the sun again shines, and the black clouds are withdrawn, sin comes again upon the man, and he becomes worse than before.

How many of the same sort of confessions, too, have we seen in times of cholera, and fever, and pestilence! Then our churches have been crammed with hearers who, because so many funerals have passed their doors, or so many have died in the street, could not refrain from going up to God's house to confess their sins. And under that visitation, when one, two, and three have been lying dead in the house, or next door, how many have thought they would really turn to God! But, alas! when the pestilence had done its work, conviction ceased; and when the bell had tolled the last time for a death caused by cholera, then their hearts ceased to beat with repentance, and their tears did flow no more.

Have I any such here this morning? I doubt not I have hardened persons who would scorn the very idea of religion, who would count me a twitterer and a hypocrite if I should endeavor to press it home upon them, but who know right well that religion is true, and who feel it in their times of terror! If I have such here this morning, let me solemnly say to them, "Sirs, you have forgotten the feelings you had in your hours of alarm; but remember, God has not forgotten the vows you then made."

Sailor, you said if God would spare you to see the land again, you would be his servant, but you are not so; you have lied against God, you have made him a false promise, for you have never kept the vow which your lips did utter. You said, on a bed of sickness, that if he would spare your life you would never again sin as you did before; but here you are, and this week's sins shall speak for themselves. You are no better than you were before your sickness.

Could you lie to your fellow man, and yet go unrebuked? And do you think that you will lie against God, and yet go unpunished? No; the vow, however rashly made, is registered in heaven; and though it be a vow that man cannot perform, yet, as it is a vow that he has made himself, and made voluntarily too, he shall be punished for not keeping it; and God shall execute vengeance upon him at last, because he said he would turn from his ways, and then when the blow was removed, he did not.

A great outcry has been raised lately against pardons. I have no doubt there are some men here who before high heaven stand in the same position as the pardoned men stand before our government. They were about to die, as they thought; they promised good behavior if they might be spared, and they are here today on pardon in this world: and how have they fulfilled their promise? Justice might raise the same outcry against them as they do against the burglars so constantly let loose upon us. The avenging angel might say, "O God, these men said if they were spared, they would be so much better; if anything, they are worse. How they have violated their promise, and how they have brought down divine wrath upon their heads!" This is the first style of repentance, and it is a style I hope none of you will imitate, for it is utterly worthless. It is of no use for you to say, "I have sinned" merely under the influence of terror, and then to forget it afterwards.

The Double-Minded Man

Balaam – *I have sinned*. (Numbers 22:34)

Now for a second text. I beg to introduce to you another character – the *double-minded man* who says, *I have sinned*, and feels that he has, and feels it deeply, too, but who is so worldly-minded that he *love[s] the wages of unrighteousness* (2 Peter 2:15). The character I have chosen to illustrate this is that of Balaam. Turn to the book of Numbers, the twenty-second chapter, and the thirty-fourth verse: *And Balaam said unto the angel of the Lord, I have sinned.*

I have sinned, said Balaam; but yet he went on with his sin afterwards. One of the strangest characters of the whole world is Balaam. I have often marveled at that man; he seems really in another sense to have come up to the lines of Ralph Erskine:

> To good and evil equal bent,
> And both a devil and a saint.

He did seem to be so. At times, no man could speak more eloquently and more truthfully, and at other times he exhibited the most mean and sordid covetousness that could disgrace human nature. Imagine that you see Balaam: he stands upon the brow of the hill, and there lie the multitudes of Israel at his feet; he is bidden to curse them, and he cries, *How shall I curse, whom God hath not cursed?* (Numbers 23:8). And God opening his eyes, he begins to tell even about the coming of Christ, and he says, *I shall see him, but not now: I shall behold him, but not nigh* (Numbers 24:17). And then he winds up his oration by saying, *Let me die the death of the righteous, and let my last end be like his!* (Numbers 23:10). And you will say of that man, he is a hopeful character. Wait until he can come off the brow of the hill, and you will hear him give the most diabolical advice to the king of Moab that it was even possible for Satan himself to suggest.

Said he to the king, "You cannot overthrow these people in battle, for God is with them; try and entice them from their God." And you know how with malicious lusts they of Moab tried to entice the children of Israel from allegiance to the Lord, so that this man seemed to have the voice of an angel at one time, and yet the very soul of a devil in his bowels. He was a terrible character; he was a man of two things, a man who went all the way with two things to a very great extent. I know the Scripture says, *No man can serve two masters* (Matthew 6:24).

Now this is often misunderstood. Some read it, *No man can **serve** two* masters (emphasis added). Yes, he can; he can serve three or four. The way to read it is this: *No man can serve two **masters*** (emphasis added). They cannot both be masters. He can serve two, but they cannot both be his master. A man can serve two who are not his masters, or twenty as well; he may live for twenty different purposes, but he cannot live for more than one master purpose – there can only be one master purpose in his soul.

But Balaam labored to serve two; it was like the people of whom it was said, *They feared the Lord, and served their own gods* (2 Kings 17:33). Or like Rufus, who was a loaf of the same leaven; for you know our old King Rufus painted God on one side of his shield, and the devil on the other, and had underneath, the motto: "Ready for both; catch who you can."

There are many such, who are ready for both. They meet a minister, and how pious and holy they are. On the Sabbath they are the most respectable and upright people in the world, as you would think; indeed, they effect a drawling in their speech, which they think to be very religious. But on a weekday, if you want to find the greatest rogues and cheats, they are some of those men who are so holy in their devoutness. Now, rest assured, my friends, that no confession of sin can be genuine unless it be a wholehearted one. It is of no use for you to say, *I have sinned,* and then keep on sinning. *I have sinned,* say you, and it is a fair, fair face you show; but alas! Alas! for the sin you will go away and commit. Some men seem to be born with two characters.

I observed when in the library at Trinity College, Cambridge, a very fine statue of Lord Byron. The librarian said to me, "Stand here, sir."

I looked, and I said, "What a fine intellectual countenance! What a grand genius he was!"

"Come here," he said, "to the other side."

"Ah, what a demon! There stands the man that could defy the deity." He seemed to have such a scowl and such a dreadful malicious look on his face; even as Milton would have painted Satan when he said, "Better to reign in hell than serve in heaven." I turned away and said to the librarian, "Do you think the artist designed this?"

"Yes," he said, "he wished to picture the two characters – the great, the grand, the almost superhuman genius that he possessed, and yet the enormous mass of sin that was in his soul."

There are some men here of the same sort. I dare say, like Balaam, they would overthrow everything in argument with their enchantments; they could work miracles, and yet at the same time there is something about them that betrays a horrid character of sin, as great as that which would appear to be their character for righteousness. Balaam, you know, offered sacrifices to God upon the altar of Baal: that was just the type of his character. So do many. They offer sacrifices to God on the shrine of Wealth; and while they will give to the building of a church, and distribute to the poor, they will at the other door of their countinghouse grind the poor for bread, and press the very blood out of the widow, that they may enrich themselves. Ah! it is idle and useless for you to say, *I have sinned,* unless you mean it from your heart. That double-minded man's confession is of no benefit.

The Insincere Man

Saul – *I have sinned.* (1 Samuel 15:24)

And now a third character and a third text. In the first book of Samuel, the fifteenth chapter and the twenty-fourth verse, we read: *And Saul said unto Samuel, I have sinned.*

Here is the *insincere man* – the man who is not like Balaam, to a certain extent sincere in two things; but he is like the man who is just the opposite – who has no prominent point in his character at all, but is molded everlastingly by the circumstances that are passing over his head. Such a man was Saul. Samuel rebuked him, and he said, *I have sinned.* But he did not mean what he said; for if you read the whole verse you will find him saying, *I have sinned: for I have transgressed the commandment of the Lord, and thy words: because I feared the people,* which was a lying excuse. Saul never feared anybody; he was always ready enough to do his own will – he was the tyrant. And just before this he had pleaded another excuse, that he had saved the bullocks and lambs to offer to Jehovah; therefore, both excuses could not have been true.

You remember, my friends, that the most prominent feature in the character of Saul was his insincerity. One day he fetched David from his bed, as he thought, to put him to death in his house. Another time he declares, "God forbid that I should do anything against thee, my son David." One day, because David saved his life, he said, *Thou art more righteous than I* (1 Samuel 24:17); *I will no more do thee harm* (1 Samuel 26:21). The day before he had gone out to fight against his own son-in-law, in order to slay him. Sometimes Saul was among the prophets, easily turned into a prophet, and then afterwards among the witches; sometimes in one place, and then in another, and insincere in everything. How many such ones we have in every Christian assembly – men who are very easily molded! Say what you please to them, they always agree with you.

They have affectionate dispositions, very likely a tender conscience; but then the conscience is so remarkably tender, that when touched, it seems to give, and you are afraid to probe deeper – it heals as soon as it is wounded. I think I used the very unique comparison once before, which I must use again; there are some men who seem to have india-rubber hearts. If you do but touch them, there is an impression made at once; but then it is of no use, for it soon restores itself to its original character. You may press them whatever way you wish, they are so elastic you can always effect your purpose; but then they are not fixed in their character, and soon return to be what they were before.

O sirs, too many of you have done the same. You have bowed your heads in church and said, "We have erred and strayed from thy ways," but you did not mean what you said. You have come to your minister and said, "I repent of my sins," but you did not then feel you were a sinner; you only said it to please him. And now you attend the house of God, and there is no one more touched than you. The tear will run down your cheek in a moment, but yet, notwithstanding all that, the tear is dried as quickly as it is brought forth, and you remain for all intents and purposes the same as you were before. To say, *I have sinned* in an unmeaning manner is worse than worthless, for it is a mockery of God thus to confess with insincerity of heart.

I have been brief upon this character, for it seemed to touch upon that of Balaam; though any thinking man will at once see there was a real contrast between Saul and Balaam, even though there is a kinship between the two. Balaam was the great bad man, great in all he did. Saul was little in everything except in stature – little in his good and little in his vice; and he was too much of a fool to be desperately bad, though too wicked to be at any time good, while Balaam was great in both. He was the man who could at one time defy Jehovah, and yet at another time could say, *If Balak would give me his house full of silver and gold, I cannot go beyond the word of the Lord my God, to do less or more* (Numbers 22:18).

The Doubtful Repentant One
Achan – *I have sinned.* (Joshua 7:20)

And now I have to introduce to you a very interesting case. It is the case of the doubtful repentant one, the case of Achan, in the book of Joshua, the seventh chapter, and the twentieth verse. *And Achan answered Joshua, and said, Indeed I have sinned.*

You know that Achan stole some of the prey from the city of Jericho – that he was discovered by lot and put to death. I have singled this case out as the representative of some whose characters are doubtful on their deathbeds; who do repent apparently, but of whom the most we can say is, that we hope their souls are saved at last, but indeed we cannot tell.

Achan, you are aware, was stoned with stones for defiling Israel. But I find in the *Mishna,* an old Jewish exposition of the Bible, these words: "Joshua said to Achan, 'The Lord shall trouble thee this day.'" And the note upon it is – "He said *this* day, implying that he was only to be troubled in this life, by being stoned to death, but that God would have mercy on his soul, seeing that he had made a full confession of his sin."

And I, too, am inclined, from reading the chapter, to concur in the idea of my venerable and now-glorified predecessor, Dr. Gill, in believing that Achan really was saved, although he was put to death for the crime as an example. For you will observe how kindly Joshua spoke to him. He said, *My son, give, I pray thee, glory to the Lord God of Israel, and make confession unto him; and tell me now what thou hast done; hide it not from me* (Joshua 7:19).

And you find Achan making a very full confession. He says, *Indeed I have sinned against the Lord God of Israel, and thus and thus have I done: When I saw among the spoils a goodly Babylonish garment, and two hundred shekels of silver, and a wedge of gold of fifty shekels weight, then I coveted them, and took them; and, behold, they are hid in the earth in the midst of my tent, and the silver under it* (Joshua 7:20-21). It seems so full a confession, that if I might be allowed to judge, I would say, "I hope to meet Achan the sinner before the throne of God."

But I find Matthew Henry has no such opinion; and many other expositors consider that as his body was destroyed, so was his soul. I have, therefore, selected his case as being one of doubtful repentance. Ah! dear friends, it has been my lot to stand by many a deathbed, and to see many such a repentance as this. I have seen the man, when worn to a skeleton, sustained by pillows in his bed; and he has said, when I have talked to him of judgment to come, "Sir, I feel I have been guilty, but Christ is good; I trust in him."

And I have said within myself, "I believe the man's soul is safe." But I have always come away with the melancholy reflection that I had no proof of it beyond his own words; for it needs proof in acts and in future life, in order to sustain any firm conviction of a man's salvation. You know that great fact, that a physician once kept a record of a thousand persons who thought they were dying, and whom he thought were repentant. He wrote their names down in a book as those, who, if they had died, would go to heaven. They did not die, they lived; and he says that out of the whole thousand he had not three persons who turned out well afterwards, but they returned to their sins again, and were as bad as ever.

Ah! dear friends, I hope none of you will have such a deathbed repentance as that. I hope your minister or your parents will not have to stand by your bedside, and then go away and say, "Poor fellow, I hope he is saved. But alas! deathbed repentances are such flimsy things; such poor, such trivial grounds of hope, that I am afraid, after all, his soul may be lost."

Oh! to die with a full assurance; oh! to die with an abundant entrance, leaving a testimony behind that we have departed this life in peace. That is a far happier way than to die in a doubtful manner, lying sick, hovering between two worlds, and neither ourselves nor yet our friends knowing to which of the two worlds we are going. May God grant us grace to give in our lives evidences of true conversion, that our case may not be doubtful!

The Repentance of Despair

Judas – *I have sinned.* (Matthew 27:4)

I shall not detain you too long, I trust, but I must now give you another bad case, the worst of all. It is the repentance of despair. Will you turn to the twenty-seventh chapter of Matthew, and the fourth verse? There you have a dreadful case of the repentance of despair. You will recognize the character the moment I read the verse: *[Judas] saying, I have sinned.* Yes, Judas the traitor, who had betrayed his Master, *when he saw that he was condemned, repented himself, and brought again the thirty pieces of silver to the chief priests and elders, saying, I have sinned in that I have betrayed the innocent blood. . . . And he cast down the pieces of silver in the temple, and departed, and went –* and what? – *and hanged himself* (Matthew 27:3-5).

Here is the worst kind of repentance of all. In fact, I know not that I am justified in calling it repentance; it must be called remorse of conscience. But Judas did confess his sin, and then went and hanged himself. Oh! that dreadful, that terrible, that hideous confession of despair. Have you never seen it? If you never have, then bless God that you never were tagged to see such a sight. I have seen it once in my life; I pray God I may never see it again – the repentance of the man who sees death staring him in the face, and who says, "I have sinned." You tell him that Christ has died for sinners, and he answers, "There is no hope for me. I have cursed God to his face; I have defied him; my day of grace I know is past; my conscience is seared with a hot iron; I am dying, and I know I shall be lost!"

Such a case as that happened long ago, you know, and is on record – the case of Francis Spira – the most dreadful case, perhaps, except that of Judas, which is upon record in the memory of man. Oh! my friends, will any of you have such a repentance? If you do, it will be a beacon to all persons who sin in the future; if you have such a repentance as that, it will be a warning to generations yet to come.

In the life of Benjamin Keach – and he also was one of my predecessors – I find the case of a man who had professed religion, but had departed from the profession, and had gone into awful sin. When he came to die, Keach, with many other friends, went to see the man, but they could never stay with him for more than five minutes at a time, for he said, "Get ye gone; it is of no use your coming to me; I have sinned away the Holy Spirit. I am like Esau; I have sold my birthright, and though I seek it carefully with tears, I can never find it again."

And then he would repeat dreadful words like these: "My mouth is filled with gravel stones, and I drink wormwood day and night. Tell me not, tell me not of Christ! I know he is a Savior, but I hate him and he hates me. I know I must die; I know I must perish!" And then followed sad cries, and hideous noises, such as none could bear. They returned again in his placid moments, only to stir him up once more, and make him cry out in his despair, " I am lost! I am lost! It is of no use your telling me anything about it!"

Ah! there may be a man here who may have such a death as that. Let me warn him before he comes to it; and may God the Holy Spirit grant that that man may be turned unto God, and made a true repentant one, and then he need not have any more fear; for he who has had his sins washed away in the Savior's blood need not have any remorse for his sins, for they are pardoned through the Redeemer.

The Repentance of the Saint

Job – *I have sinned*. (Job 7:20)

And now I come into daylight. I have been taking you through dark and dreary confessions; I shall detain you there no longer, but bring you out to the two good confessions that I have read to you. The first is that of Job in the book of Job, the seventh chapter, at the twentieth verse: *I have sinned; what shall I do unto thee, O thou preserver of men?* This is the *repentance of the saint*. Job was a saint, but he sinned. This is the repentance of the man who is a child of God already, an acceptable repentance before God. But as I intend to dwell upon this later, I shall now leave it, for fear of wearying you. David was a specimen of this kind of repentance, and I would have you carefully study his psalms of repentance, the language of which is ever full of weeping humility and earnest repentance.

The Blessed Confession

The prodigal – *I have sinned*. (Luke 15:18)

I come now to the last instance that I shall mention; it is the case of the Prodigal Son. In Luke 15:18, we find the Prodigal Son saying, *Father, I have sinned*. Oh, here is *a blessed confession*! Here is that which proves a man to be a born-again character – *Father, I have sinned*. Let me picture the scene. There is the prodigal; he has run away from a good home and a kind father, and he has spent all his money on harlots, and now he has none left. He goes to his old companions and asks them for relief. They laugh him to scorn. "Oh," says he, "you have drunk my wine many a day; I have always stood as paymaster to you in all our revelries; will you not help me?"

"Get you gone," they say; and he is turned out of doors.

He goes to all his friends with whom he had associated, but no man gives him anything. At last a certain citizen of the country says, "You want something to do, do you? Well, go and feed my swine." The poor prodigal, the son of a rich landowner who had a great fortune of his own, has to go out to feed swine; and he a Jew, too! – the worst employment (to his mind) to which he could be put. See him there, in squalid rags, feeding swine; and what are his wages? Why, so little, that *he would fain have filled his belly with the husks that the swine did eat: and no man*

gave unto him (Luke 15:16). Look, there he is, with the fellow common-
ers of the pigpen, in all his mire and filthiness.

Suddenly a thought put there by the good Spirit strikes his mind.
"How is it," says he, "that in my father's house there is *bread enough
and to spare, and I perish with hunger! I will arise and go to my father,
and will say unto him, Father, I have sinned against heaven, and before
thee, and am no more worthy to be called thy son: make me as one of
thy hired servants* (Luke 15:17-19). Off he goes. He begs his way from
town to town. Sometimes he gets a lift on a coach, perhaps, but at other
times he goes trudging his way up barren hills and down desolate val-
leys, all alone.

And now at last he comes to the hill outside the village, and sees
his father's house down below. There it is; the old poplar tree against
it, and there are the stacks around which he and his brother used to
run and play; and at the sight of the old homestead all the feelings and
associations of his former life rush upon him, and tears run down his
cheeks, and he is almost ready to run away again. He says, "I wonder
whether father's dead. I daresay mother broke her heart when I went
away; I always was her favorite. And if they are either of them alive,
they will never see me again; they will shut the door in my face. What
am I to do? I cannot go back, I am afraid to go forward." And while he
was thus deliberating, his father had been walking on the housetop,
looking out for his son; and though he could not see his father, his
father could see him.

Well, the father comes downstairs with all his might, runs up to
him, and while he is thinking of running away, his father's arms are
around his neck, and he begins vigorously kissing him, like a loving
father indeed, and then the son begins – *Father, I have sinned against
heaven, and in thy sight, and am no more worthy to be called thy son*
(Luke 15:21); and he was going to say, *Make me as one of thy hired servants* (Luke 15:19).

But his father puts his hand on his mouth. "No more of that," says
he. " I forgive you all; you shall not say anything about being a hired
servant – I will have none of that. Come along," says he, "come in, poor
prodigal. Ho!" says he to the servants, "*bring forth the best robe, and
put it on him;* and put shoes on his poor bleeding feet; *and bring hither*

the fatted calf, and kill it; and let us eat, and be merry: For this my son was dead, and is alive again; he was lost, and is found. And they began to be merry (Luke 15:22-24). Oh, what a precious reception for one of the chief of sinners!

Good Matthew Henry says, "His father saw him, there were eyes of mercy; he ran to meet him, there were legs of mercy; he put his arms around his neck, there were arms of mercy; he kissed him, there were kisses of mercy; he said to him – there were words of mercy – *Bring forth the best robe;* there were deeds of mercy, wonders of mercy – all mercy. Oh, what a God of mercy he is."

Now, prodigal, you do the same. Has God put it into your heart? There are many who have been running away for a long time now. Does God say, "Return"? Oh, I bid you to return, then, for as surely as ever you do return, he will take you in. There never was a poor sinner yet who came to Christ, whom Christ turned away. If he turns you away, you will be the first. Oh, if you could but try him! "Ah, sir, I am so wicked, so filthy, so vile." Well, come along with you – you cannot be more wicked than the prodigal. Come to your Father's house, and as surely as he is God, he will keep his word – *Him that cometh to me I will in no wise cast out.*

Oh, if I might hear that some had come to Christ this morning, I would indeed bless God! I must tell here, for the honor of God and Christ, one remarkable circumstance, and then I will be done. You will remember that one morning I mentioned the case of an infidel who had been a scorner and scoffer, but who, through reading one of my printed sermons, had been brought to God's house and then to God's feet.

Well, last Christmas Day, the same infidel gathered together all his books, and went into the marketplace at Norwich, and there made a public recantation of all his errors, and a profession of Christ; and then taking up all his books that he had written and had in his house, on evil subjects, burned them in the sight of the people. I have blessed God for such a wonder of grace as that, and pray that there may be many more such, who, though they be born prodigals, will yet return home, saying, *I have sinned.*

Chapter 16

The Turning Point

And he arose, and came to his father. (Luke 15:20)

This sentence expresses the true turning point in the prodigal's life story. Many other matters led up to it, and before he came to it there was much in him that was very hopeful; but this was the point itself, and had he never reached it he would have remained a prodigal, but would never have been the prodigal restored, and his life would have been a warning rather than an instruction to us. *He arose, and came to his father.* Speaking, as I do, in extreme weakness, I have no words to spare; and while my voice holds out, I shall speak straight to the point, and I pray the Lord to make every syllable practical and powerful by his Holy Spirit.

We shall begin by noticing that here was action – *He arose, and came to his father.* He had already been in a state of thoughtfulness; he had come to himself, but now he was to go further, and come to his father. He had considered the past, and weighed it up, and had seen the hollowness of all the world's pleasures; he had seen his condition in reference to his father, and his prospects if he remained in the far-off country; he had thought upon what he ought to do, and what would be the probable result of such a course; but now he passed beyond the dreaminess of thought into matter-of-fact acting and doing. How long will it be, dear friends, before you will do the same?

We are glad to have you thoughtful; we hope that a great point is gained when you are led to consider your ways, to ponder your condition, and to look earnestly into the future, for thoughtlessness is the ruin of many a traveler to eternity, and by its means the unwary fall into the deep pit of carnal security and perish therein. But some of you have been among the "thoughtful" quite long enough; it is time you passed into a more practical stage. It is high time that you came to action; it would have been better if you had acted already, for, in the matter of reconciliation to God, first thoughts are best.

When a man's life hangs on a thread, and hell is just before him, his path is clear, and a second thought is superfluous. The first impulse to escape from danger and lay hold on Christ is that which you would be wise to follow. Some of you whom I now address have been thinking, and thinking, and thinking, until I fear that you will think yourselves into hell. May you, by divine grace, be turned from thinking to believing, or else your thoughts will become the undying worm of your torment.

The prodigal had also passed beyond mere regret. He was deeply grieved that he had left his father's house, he lamented his lavish expenditure upon unruliness and reveling, and he mourned that the son of such a father should be degraded into a swineherd in a foreign land. But he now proceeded from regret to repentance, and roused himself to escape from the condition over which he mourned. What is the use of regret if we continue in sin? By all means pull up the floodgates of your grief if the floods will turn the wheel of action, but you may as well reserve your tears if they mean no more than idle sentimentalism. What does it benefit a man to say he repents of his misconduct if he still perseveres in it?

We are glad when sinners repent of their sin and mourn the condition into which sin has brought them, but if they go no further, their regrets will only prepare them for eternal remorse. Had the prodigal become inactive through despondency, or unemotional through sullen grief, he would have perished, far away from his father's home, as it is to be feared that many will whose sorrow for sin leads them into a proud unbelief and willful despair of God's love. But he was wise, for he shook off the drowsiness of his despondency, and, with resolute determination, *arose, and came to his father.* Oh, when will you sad ones be wise enough to do the same? When will your thinking and your sorrowing give place to practical obedience to the gospel?

The prodigal also pressed beyond mere resolving. That is a sweet verse that says, *I will arise;* but that is a far better verse that says, *And he arose.* Resolves are good, like blossoms, but actions are better, for they are the fruits. We are glad to hear from you the resolution, "I will turn to God," but holy angels in heaven do not rejoice over resolutions; they reserve their music for sinners who actually repent. Many of you like the son in the parable have said, *I go, sir,* but you have not gone. You are as ready to forget as you are to resolve. Every earnest sermon, every death in your family, every funeral chime for a neighbor, every pricking of conscience, every touch of sickness sets you a resolving to amend, but your promissory notes are never honored, and your repentance ends in words.

Your goodness is as the dew, which at early dawn hangs each blade of grass with gems, but leaves the fields all parched and dry when the sun's burning heat is poured upon the pasture. You mock your friends, and trifle with your own souls. You have often in this house said, "Let me reach my bedroom and I will fall upon my knees," but on the way home you have forgotten what manner of men you were, and sin has confirmed its tottering throne.

Have you not dallied long enough? Have you not lied unto God sufficiently? Should you not now give over resolving and proceed to the solemn business of your souls like men of common sense? You are in a sinking vessel, and the lifeboat is near, but your mere resolve to enter it will not prevent your going down with the sinking craft; as sure as you are a living man, you will drown unless you take the actual leap for life.

He arose, and came to his father. Now, observe that *this action of the prodigal was immediate,* and without further discussion. He did not go back to the citizen of that country and say, "Will you raise my wages? If not, I must leave." Had he consulted about this, he would have been lost; but he gave his old master no notice, and he canceled his contracts by running away. I would that sinners here would break their league with death, and violate their covenant with hell by escaping for their lives to Jesus, who receives all such runaways. We lack neither leave nor license for quitting the service of sin and Satan, neither is it a subject which demands a month's consideration: in this matter instantaneous action is the surest wisdom.

Lot did not stop to consult the king of Sodom as to whether he might leave his dominions, neither did he consult the parish officers as to the propriety of speedily deserting his home; but with the angel's hand pressing them, he and his family fled from the city. No, one fled not; she looked and lingered, and that lingering cost her life! That pillar of salt is the eloquent monitor to us to avoid delays when we are bidden to flee for our lives. Sinner, do you wish to be a pillar of salt? Will you halt between two opinions, until God's anger shall doom you to final unrepentance? Will you trifle with mercy until justice strikes you? Up, man, and while your day of grace continues, fly into the arms of love.

The text implies that *the prodigal aroused himself* and put forth all his energies. It is said, *he **arose*** (emphasis added); the word suggests that he had until then been asleep upon the bed of sloth, or the couch of presumption. Like Samson in Delilah's lap, he had been leaning backwards, inactive, and unstable; but now, startled from his lethargy, he lifts up his eyes, he girds up his loins, he shakes off the spell that had enthralled him, he puts forth every power, he arouses his whole nature, and he spares no exertion until he returns to his father.

Men are not saved between sleeping and waking. *The kingdom of heaven suffereth violence, and the violent take it by force* (Matthew 11:12). Grace does not surprise us, but it arouses us. Surely, sirs, it is worthwhile making an awful effort to escape from eternal wrath. It is worthwhile summoning up every faculty and power and emotion and passion of your being, and saying to yourself, "I cannot be lost; I will not be lost. I am resolved that I will find mercy through Jesus Christ." The worst of it is, O sinners, that you are so sluggish, so indifferent, so ready to let things happen as they may. Sin has bewitched and benumbed you. You sleep as on beds of down and forget that you are in danger of hellfire.

You cry, "A little more rest, and a little more slumber, and a little more folding of the arms to sleep," and so you sleep on, though your damnation slumbers not. Would to God you could be awakened. It is not in the power of my voice to arouse you; but may the Lord Himself alarm you, for never were men more in danger. Let but your breath fail, or your blood pause, and you are lost forever. Frailer than a cobweb is that life on which your eternal destiny depends.

If you were wise you would not give sleep to your eyes, nor slumber to your eyelids, until you had found your God and been forgiven. Oh, when will you come to a real action? How long will it be before you believe in Jesus? How long will you frolic between the jaws of hell? How long dare you provoke the living God?

Secondly, here was a soul coming into actual contact with God – *He arose, and came to his father.* It would have been of no benefit for him to have arisen if he had not come to his father. This is what the sinner has to do, and what the Spirit enables him to do, namely, to come straight away to his God. But alas! very commonly, when men begin to be anxious, they go round about and hasten to a friend to tell him about it, or they even resort to a deceitful priest, and seek help from him. They fly to a saint or a virgin, and ask these to be mediators for them, instead of accepting the only Mediator, Jesus Christ, and going to God at once by him. They fly to outward forms and ceremonies, or they turn to their Bibles, their prayers, their repentances, or their sermon-hearings; in fact, to anything rather than their God. But the prodigal knew better; he went to his father, and it will be a grand day for you, O sinner, when you do the same.

Go straight away to your God in Christ Jesus. "Come here," says the priest. Pass that fellow by. Get away to your Father. Reject an angel from heaven if he would detain you from the Lord. Go personally, directly, and at once to God in Christ Jesus. But surely, I must perform some ceremony first? Not so did the prodigal; he arose and went at once to his father. Sinner, you must come to God, and Jesus is the way; go to him then, tell him you have done wrong, confess your sins to him, and yield yourself to him. Cry, "Father, I have sinned; forgive me, for Jesus' sake."

Alas! there are many anxious souls who do not go to others, but they look to themselves. They sit down and cry, "I want to repent; I want to feel my need; I want to be humble." O man, get up! What are you at? Leave yourself and go to your Father. "Oh, but I have so little hope; my faith is very weak, and I am full of fears." What causes your hopes or your fears while you are away from your Father? Your salvation does not lie within yourself, but in the Lord's good will to you. You will never be at peace until, leaving all your doubts and your hopes, you come to your God and rest in his bosom. "Oh, but I want to conquer my propensities to sin, I want to roast my strong temptations."

I know what it is you want. You want the best robe without your Father's giving it to you, and shoes on your feet of your own procuring; you do not like going in a beggar's suit and receiving all from the Lord's loving hand; but this pride of yours must be given up, and you must get away to God, or perish forever. You must forget yourself, or only remember yourself so as to feel that you are bad throughout, and no more worthy to be called God's son. Give yourself up as a sinking vessel that is not worth pumping, but must be left to go down, and get yourself into the lifeboat of free grace.

Think of God your Father – of him, I say, and of his dear Son, the one Mediator and Redeemer of the sons of men. There is your hope – to fly away from self and to reach your Father.

Do I hear you say, "Well, I shall continue in the means of grace, and I hope there to find my God." I tell you, if you do that, and refuse to go to God, the means of grace will be the means of damnation to you. "I must wait at the pool," says one. Then I solemnly warn you that you will lie there and die, for Jesus does not command you to lie there; his bidding is, *Take up thy bed, and walk* (John 5:8). *Believe on the Lord Jesus Christ, and thou shalt be saved* (Acts 16:31). You have to go unto your Father, and not to the pool of Bethesda, or any other pool of ordinances or means of grace. "But I mean to pray," says one. What would you pray for? Can you expect the Lord to hear you while you will not hear him? You will pray best with your head in your Father's bosom, but the prayers of an unyielding, disobedient, unbelieving heart are mockeries. Prayers themselves will ruin you if they are made a substitute for going at once to God.

Suppose the prodigal had sat down at the swine trough and said, "I will pray here"; what would it have profited him? Or suppose he had wept there; what good would have come of it? Praying and weeping were good enough when he had come to his father, but they could not have been substituted for it.

Sinner, your business is with God. Hasten to him at once. You have nothing to do with yourself, or your own doings, or what others can do for you; the turning point of salvation is: *He arose, and came to his father*. There must be a real, living, and earnest contact of your poor guilty soul with God, a recognition that there is a God, and that God can be spoken to, and an actual speech of your soul to him, through Jesus Christ; for it is only God in Christ Jesus who is accessible at all.

Going thus to God, we tell him that we are all wrong and want to be set right; we tell him we wish to be reconciled to him, and are ashamed that we have sinned against him; we then put our trust in his Son, and we are saved. O soul, go to God. It matters not though the prayer you come with may be a very broken prayer, or even if it has mistakes in it, as the prodigal's prayer had when he said, *Make me as one of thy hired servants.* The language of the prayer will not matter so long as you really approach God with it. *Him that cometh to me,* says Jesus, *I will in no wise cast out,* and Jesus *ever liveth to make intercession for them* that come to God through him.

Here, then, is the great Protestant doctrine. The Roman Catholic doctrine says you must go around by the back door, and half a dozen of the Lord's servants must knock for you, and even then you may never be heard. But the grand old Protestant doctrine is: Come to God yourself; come with no other mediator than Jesus Christ; come just as you are without merits and good works; trust in Jesus and your sins will be forgiven you.

There is my second point: There was action, and that action was contact with God.

Now, thirdly, in that action there was an entire yielding up of himself. In the prodigal's case, his proud independence and self-will were gone. In other days he demanded his portion, and resolved to spend it as he pleased; but now he is willing to be as much under rule as a hired servant; he has had enough of being his own master, and he is weary of the distance from God that self-will always creates. He longs to get into a child's true place, namely, that of dependence and loving submission. The great mischief of all was his distance from his father, and he now feels it to be so. His great thought is to remove that distance by humbly returning, for then he feels that all other ills will come to an end. He yields up his cherished freedom, his boasted independence, his liberty to think and do and say whatever he chose, and he longs to come under loving rule and wise guidance. Sinner, are you ready for this? If so, come, and welcome; your father longs to press you to his bosom!

He gave up all idea of self-justification, for he said, *I have sinned.*

Before, he would have said, "I have a right to do as I like with my own; who is to dictate how I shall spend my own money? If I do sow a few wild oats, every young man does the same. I have been very generous, if nothing else; nobody can call me greedy. I am no hypocrite. Look at your affectedly pious Methodists, how they deceive people! There's nothing of that in me, I'll warrant you; I am an outspoken man of the world, and after all, a good deal better in disposition than my elder brother, fine fellow though he pretends to be." But now the prodigal boasts no longer. Not a syllable of self-praise falls from his lips; he mournfully confesses, *I have sinned against heaven, and before thee.*

Sinner, if you would be saved, you also must come down from your high places and acknowledge your iniquity. Confess that you have done wrong, and do not try to excuse your offense; do not offer apologies and make your case better than it is, but humbly plead guilty and leave your soul in Jesus' hands. Of two things – to sin or to deny the sin – probably to deny the sin is the worst of the two and shows a blacker heart. Acknowledge your fault, man, and tell your heavenly Father that if it were not for his mercy you would have been in hell, and that as it is, you richly deserve to be there even now.

Make your case rather wickeder than it is if you can; this I say because I know you cannot do any such thing. When a man is in the hospital, it cannot be of any service to him to pretend to be better than he is; he will not receive any more medical attention on that account, but rather the other way around; for the worse his case, the more likely is the physician to give him special notice. Oh sinner, lay bare before God your sores, your putrefying sores of sin, the horrid ulcers of your deep depravity, and cry, "O Lord, have mercy upon me." This is the way of wisdom. Be done with pride and self-righteousness and make your appeal to the undeserved pity of the Lord, and you will succeed.

Observe that the prodigal yielded up himself so thoroughly that he acknowledged his father's love for him to be an aggravation of his guilt; so I take it that he means it when he says, *Father, I have sinned.* It adds an emphasis to the *I have sinned,* when it follows after the word *Father.* "You good God, I have broken your good laws; you loving, tender, merciful God, I have done wrong maliciously and wickedly against you. You have been a very loving Father to me, and I have been a most ungenerous and shameless traitor to you, rebelling without cause. I confess this frankly and humbly, and with many tears. Ah! had you been a tyrant, I might have gathered some apology from your severity, but you have been a Father, and this makes it worse that I should sin against you." It is sweet to hear such a confession as this poured out into the Father's bosom.

The repentant son also yielded up all his supposed rights and claims upon his father, saying, *I . . . am no more worthy to be called thy son.* He might have said, "I have sinned, but still I am your child," and most of us would have thought it a very justifiable argument; but he does not say so, he is too humble for that. He admits, *I . . . am no more worthy to be called thy son.* A sinner is really broken down when he acknowledges that if God would have no mercy on him, but casts him away for forever, it would be no more than justice.

> Should sudden vengeance seize my breath,
>   I must pronounce thee just in death;
> And, if my soul were sent to hell,
>   Thy righteous law approves it well.

That soul is not far from peace which has ceased arguing and submits to the sentence. Oh sinner, I urge you, if you would find speedy rest, go and throw yourself at the foot of the cross where God meets such as you are, and say, "Lord, here I am; do what you will with me. Never a word of excuse will I offer, nor one single plea by way of partial justification. I am a mass of guilt and misery, but pity me, oh, pity me! No rights or claims have I; I have forfeited the rights of creatureship by becoming a rebel against you. I am lost and utterly undone before the bar of your justice. From that justice I flee and hide myself in the wounds of your Son. According to the multitude of your tender mercies, blot out my transgressions!"

Once again, here was such a yielding up of himself to his father that no terms or conditions are mentioned or implied. He begs to be received, but a servant's place is good enough for him; among the helpers in the kitchen he is content to take his place, so long as he may be forgiven. He does not ask for a little liberty to sin nor stipulate for a little self-righteousness wherein he may boast; he gives all up. He is willing to be anything or nothing, just as his father pleases, so that he may but be numbered with his household. No weapons of rebellion are in his hands now. No secret opposition to his father's rule lingers in his soul; he is completely subdued, and lies at his father's feet.

Our Lord never crushed a soul yet that lay prostrate at his feet, and he never will. He will stoop down and say, "Rise, my child, rise, for I have forgiven you. Go and sin no more. I have loved you with an everlasting love." Come and let us return unto the Lord, for he has torn, and he will heal us; he has struck, and he will bind us up. He will not break the bruised reed, nor quench the smoking flax.

Notice further, and fourthly, that in this act there was a measure of faith in his father – a measure, I say, meaning thereby not much faith, but some. A little faith saves the soul. There was faith in his father's power. He said, "In my father's house there is *bread enough and to spare*."

Sinner, do you not believe that God is able to save you; that through Jesus Christ he is able to supply your soul's needs? Can you not get as far as this: *Lord, if thou wilt, thou canst make me clean* (Luke 5:12)? The prodigal also had some faith in his father's readiness to pardon; for if he had not so hoped, he would never have returned to his father at all. If he had been sure that his father would never smile upon him, he would never have returned to him.

Sinner, believe that God is merciful, for so he is. Believe, through Jesus Christ, that he desires not the death of the sinner, but rather that he would turn to him and live; for as surely as God lives, this is truth, and do not believe a lie concerning your God. The Lord is not hard or harsh, but he rejoices to pardon great transgressions. The prodigal also believed in his father's readiness to bless him. He felt sure that his father would go as far as propriety would permit, for he said, "I am not worthy to be called your son, but make me at least your servant." In this also he admitted that his father was so good, that even to be his servant would be a great matter. He was content even to get the lowest place, so long as he might be under the shade of so good a protector.

Ah, poor sinner, do you not believe that God will have mercy on you if he can do so consistently with his justice? If you believe that, I have good news to tell you. Jesus Christ, his Son, has offered such an atonement, so that God can be just, and yet the justifier of him that believes; he has mercy upon the vilest, and justifies the ungodly, and accepts the very chief of sinners through his dear Son.

Oh soul, have faith in the atonement. The atonement made by the personal sacrifice of the Son of God must be infinitely precious; believe that there is effectualness enough in it for you. It is your safety to fly to that atonement and cling to the cross of Christ, and you will honor God by doing so; it is the only way in which you can honor him. You can honor him by believing that he can save you, even you.

The truest faith is that which believes in the mercy of God in the teeth of conscious unworthiness. The repentant son in the parable went to his father as too unworthy to be called his son, and yet he said, *My father.* Faith has a way of seeing the blackness of sin, and yet believing that God can make the soul as white as snow. It is not faith that says, "I am a little sinner, and therefore God can forgive me"; but that is faith that cries, "I am a great sinner, an accursed and condemned sinner, and yet, for all that, God's infinite mercy can forgive me, and the blood of Christ can make me clean."

Believe in the teeth of your feelings, and in spite of your conscience; believe in God, though everything within you seems to say, "He cannot save you; he will not save you." Believe in God, sinner, over the tops of mountainous sins.

Do as John Bunyan says he did, for he was so afraid of his sins and of the punishment thereof, that he could not but run into God's arms, and he said, "Though he had held a drawn sword in his hands, I would have run on the very point of it, rather than have kept away from him." So do the same, poor sinner. Believe your God. Believe in nothing else, but trust your God, and you will get the blessing. It is wonderful the power of faith over God; it binds his justice and constrains his grace.

I do not know how to illustrate it better than by a little story. When I walked down my garden some time ago, I found a dog amusing himself among the flowers. I knew that he was not a good gardener, and was no dog of mine, so I threw a stick at him and bade him to be gone. After I had done so, he conquered me, and made me ashamed of having spoken roughly to him, for he picked up my stick, and, wagging his tail very pleasantly, he brought the stick to me, and dropped it at my feet. Do you think I could strike him or drive him away after that? No, I patted him and called him good names. The dog had conquered the man.

And if you, poor sinner, dog as you are, can have confidence enough in God to come to him just as you are, it is not in his heart to reject you. There is an omnipotence in simple faith that will conquer even the divine Being himself. Only do but trust him as he reveals himself in Jesus, and you shall find salvation.

I have not time or strength to dwell longer here, and so I must notice, fifthly, that this act of coming into contact with God is performed by the sinner just as he is. I do not know how wretched the prodigal's appearance may have been, but I will be bound to say he had grown none the sweeter by having fed swine, nor do I suppose his garments had been very sumptuously embroidered by gathering husks for them from the trees. Yet, just as he was, he came. Surely, he might have spent an hour profitably in cleansing his flesh and his clothes. But no; he said, *I will arise,* and no sooner said than done! he did arise, and he came to his father.

Every moment that a sinner steps away from God in order to get better he is but adding to his sin, for the most radical sin of all is his being away from God, and the longer he stays in it the more he sins. The attempt to perform good works apart from God is like the effort of a thief to set his stolen goods in order; his sole duty is to return them at once. The very same pride that leads men away from God may be seen in their self-conceited notion that they can improve themselves while still they refuse to return to him. The essence of their fault is that they are far-off from God, and whatever they do, so long as that distance remains, nothing is effectively done. I say the root of the whole matter is distance from God, and therefore the commencement of setting matters right lies in arising and returning to him from whom they have departed.

The prodigal was bound to go home just as he was, for there was nothing that he could do. He was reduced to such extremities that he could not purchase a fresh piece of cloth to mend his garments, nor a farthing's worth of soap with which to cleanse his flesh. And it is a great mercy when a man is so spiritually reduced that he cannot do anything but go to his God as a beggar, when he is so bankrupt that he cannot pay a farthing in the pound, and when he is so lost that he cannot even repent or believe apart from God, but feels that he is forever undone unless the Lord shall intercede. It is our wisdom to go to God for everything.

Moreover, there was nothing needed from the prodigal but to return to his father. When a child who has done wrong comes back, the more its face is blurred with tears the better. When a beggar asks for charity, the more his clothes are in rags the better. Are not rags and sores the very garb of beggars? I once gave a man a pair of shoes because he said he was in need of them; but after he had put them on and gone a little way, I overtook him in a gateway taking them off in order to go barefoot again. I think they were patent leather, and what should a beggar do in such attire? He was changing them for *old shoes and clouted* [patched] (Joshua 9:5), for those were suitable to his business. A sinner is never so well arrayed for pleading as when he comes in rags.

At his worst, the sinner, for making an appeal to mercy, is at his best. And so, sinners, there is no need for you to linger; come just as you are. "But must we not wait for the Holy Spirit?" Ah, beloved, he who is willing to arise and go to his Father has the Holy Spirit. It is the Holy Spirit who moves us to return to God, and it is the spirit of the flesh or of the devil that would bid us to wait.

How now, sinners? Some of you are sitting in those pews; where are you? I cannot find you out, but my Master can; he has made this message on purpose for you. "Well, but I would like to get home and pray." Pray where you are, in the pew. "But I cannot speak out aloud." You may if you like; I won't stop you. "But I would not like." Well, don't then. God can hear you without a sound, though I wish sometimes we did hear people cry out, *What must I do to be saved?* I would gladly hear the prayer: *God be merciful to me a sinner.* But if men cannot hear you, the Lord can hear the cries of their hearts.

Now, just sit still a minute, and say, "My God, I must come to you. You are in Jesus Christ, and in him you have already come a great way to meet me. My soul wants you; take me now, and make me what I ought to be. Forgive me and accept me." It is the turning point of a man's life when that is done, wherever it is; whether in a workshop, or in a sawpit, in a church, or in a tabernacle, it does not matter where. There is the point – the getting to God in Christ, giving all up, and by faith resting in the mercy of God.

The last point of all is this – that act effected the greatest conceivable change in the man. He was a new man after that. Harlots, winebibbers, you have lost your old companion now! He has gone to his Father, and his Father's company and yours will never agree. A man's return to his God means his leaving the chambers of corruption and the tables of riot. You may depend upon it whenever you hear of a professing Christian living in uncleanness, that he has not been living anywhere near his God. He may have talked a great deal about it, but God and impurity never agree; if you have friendship with God you will have no fellowship with the unfruitful works of darkness.

Now, too, the repentant son is done with all degrading works to support himself. You will not find him feeding swine anymore, or making a swine of himself either by trusting in priests or sacraments; he will not confess to a priest again, or pay a penny to get his mother out of purgatory; he is not such a fool as that anymore. He has been to his God on his own account, and he does not want any of these priests to go to God for him. He has gotten away from that bondage. No more pig-feeding; no more superstition for him! "Why," says he, "I have access with boldness to the mercy seat, and what have I to do with the priests of Rome?"

There is a change in him in all ways. Now that he has come to his father, his pride is broken down. He no longer glories in that which he calls his own; all his glory is in his father's free, pardoning love. He never boasts of what he has, for he admits that he has nothing but what his father gives him; and though he is far better off than ever he was in his spendthrift days, yet he is as unassuming as a little child. He is a gentleman-commoner upon the bounty of his God, and lives from day to day by a royal grant from the table of the King of Kings. Pride is gone, but contentment fills its room. He would have been contented to be one of the servants of the house, but much more satisfied is he to be a child.

He loves his father with a new love; he cannot even mention his name without saying, "And he forgave me. He forgave me freely, he forgave me all, and he said, *Bring forth the best robe, and put it on him; and put a ring on his hand, and shoes on his feet.*" From the day of his restoration the prodigal is bound to his father's home, and reckons it to be one of his greatest blessings that it is written in the covenant of grace: *I will put my fear in their hearts, that they shall not depart from me* (Jeremiah 32:40).

This morning I believe that God in his mercy means to call many sinners to himself. I am often very much surprised to find how the Lord guides my words according to the persons before me. Last Sunday there came here a young son of a gentleman, a foreigner, from a distant land, under considerable impressions as to the truth of the Christian religion. His father is a follower of one of the ancient religions of the East, and this young gentleman naturally felt it a great difficulty that he would probably make his father angry if he became a Christian.

Judge, then, how closely the message of last Sabbath came home to him, when the text was: "What if your father answers you roughly?" He came to tell me that he thanked God for that message, and he hoped to bear up under the trial, should persecution arise. I feel that I am with equal plainness speaking to some of you. I know I am. You are saying, "May I now go to God just as I am, and through Jesus Christ yield myself up; and will he forgive me?"

Dear brother, or dear sister, wherever you may be, *try it*. That is the best thing to do: *try it*; and, if the angels do not set the bells in heaven ringing, God has changed from what he was last week, for I know he received poor sinners then, and he will receive them now.

The worst thing I dread about you is that you would say, "I will think about it." *Don't* think about it. *Do it!* Concerning this, no more thinking is needed, but just do it. Get away to God. Is it not according to nature that the creature should be at peace with its Creator? Is it not according to your conscience? Is there not something within you that cries, "Go to God in Christ Jesus." In the case of that poor prodigal, the famine said to him, "Go home!" Bread and meat were scarce, he was hungry, and every pang of need said, "Go home! Go home!"

When he went to his old friend the citizen, and he asked him for help, his scowling looks said, "Why don't you go home?" There is a time with sinners when even their old companions seem to say, "We do not want you. You are too miserable and melancholy. Why don't you go home?" They sent him to feed swine, and the very hogs grunted, "Go home." When he picked up those carob husks and tried to eat them, they crackled, "Go home." He looked upon his rags, and they gaped at him, saying, "Go home." His hungry belly and his faintness cried, "Go home." Then he thought of his father's face, and how kindly it had looked at him, and it seemed to say, "Come home!" He remembered the *bread enough and to spare,* and every morsel seemed to say, "Come home!" He pictured the servants sitting down to dinner and feasting to the full, and every one of them seemed to look right away over the wilderness to him and to say, "Come home! Your father feeds us well. Come home!"

Everything said, "Come home!" Only the devil whispered, "Never go back. Fight it out! Better starve than yield! Die game!" But then he had gotten away from the devil this once, for he had come to himself, and he said, "No; *I will arise and go to my father.*" Oh, that you would be equally wise.

Sinner, what is the use of being damned for the sake of a little pride? Yield yourself, man! Down with your pride! You will not find it so hard to submit if you remember that dear Father who loved us and gave himself for us in the person of his own dear Son. You will find it sweet to yield to such a friend. And when you get your head in his bosom, and feel his warm kisses on your cheek, you will soon feel that it is sweet to weep for sin – sweet to confess your wrongdoing, and sweeter still to hear him say, *I have blotted out, as a thick cloud, thy transgressions, and, as a cloud, thy sins* (Isaiah 44:22). *Though your sins be as scarlet, they shall be as white as snow; though they be red like crimson, they shall be as wool* (Isaiah 1:18).

God Almighty grant this may be the case with hundreds of you this morning. He shall have all the glory of it, but my heart shall be very glad, for I feel nothing of the spirit of the elder brother within me, but the greatest conceivable joy at the thought of making merry with you by and by, when you come to acknowledge my Lord and Master, and we sit together at the sacramental feast, rejoicing in his love. God bless you, for his sake. Amen.

Charles H. Spurgeon – A Brief Biography

Charles Haddon Spurgeon was born on June 19, 1834, in Kelvedon, Essex, England. He was one of seventeen children in his family (nine of whom died in infancy). His father and grandfather were Nonconformist ministers in England. Due to economic difficulties, eighteen-month-old Charles was sent to live with his grandfather, who helped teach Charles the ways of God. Later in life, Charles remembered looking at the pictures in *Pilgrim's Progress* and in *Foxe's Book of Martyrs* as a young boy.

Charles did not have much of a formal education and never went to college. He read much throughout his life though, especially books by Puritan authors.

Even with godly parents and grandparents, young Charles resisted giving in to God. It was not until he was fifteen years old that he was born again. He was on his way to his usual church, but when a heavy snowstorm prevented him from getting there, he turned in at a little Primitive Methodist chapel. Though there were only about fifteen people in attendance, the preacher spoke from Isaiah 45:22: *Look unto me, and be ye saved, all the ends of the earth.* Charles Spurgeon's eyes were opened and the Lord converted his soul.

He began attending a Baptist church and teaching Sunday school. He soon preached his first sermon, and then when he was sixteen years old, he became the pastor of a small Baptist church in Cambridge. The church soon grew to over four hundred people, and Charles Spurgeon, at the age of nineteen, moved on to become the pastor of the New Park Street Church in London. The church grew from a few hundred attenders to a few thousand. They built an addition to the church, but still needed more room to accommodate the congregation. The Metropolitan Tabernacle was built in London in 1861, seating more than 5,000 people. Pastor Spurgeon preached the simple message of the cross, and thereby attracted many people who wanted to hear God's Word preached in the power of the Holy Spirit.

On January 9, 1856, Charles married Susannah Thompson. They had twin boys, Charles and Thomas. Charles and Susannah loved each other deeply, even amidst the difficulties and troubles that they faced in life, including health problems. They helped each other spiritually, and often together read the writings of Jonathan Edwards, Richard Baxter, and other Puritan writers.

Charles Spurgeon was a friend of all Christians, but he stood firmly on the Scriptures, and it didn't please all who heard him. Spurgeon believed in and preached on the sovereignty of God, heaven and hell, repentance, revival, holiness, salvation through Jesus Christ alone, and the infallibility and necessity of the Word of God. He spoke against worldliness and hypocrisy among Christians, and against Roman Catholicism, ritualism, and modernism.

One of the biggest controversies in his life was known as the "Down-Grade Controversy." Charles Spurgeon believed that some pastors of his time were "down-grading" the faith by compromising with the world or the new ideas of the age. He said that some pastors were denying the inspiration of the Bible, salvation by faith alone, and the truth of the Bible in other areas, such as creation. Many pastors who believed what Spurgeon condemned were not happy about this, and Spurgeon eventually resigned from the Baptist Union.

Despite some difficulties, Spurgeon became known as the "Prince of Preachers." He opposed slavery, started a pastors' college, opened an orphanage, led in helping feed and clothe the poor, had a book fund for pastors who could not afford books, and more.

Charles Spurgeon remains one of the most published preachers in history. His sermons were printed each week (even in the newspapers), and then the sermons for the year were re-issued as a book at the end of the year. The first six volumes, from 1855-1860, are known as *The Park Street Pulpit*, while the next fifty-seven volumes, from 1861-1917 (his sermons continued to be published long after his death), are known as *The Metropolitan Tabernacle Pulpit*. He also oversaw a monthly magazine-type publication called *The Sword and the Trowel*, and Spurgeon wrote many books, including *Lectures to My Students*, *All of Grace*, *Around the Wicket Gate*, *Advice for Seekers*, *John Ploughman's Talks*, *The Soul Winner*, *Words of Counsel for Christian Workers*, *Cheque Book of the Bank of Faith*, *Morning and Evening*, his autobiography, and more, including some commentaries, such as his twenty-year study on the Psalms – *The Treasury of David*.

Charles Spurgeon often preached ten times a week, preaching to an estimated ten million people during his lifetime. He usually preached from only one page of notes, and often from just an outline. He read about six books each week. During his lifetime, he had read *The Pilgrim's Progress* through more than one hundred times. When he died, his personal library consisted of more than 12,000 books. However, the Bible always remained the most important book to him.

Spurgeon was able to do what he did in the power of God's Holy Spirit because he followed his own advice – he met with God every morning before meeting with others, and he continued in communion with God throughout the day.

Charles Spurgeon suffered from gout, rheumatism, and some depression, among other health problems. He often went to Menton, France, to recuperate and rest. He preached his final sermon at the Metropolitan Tabernacle on June 7, 1891, and died in France on January 31, 1892, at the age of fifty-seven. He was buried in Norwood Cemetery in London.

Charles Haddon Spurgeon lived a life devoted to God. His sermons and writings continue to influence Christians all over the world.

Other Similar Titles

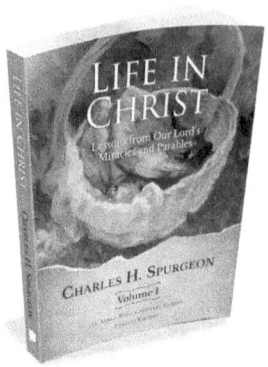

Life in Christ (Vol. 1 - 12),
by Charles H. Spurgeon

Men who were led by the hand or groped their way along the wall to reach Jesus were touched by his finger and went home without a guide, rejoicing that Jesus Christ had opened their eyes. Jesus is still able to perform such miracles. And, with the power of the Holy Spirit, his Word will be expounded and we'll watch for the signs to follow, expecting to see them at once. Why shouldn't those who read this be blessed with the light of heaven? This is my heart's inmost desire.

– Charles H. Spurgeon

Available where books are sold.

Jesus Came to Save Sinners, by Charles H. Spurgeon

This is a heart-level conversation with you, the reader. Every excuse, reason, and roadblock for not coming to Christ is examined and duly dealt with. If you think you may be too bad, or if perhaps you really are bad and you sin either openly or behind closed doors, you will discover that life in Christ is for you too. You can reject the message of salvation by faith, or you can choose to live a life of sin after professing faith in Christ, but you cannot change the truth as it is, either for yourself or for others. As such, it behooves you and your family to embrace truth, claim it for your own, and be genuinely set free for now and eternity. Come and embrace this free gift of God, and live a victorious life for Him.

Available where books are sold.

Words of Warning,
by Charles H. Spurgeon

This book, _Words of Warning_, is an analysis of people and the gospel of Christ. Under inspiration of the Holy Spirit, Charles H. Spurgeon sheds light on the many ways people may refuse to come to Christ, but he also shines a brilliant light on how we can be saved. Unsaved or wavering individuals will be convicted, and if they allow it, they will be led to Christ. Sincere Christians will be happy and blessed as they consider the great salvation with which they have been saved.

Available where books are sold.

According to Promise,
by Charles H. Spurgeon

The first part of this book is meant to be a sieve to separate the chaff from the wheat. Use it on your own soul. It may be the most profitable and beneficial work you have ever done. He who looked into his accounts and found that his business was losing money was saved from bankruptcy.

The second part of this book examines God's promises to His children. The promises of God not only exceed all precedent, but they also exceed all imitation. No one has been able to compete with God in the language of liberality. The promises of God are as much above all other promises as the heavens are above the earth.

Available where books are sold.

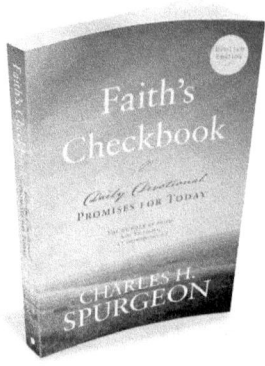

Faith's Checkbook, by Charles H. Spurgeon

Faith's Checkbook is a one-year devotional meant to encourage you to take God at His Word – to take hold of God's promises by faith. Each day you will be presented with a specific promise from the Bible, along with accompanying exhortation by Charles Spurgeon.

This is your "spiritual checkbook," if you will. God's bank account of provision is ample, and it cannot be overdrawn. Every situation you might face is equally met with a promise that, if accepted, will sufficiently see you through.

"God has given no promise that He will not redeem. He does not offer hope that He will not fulfill. To help my brethren believe this, I have prepared this little volume."
– Charles H. Spurgeon

Available where books are sold.

Morning by Morning, by Charles H. Spurgeon

Charles H. Spurgeon's devotionals _Morning by Morning_ and _Evening by Evening_ have inspired, encouraged, and challenged Christians for generations. Spurgeon, with his masterful hand, carefully selected his text from throughout the Bible and covered a broad range of topics, in order to present a well-balanced and fruitful daily devotional for readers both young and old.

Now updated into more-modern English for today's readers, and again separated into two volumes as originally published, with morning devotionals in one volume and evening devotionals in the second. We chose a 11-point font for the sake of legibility, and formatted the devotionals so each fits on a single page.

Available where books are sold.

www.ingramcontent.com/pod-product-compliance
Lightning Source LLC
Chambersburg PA
CBHW071145130626

46553CB00004B/1531